cilantro

W9-BBY-608

MANGO

PAPAYA

Plantain

¡Cuba Cocina!

The Tantalizing World

of Cuban Cooking—

Yesterday, Today,

and Tomorrow

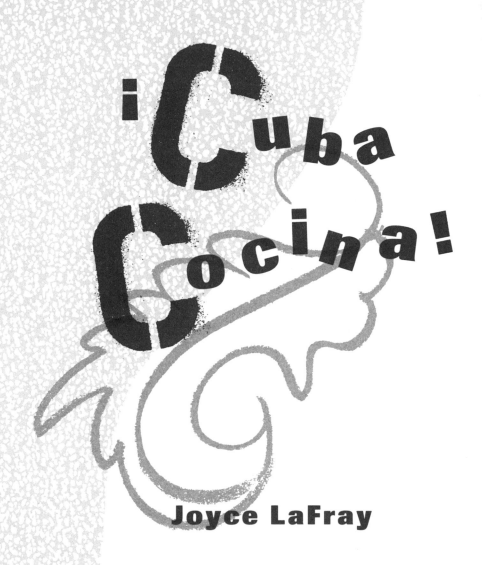

¡Cuba Cocina!

Joyce LaFray

Illustrations by Ann Field

Hearst Books

New York

It is the policy of William Morrow and Company, Inc., and its imprints and affiliates, recognizing the importance of preserving what has been written, to print the books we publish on acid-free paper, and we exert our best efforts to that end.

Library of Congress Cataloging-in-Publication Data

LaFray, Joyce.
    ¡Cuba Cocina! : the tantalizing world of Cuban cooking—yesterday, today, and tomorrow / Joyce LaFray.
        p.   cm.
    Includes indexes.
    ISBN 0-688-11067-3
    1. Cookery, Cuban.   I. Title.
TX716.C8L33   1994
641.597291—dc20   94-1594
                                                            CIP

Printed in the United States of America

First Edition

1 2 3 4 5 6 7 8 9 10

BOOK DESIGN BY RICHARD ORIOLO

This book is dedicated
to my great friend and confidant,
William Richard Young,
whose support and faith throughout
this four-year project is
gratefully appreciated.

Acknowledgments

Recomocimiento

Many thanks to those who contributed to *¡Cuba Cocina!*:

Joan Whitman, for her broad knowledge of cuisine and her copyediting prowess.

Bob Schoolsky, for superb editorial input, support, and friendship.

Jennifer Bistyga, photographer extraordinaire, for help in documenting the herbs, spices, fruits, and vegetables.

Julie and Christy LaFray, my daughters, who lent great support and encouragement.

Leanore Cornyn, my mother, for giving me my first lessons in baking.

John Cornyn, my father, who taught me how to make the best sandwiches on earth and, best of all, to enjoy fine foods.

Maria Elena Cardenas, La Condesa de la Buena Mesa, Miami culinarian, for her expertise in the art of the old and new Cuban cuisine and her exacting translations.

Jackie Guldris and Miren Sexauer, for help in Spanish translations.

Richard Chiavari, executive chef at aMano Restaurant in Miami, for his help.

Carmen Gonzalez, chef extraordinaire, for her input and insight.

All of the talented Florida and Caribbean chefs who shared their recipes and insight into the classic as well as the *nuevo Cubano* cuisine.

Linda Smith, for help in testing all of these recipes over and over and over.

Ann Warner, for help in typing this manuscript.

Nano Riley, for her input.

Sherry Funt and Merrily Davis, for their steadfast support.

My cousin Marjorie McNaughton, for her undying enthusiasm.

"Vivi," who helped me explore cuisine in Cuba and for helping me drive in the dark.

Cav. Enrico Garzaroli and his lovely wife, Ann Marie, Nassau, for help on my trip and in Cuba.

Juan Vicente Gomez Moya, director of Asoliva, Madrid, Spain, for his help.

Novel and Alicia Penabad, Miamians, for support and recipes.

Julia and Angel Suarez of Hialeah, for inspiration.

Willy Gort, county commissioner, Miami, for his insight into the Cuban community.

Pedro Diaz, director, Empresa Turistica Habana, who introduced me to many of Cuba's fine chefs and helped me tour their kitchens.

Stuart Bornstein, for his kind hospitality at Hotel St. Michel, in Coral Gables.

Eduardo Alonso Triana, who showed me the art of Cuban home cookery.

Gustavo Herrara, who showed me how to make great black beans and *mojo* with a minimum of ingredients.

Antonio Meilan, Hemingway's favorite bartender, Restaurante Floridita, for help in understanding the Cuban people.

José Cartaya, manager, Cabaret Tropicana, who showed me how to make the world's best daiquiri.

Sergio Cabrera, Manuel Trasancos Hernandez, José Ignacio Elosegui, Reynaldo Vereier Clanco, and Antonio Hevia Martinez, for their valuable insight into present-day Cuba and the cuisine that exists today on the island.

And finally, to my cairn terrier, Miss Nelly, whose enthusiasm for leftovers and failed recipes never waned.

Contents

Foreword

Prefacio

by Barbara Kafka

Joyce LaFray is a warm and enthusiastic person and eater. In South Florida, as restaurant reviewer, local booster, publisher, and ardent friend to cooks, she has become deeply knowledgeable about local Cuban food, that of the Cubans who in the last twenty years have brought their splendid foods with them and those, like the inhabitants of Tampa, who have maintained their traditions for generations.

I have gone with her to stand-up coffee bars, raunchy nightclubs, elegant restaurants, sandwich shops, markets where there were wonderful ingredients as well as take-out foods for local workers, empanada shops, bakeries, greasy spoons, family restaurants without a word of English, brilliantly festive banquets, family dinners, and elegant celebrations. At every meal, her knowledge and friendships increased.

As she became more interested in this vibrant cooking, she talked with experts, worked with chefs in their kitchens, and finally made visits to Cuba to see what was actually being cooked today. She has indeed become an expert on Cuban cooking. Along the way she has uncovered, in addition to wonderful recipes, numerous techniques that make the food better—both techniques of cooks at home and those of restaurant chefs. She has learned how to get the most from beans, how home cooks lighten sauces by using products like low-fat mayonnaise thinned with milk and seemingly endless variations on the basic cooking mixtures like *mojo*, *salsa*, and *sofrito*.

This is food that is savory and full bodied without being searingly hot. It is food for every day and for holidays. Welcome Joyce and her many pleasures into your kitchen. You won't regret it.

Introduction

As the Cuban population in the United States has grown, especially in Florida, New York, New Jersey, and California, so has my interest in the delicious and distinctive island food about which very little has been written. While many people are enthusiastic about Cuban cuisine, others are puzzled by some of the ingredients. Questions such as "What do I do with this strange-looking vegetable?" are commonly overheard in supermarkets whose regular stock includes unusual and exotic fruits and vegetables.

Living in Florida for the past twenty years gave me a ringside seat to watch the development and impact of Cuban cooking in the South, and allowed me to track its progress throughout the United States. The food gained much public acceptance long before being acclaimed by food journalists.

My very first introduction to Cuban foods came many years ago in Hialeah, a predominantly Hispanic section of Miami. I worked in a print shop across the street from a little hole-in-the-wall with four tables, Angel's Restaurant, owned by Angel and Julia Suarez. Julia was an excellent cook. In her family-style kitchen, far removed from the tourist beat, I learned to enjoy Cuban cooking; her *lechón asado,* or roast pig, and *tamal en hoja,* or handmade tamales, are the best I have sampled.

What started as my fondness for such dishes became a devoted quest to assimilate the Cuban style of cooking, which is simple in concept but complex in flavor. Ad lib sessions with Cuban friends led to formal educational forays into the kitchens of many of Miami's Cuban restaurants and home kitchens.

As a restaurant critic for fifteen years, I immersed myself in the Cuban way of life, which focuses on working hard and eating well. It was not long before store owners began inviting me into their establishments to give recipe demonstrations for the *Norte Americanos,* as well as the local Hispanic population.

All of this was a prelude to my visit to Cuba, where I was able to fine tune much of what I had absorbed over the years. Finally, I was able to see the food prepared where it evolved, and I came to know the subtle variations in style from one province to another, and from Cuba to the United States. What I have learned and observed during this lengthy journey of discovery has been carefully recorded in the pages of this cookbook.

Considering the number of cookbooks published annually, very little has been written on the subject of Cuban cuisine, perhaps because few people have taken the time to write down or translate the best recipes. Another reason is that most North Americans often confuse Cuban cooking with Spanish cooking, not realizing that it has an identity of its own.

Despite a strong Spanish influence, however, Cuban food also owes much to the heritage and traditions of the slaves imported from Africa and neighboring Caribbean cultures, and the basic ingredients of the New World. From this mélange, two distinctive styles have emerged: the classic, featuring techniques and ingredients in long use across all regions of the island, and the "new" Cuban cuisine, or *nuevo Cubano,* which adds a variety of herbs and spices from other cuisines, cooking techniques borrowed from other cultures, and fearlessly beautiful presentations.

An alligator-shaped island located in the heart of the Greater Antilles, Cuba is the largest island in the entire West Indies archipelago—a 700-mile-long natural paradise. Its people are proud of this splendor, acclaimed by Columbus who observed it to be "the most beautiful land I have ever seen."

On a clear day on the island one can see from Cayo Confites to Cayo Lobo in the Bahamas, from Punta Maisi to the Haitian mountains of St. Nicholas, and from the southern slopes of the breathtaking Sierra Maestra mountains to the mystical Blue Mountains of neighboring Jamaica. To the north, it is bounded by the Straits of Florida, to the south the nearest land is Jamaica, to the west lies the Yucatan channel, and far to the east is Africa.

Before the arrival of Columbus and the Spanish caravels, the land was inhabited by the Carib and Arawak natives. Their fish-based diet was supplemented by game, yuca, and corn. The Caribs were a fierce group, the Arawaks a peaceful lot. The Arawaks, an agricultural society, cultivated many fruits and vegetables such as corn, tomatoes, and squash that were either unknown or considered poisonous by the Europeans.

In 1511, the Spanish erected their first settlement. A year later the first permanent town was founded at Baracoa. This led to the rapid development of additional settlements, including Santiago de Cuba and Batabano. San Cristobal de la Habana was founded near Batabano and the name was eventually shortened to Habana, known to us today as Havana.

African slaves were brought in as laborers for the thriving Spanish colony after the conquistadores decimated the native population. Those unwilling immigrants brought with them memories of their traditional foods and cooking methods, adapting them to the ingredients of their new home.

By the mid 1500s, agriculture was bolstered by the cultivation of sugarcane, cocoa, and coffee from nearby islands such as Jamaica, Haiti, Puerto Rico, and Dominica. Because of its central location, Cuba became a trade center for the Spanish fleet. By 1558, Havana was the official capital and one of the most important commercial centers in the New World. About two decades later, tobacco was first grown in commercial quantities. Trade in that commodity substantially increased the already flourishing economy and its importance to the Spanish empire.

When sugarcane became the country's main crop, some 300 years after Columbus, nearly 100,000 additional slaves were imported to harvest the crop.

The island's political and military importance made it a strategic pawn in Spain's battles with the other European powers jealous of Spanish prominence in the New World. Cuba entered into a period of struggle that saw conquerors come and go.

For many years, thousands of Spaniards arrived from all regions of their homeland, many from the provinces of Asturias and Galicia. The now native Cubans embraced the methods and traditions of the Spanish provinces, but interpreted them in their own special way, using the products indigenous to the beautiful island.

Other immigrants to the island included many from China. Although there are a number of popular "Chino-Latino" eateries today in the United States and particularly in New York City, the Chinese did not contribute significantly to the cuisine of the island. Rather, as farmers and great fishermen, they helped supply local markets with fresh fish, fruits, and vegetables. Probably their most notable contribution, according to Victor del Corral, owner of Victor's Café in New York City and Miami, was the Chinese bok choy, or white cabbage, together with the fried rice, which became more elaborate as a paella-style dish served with plantains.

The province of Oriente in Cuba attracted many immigrants from Haiti and Jamaica, beginning in the 1790s and reaching large proportions in the 1930s. This province is well known for its contribution of spicier, more robust dishes to the cuisine of the island.

Today in Cuba, under the austerity regime of Fidel Castro, food is rationed. Few ingredients are widely available, but in my travels throughout Cuba I found the native cuisine, which is carefully prepared, preserved both in the homes and restaurants of the nation. Cubans in the countryside told me that they could cultivate small crops, and often were able to grow those things not available to much of the population.

When my Havana-born Vassar-educated friend, Maria Elena Cardenas, heard that I was compiling this book, she pointed her finger at me and said, "Don't you fool with our classic recipes. This is the way we do it, and we don't use black pepper!" I have not forgotten her pleas. And yet, Maria Elena knows that Cuban cooking is evolving into an even greater taste sensation than she herself had previously experienced.

For instance, in the States, Cubans not only enjoy white and black pepper in many of their dishes, but increasingly choose hot peppers like the blazing Scotch bonnet and serranos. In Miami, chefs introduce novel recipes for black bean salsa, while their colleagues in Los Angeles create an amalgam of new applications for the plantain.

In the following collection, each recipe has been tested in my home kitchen to ensure your success. Where traditional recipes included excess fat, sodium, or sugar, I have adjusted them to healthful measures without sacrificing taste or texture. I think you'll enjoy the diverse and delectable dining experience it will bring to your own table.

Truly, this cookbook has been more than a labor of love. It has been an exciting voyage of discovery.

Ingredients and Techniques

Ingredientes y Técnicas

Glossary

Aceituna (*Olea europaea*) See olive.

Achiote (*Bixa orellana*) See annatto.

Adobo A marinade used for fish, meat, and game that consists of an acid (vinegar, sour orange, lime or lemon juice) and garlic, seasonings, herbs and spices (cilantro, cumin, oregano, allspice, and thyme).

Aguacate (*Persea americana*) See avocado.

Ajiaco The Cuban national dish. There are many variations, but basically it is a thick soup or stew that contains tubers, vegetables, and meats seasoned with herbs and spices.

Ají Cachucha (*Capsicum annum*) Small fiery peppers, similar in heat to the Scotch bonnet pepper.

Ají Picante A hot pepper substitute, such as Tabasco or *peguin*.

Ají Sazonador (*Capsicum annum*) Hot seasoning pepper.

Ajo Garlic.

Annatto (*Bixa orellana*) The rusty red, musky-flavored seed of the annatto tree, also called *achiote* or *urucu*. In its powdered form it is used to color butter, margarine, cheeses, and smoked fish. Use fresh. When browned from age, the flavor will be impaired.

Annona (*Annona muricota*) A genus of tropical fruit trees that includes the soursop.

Arroz Rice, a staple in Cuban cookery. A long-grain rice is commonly used.

Asado Roasted or barbecued meat.

Atemoya (*Annona hybrid*) A pale green bumpy-skinned fruit with white pulp that is sweet and puddinglike. It's good eaten fresh, in fruit salads, mousses, or in chilled fruit *batidos*.

Buying. The fruit is ready when the skin has separated from the stem. Choose pale green tender fruits void of spots or blemishes.

Availability. August to November.

Storing. Keep at room temperature until ripe, then refrigerate. Will keep refrigerated for 3 to 4 days.

Freezing. Freeze juice.

Avocado (*Persea americana*) A leather-skinned fruit with rich buttery flesh that tastes much like a vegetable. It ripens just as well off the tree as on, so any avocado can be delicious if handled properly. There are two types you will likely encounter: the Haas, a plump, pebbly-skinned variety that turns black as it ripens, and Fuerte, a pear-shaped avocado with a thin green skin.

Buying. Look for fruit that feels heavy for its size. Watch for soft dark spots that are signs of bruised or damaged flesh.

Availability. Year-round.

Storing. To ripen very firm fruit, place in a paper bag that is folded and closed with a paper clip. Leave at room temperature for 4 to 5 days. Never store unripe fruit in the refrigerator. As soon as they are fully ripe, store in the vegetable drawer in refrigerator. They should last about 10 days.

Freezing. Purée the flesh, add 1 tablespoon lemon juice for every 2 avocados, then pack in rigid containers with ½-inch headspace. Seal, label, and freeze. It will keep 3 to 6 months.

Ayacas Also spelled *hallacas*. Corn tamales wrapped in corn husks.

Bacalao See salt-dried codfish.

Bacalaito Small fritters prepared with salt-dried codfish, known as bacalao.

Banana (*Musa* hybrids, particularly *Musa sapientum*) Just about the most popular fresh fruit, widely used for dessert or eaten raw. Bananas are best when ripened to yellowish black. Plantains, their versatile big brothers, are used most often in Cuban cuisine. Red Cuban bananas are a red-purple color, small and chunky, and possess a creamier flesh than the yellow variety. *Chicaditas,* or ladyfinger bananas, are tiny yellow bananas.

Barbacoa A sixteenth-century Spanish term that referred to the wooden racks on which the Taino Indians grilled over an open flame. In English, we call it barbecue.

Batido A luscious tropical drink very popular with the Cuban people that is similar to the American milkshake. It is usually made with milk and fresh fruit juices.

Bay Leaves (*Laurus nobilis*) Sometimes called laurel leaf or bay laurel, this very aromatic herb is from the evergreen bay laurel tree, which is native to the Mediterranean. Dried bay leaves are the easiest to find and add flavor to stews, soups, meat, and vegetable dishes. Store in a cool dark place and they will keep for about 6 months.

Beans (*Phaseolus vulgaris*) These seeded pods of various legumes can be purchased fresh, dried, or canned. Dried black and red beans are the most popular in Cuban cuisine.

Bijol, Bija-Bekal A condiment that is used instead of saffron to color rice. It is made up of corn flour, cumin, and food dye.

Bitter Orange (*Citrus aurantium*) See Sour Orange.

Boniato (*Ipomoea batatas*) This versatile tuber looks like a sweet potato with white or yellow flesh, but it is drier and fluffier than a sweet potato and a little less sweet. Like an Irish potato, it can be boiled and served with butter or olive oil, salt, and pepper; or baked, deep-fried, boiled, roasted, steamed, or sautéed. After cutting, immediately place in cold water. Also known as *batata,* Cuban sweet potato, *batata dulce,* or *camote.*

Buying. Choose firm tubers with no breakage or deep dents in skin.

Availability. Year-round, although not plentiful in February and March.

Storing. Keep at room temperature or in a cool dark place. After peeling, keep covered with water and refrigerate.

Freezing. Does not freeze well.

Bread Cuban bread is usually formed into loaves that can be 3 feet long. The texture is coarse compared to Italian or French bread.

Buñuelo A doughnut-like fritter that is typically served with a light sugar syrup.

CALABAZA

Cacerola A casserole or large saucepan.

Calabaza (*Cucurbita moschata*) This vegetable is similar to the pumpkin with its round or sometimes pear-shaped body. The peel is most often orange-colored, but there also are green and striped variations. It possesses a wonderful flavor that is particularly savored when made into a soup or as part of a stew.

Buying. Purchase those that are heavy, as light squash have often lost moisture due to evaporation. Test with your knuckle to look for soft spots since the skin should feel firm and hard. Look for dull rinds; it usually means it was picked when ripe. Often, these vegetables are so large that they are sold by the rough-cut piece. Be certain that the flesh is grainy and moist and essentially stringless.

Availability. Year-round.

Storing. Will keep for months at room temperature.

Freezing. Cook completely, whether by boiling or baking. Cut into pieces, remove skin, and purée the pulp or cut into small chunks. Seal in airtight plastic bags. Will keep 10 to 12 months.

Caldo A broth or soup.

Callaloo (*Xanthosma hastifolium*) Also spelled *callalou.* A vegetable that looks like kale or spinach that was a favorite of the African slaves brought to Cuba. They substituted malanga leaves for these greens, which are available in some Jamaican markets, where the vegetable is most popular. Spinach or kale is a good substitute.

Camarón Shrimp.

Carambola (*Averrhoa carambola*) A stunning, colorful fruit often used as a garnish in *nuevo Cubano* cuisine, and is sometimes called star fruit or five-angled fruit because of its unique shape. It has an ellipsoid surface with five ribs that form star shapes when sliced. The fruit is usually yellow with a thin, slightly waxy skin.

Buying. Look for firm full fruits from 2 to 5 inches long. Avoid those with browned, shriveled ribs. The fruit should ripen at room temperature until it is intensely yellow.

Availability. Year-round, but main season is late summer, fall, and winter.

Storing. Keep at room temperature until ripe, 1 or 2 days, then refrigerate for no longer than 2 weeks.

Freezing. Does not freeze well.

Carne Meat.

Carne Seca Sun-dried salted beef, often called beef jerky.

Carnitas   Crisply roasted cubes of pork with little fat.

Cassava   (*Manihot esculenta*)   See Yuca.

Cazuelitas.   Small casserole dishes made of glazed earthenware.

Ceviche   See Seviche.

Chayote   (*Sechium edule*)   A versatile pear-shaped fruit with smooth to slightly spiny skin. It tastes like a blend of cucumber and squash.

Buying. Look for firm vegetables with no soft or deep brown spots. Small ones tend to be more tender.

Availability. Year-round.

Storing. Refrigerate in vegetable bin. Will keep up to 4 weeks.

Freezing. Does not freeze well.

Cherna or Mero   Grouper.

Chiles   (*Capsicum annum*)   See individual peppers.

Chorizo.   This spicy dry Spanish sausage comes in a variety of styles, but basically it is prepared with pork and seasoned with juniper berries, garlic, paprika, or cayenne pepper. It is a frequent ingredient in paellas and stews, and is popular grilled. Available in different sizes, ranging from 2 to 8 inches, they are usually packaged in cellophane, sometimes in lard.

Christophine   (*Sechium edule*)   See Chayote.

Chuletas   Cutlets or chops.

Cidra   A cider-type wine of Cuba.

Cilantro   (*Coriandrum satirum*)   The roundish and lobed leaves of the coriander plant that possess a bold, robust, sagelike flavor with citrus overtones.

Cinnamon   (*Cinnamonum lauraceae*)   This delightful spice comes from the bark of the cinnamon tree, and grinding your own produces an exceptional flavor.

Cocina   The Spanish word for kitchen, cuisine, and culinary arts.

Coconut   (*Cocos nucifera*)   A round fruit with a hairy brown skin and milk-white flesh that is eaten raw or used to flavor desserts, sauces, stews, and main dishes. The coconut water inside is a refreshing drink. See also Water Coconut.

Buying. Select those that make a sloshing sound when gently shaken; the more water, the fresher the nut. Avoid those with cracked shells and mold in the eyes.

Availability. Year-round.

Storing. A fresh nut will keep up to about 4 weeks refrigerated. Once opened, cover the meat tightly and refrigerate for up to 5 days. The water and prepared coconut milk should be used in 48 hours. Canned coconut will keep almost a week after opening. Dried coconut, tightly covered and refrigerated, will keep 4 to 6 weeks.

Conch   Pronounced "konk." A large delicious mollusk that needs a lot of tenderizing. Serve as *seviche* with bell peppers, onions, and a lime vinaigrette dressing, or breaded and fried until golden brown. When fresh conch is available, it is sold by the piece or the pound. In the United States, it is usually sold in 5-pound frozen packages.

Buying. Conch can be purchased cooked, partially cooked, or uncooked by the piece or by the pound. Estimate two conch per person. Avoid pieces that appear yellowed or freezer burned.

Availability. Frozen at many seafood markets year-round. Fresh in the Caribbean.

Storing. Fresh conch should be used in 24 hours or frozen. Frozen conch will keep well up to 6 months or more.

Freezing. Freezes extremely well.

Coo-coo   A cornmeal mush and okra dish of African origin.

Coriander   (*Coriandrum sativum*)   Use of this term usually refers to the seeds of the coriander plant, which are sold either whole or ground. The fruit are the seeds, which are brownish yellow and lack the sagelike flavor like the leaves, but have the flavor of citrus. The leaves are most often called *cilantro* and are popular as a seasoning and a garnish.

Corn Husks   The inner leaves are used as wrapping for tamales. Dried husks can be purchased and soaked in water to add moisture.

Cracker Meal Finely ground meal processed from crushed saltine crackers. Can be purchased in supermarkets, or make your own. When ground in food processor, 3 dozen crackers make about 1 cup.

Cubanella Pepper (*Capsicum annum*) A mild lemon-yellow pepper available at most Hispanic markets. They are grown almost to the size of a green bell pepper, with an average weight of 3 ounces.

Culantro A flat-leaf herb, similar in taste to cilantro, that is especially good for seasoning bean dishes and prized by many Cuban chefs.

Cumin (*Cominum cyminum*) This spice is used whole or ground in Cuban cooking. The flavor is similar to caraway, but slightly bitter and somewhat hot. A little goes a long way. Whole seeds are spicier than the more commonly found ground spice.

Dasheen See Malanga.

Empanada A delicious pastry turnover, usually crescent shaped and filled with a variety of meat, fish, poultry, or fruit fillings.

Escabeche A pickling method, usually for fish. Fatty full-flavored fish is first sautéed in oil with herbs, spices, and vegetables and then vinegar and oil are added.

Flan A popular custard prepared in many ways and usually served with a caramelized topping.

Frijoles Beans.

Frijoles Colorados Red beans, including kidney beans.

Frijoles Negros Black beans.

Fruta Fruit.

Fruta Bomba See Papaya.

Gallego Refers to the Galician region of Spain.

Garbanzos (*Cicer arietinum*) Beige-colored small beans, also called chick-peas. One of the most popular beans in Cuban cooking.

Garlic (*Allium sativum*) Known as *ajo, sudulunu,* and *vellavengam.* A member of the lily family and a relative of onions, shallots, chives, and leeks, it has a strong and pungent flavor, especially when raw, and is used extensively in Cuban cookery. Frying makes it sweet; when boiled or baked, it becomes mild and creamy. Properly stored, in a cool dark place, it will keep up to 2 months.

Guanábana (*Annona muricata*) See Soursop.

Guava Pineapple quava (*Feijoa sellowiana*); Strawberry guava (*Psidium cattleianum*); Cattley guava (*Psidium guajava*) A pale green very aromatic fruit grown in tropical and subtropical areas such as Florida, Cuba, and Hawaii. It is oval shaped with a thick skin, ranges in size from 2 to 4 inches, and has pink or yellow flesh. Seeds, though bothersome, are edible.

Buying. Purchase those with a strong flowery scent, a smoothness of skin, and a firm give when pressed upon.

Availability. January, February, and May through October.

Storing. Allow to ripen at room temperature for 1 to 2 days. Use ripened fruit within 2 to 3 days.

Freezing. Best frozen as a purée, cooked or not. Place in ice cube trays and freeze, then remove to plastic freezer bags.

Guava Paste *Ate de Guayaba.* A sweet preserve that is made by boiling the pulp until it becomes a solid mass that can be sliced. Used often in baking desserts and pastries. It is sold canned or in 13- to 18-ounce loaves and in most Hispanic markets.

Guinea Hen A West African exotic with a delicious, dry, gamey flavor somewhat like pheasant. Guinea hens typically weigh between 2 and 4 pounds and are prepared much like chicken. They are cooked by many as part of a Santeria ritual.

Harina de Maíz Fine-ground kernels of dried corn. It is often eaten as a porridge, combined with meats and fish, or baked.

Huevos Eggs.

Jamón Ham. *Jamón de cocina,* or cooking ham, is sold at most Hispanic markets in large slices or chunks.

Jícama (*Pachyrrhizus erosus*) This large tuberous tropical plant root looks similar to a huge turnip with a tough outer skin that should be peeled off. It is most often used raw in the more innovative Cuban cooking, especially in salads and salsas where it has a pleasing crunchy texture.

Key Lime, Mexican Lime, West Indian Lime (*Citrus aurantifolia*) Also known as West Indian or Mexican lime. A small yellow-green lime with very tart pulp. The tree grows much slower than that of the Persian lime, so it is difficult to grow commercially and hence, difficult to find. It is used mostly for pies, but is also a substitute for Persian lime on the islands of the Caribbean.

Langosta Also known as *langouste* and spiny lobster. There are no pincer claws on this juicy shellfish, which can be boiled, broiled, or stuffed.

Leche Milk.

Legumbre A pod vegetable. Beans.

Lime, Tahitian, Persian (*Citrus latifolia*) Called *limon* in Spanish, this versatile citrus fruit is used in many ways. When sprinkled on fish or fruits, lime brings out the flavor in the food. When sprinkled on apples, bananas, avocados, and pears it prevents discoloring. Also an attractive garnish. Cubans often call limes "lemons" when speaking.

To get the most juice out of limes, keep at room temperature for at least 1 hour before squeezing. Slice lengthwise to get the best yield. One medium lime contains about ¼ cup juice.

Malanga (*Xanthosoma sagittifolium*) A starchy tuber that has a thin, hairlike brown skin. It is similar to a yam and can weigh from ½ to 2 pounds. The flesh is yellow, beige, or red and the cooked taste is nuttier than a sweet potato. Used like a potato, it is delicious as chips, boiled with butter, or in a variety of soups and stews. When boiled, it turns slightly gray. It is the favorite vegetable of Cuban children.

Malta (Most often the Hatuey brand) Often used in Cuban cooking, it is not readily available except in Hispanic supermarkets. Malta is a non-alcoholic grain-based beverage brewed from water and choice malt, sugar, corn, and hops. It imparts a nice flavor to roasted meats, but it also is widely drunk as a beverage.

Mamey Sapote (*Pouteria sapota*) Fruits are very large, shaped like footballs, and covered with a rough brown skin. Its flesh, when ripe, is bright salmon in color, very sweet and granular. Often used in ice cream and blender recipes.
Buying. Scratch the surface of the skin to determine the color of the flesh just beneath the surface. It should be pink. In 1 or 2 days at room temperature, it will be soft and ready to eat.
Availability. Year-round, but irregular.
Storing. Sapote ripens at room temperature. Store in refrigerator 3 to 5 days after ripening.
Freezing. Puréed fruit will last up to a year in the freezer.

Mango (*Manifera indica*) A sweet fruit of which there are many varieties. It's intensely aromatic when ripe and used much like a peach. When green, often used in stews or chutneys. Most are grown in Florida, California, and Hawaii.
Buying. Skin should be smooth with no pits. When ripe, it will yield to slight pressure, much like the avocado, and ends will have a perfumed aroma. Sizes range from a few ounces to 5 pounds.
Availability. June to September.
Storing. Mango ripens best at room temperature in a closed brown paper bag. When ripe, store in the refrigerator, where it will keep up to a week. When cut, fruit should be tightly sealed.
Freezing. Purée fruit; it keeps 2 to 3 months.

Mangrove snapper A delicious variety of red snapper that is found in the Caribbean sea.

Marisco Shellfish.

Mayonesa Mayonnaise.

Mint (*Minta spicata*) A leafy green plant most often used as a garnish, but it also adds savor to salads and fruit dishes. It is a necessary component of the *mojito,* the famous Cuban rum drink that combines rum with sugar and lime juice and is crowned with copious sprigs of fresh mint.

Mojo A sauce, containing juice, that is prepared both hot and cold and combined with vegetables and other foods. In the hot version, garlic is sautéed in olive oil and mixed with sour orange or lime juice and other seasonings.

Moro Crab A large meaty saltwater crab much enjoyed by the people of Cuba.

Moros y Cristianos The Spanish phrase for the mixture of black beans and white rice, which means "Moors and Christians."

Namé (*Dioscorea alata*) Pronounced "ny-AH-may," a brown-black tropical tuber yam, near in taste to the Irish potato but with a coarser, drier texture. Flesh may be ivory colored, white, or yellow. It's best fried, boiled, sautéed, or puréed. Flavor is more bland than with most tubers and flesh has a very coarse texture. They grow to extremely large lengths.

Buying. Select firm hard tubers with no cracks or soft spots.

Availability. Year-round.

Storing. Will keep for about a week at room temperature. When you use part of a large tuber, cut off an end piece. The cut end will automatically seal itself with the latex-like juices. After peeling, store in the refrigerator in water to which a little lemon juice has been added.

Freezing. Does not freeze well.

Naranja (*Solanum quitosense*) Orange.

OKRA

Okra (*Hibiscus esculentus*) Of African origin, this lime-green small, rocket-shaped vegetable has a furry velvety skin with small seeds in a slippery sack. It's good pickled, fried, and boiled.

Buying. Purchase pods that are about 3 inches long. The longer they get the tougher they are. Choose firm nonshriveled pods with little reddish coloring on their skin. When broken, fresh pods will have a quick snap.

Availability. Year-round. Peak at midsummer.

Storage. Extremely perishable. Buy the day of use or a day before. Cut off stems just before use.

Freezing. Wash and trim off stems. Blanch, chill, and drain. Frozen whole or sliced in airtight plastic bags, okra will keep for 10 to 12 months.

Olive (*Olea europaea*) This small oval fruit, known as *aceituna* or *oliva* in Spanish, is bitter and green when first picked. Curing eliminates the bitterness and produces a variety of flavors, depending on the ripeness of the olive. The smaller olives, called *manzanillas,* are used more frequently in Cuban cooking than the larger ones, called "queens." Both are delicious, yet the manzanilla olive seems to have a more intense flavor.

Ostiónes Juicy small oysters that are typically cooked in *sofrito* sauces.

Plantain

Paella A popular yellow rice dish made with saffron that originated in Spain and contains a variety of ingredients, depending on the region where it is made: shellfish, fish, chicken, and sausage.

Papas or Patatas Potatoes.

Papaya (*Carica papaya*) A sweet, tender melonlike fruit that often has a bright orange flesh. The seeds of the papaya are delicious combined in salad dressings. Good raw or in chutneys, grilled, or in desserts. Green papaya must be cooked and is eaten as a vegetable or in chutneys. The unripe fruit contains papain, a good meat tenderizer. When cooked with roasts in a slow oven, it tenderizes and flavors the meat.
Buying. The fruit should have a little give when pressed.
Availability. Year-round.
Storing. Nonripe fruit will ripen in a warm environment. When ripe, it will keep refrigerated for a few days.
Freezing. Seed and cut into cubes. Pack chunks in a heavy plastic container and cover with a 30 percent sugar syrup. Allow at least ½ inch at the top for expansion. Freezes well for about 10 months.

Paprika Cubans use Spanish paprika, called *pimentón*, which is milder than most. Store in a cool dark place.

Passion Fruit (*Passiflora edulis* [purple]; *Passiflora edulis var. flavicarpa* [yellow]) A small round fruit that resembles a strong brittle-skinned yellow or purple plum with a very aromatic flavor. Its juice is often used in punches, sauces, and sorbets, and is the main taste in the popular Hawaiian Punch. To flavor foods, scoop out the pulp, strain, and add a very little. Also known as purple passion fruit, yellow passion fruit, *maracudja,* and purple granadilla.
Buying. Buy when it is creased but skin is still firm; do not purchase fruits that are cracked or mushy.
Availability. July to March.
Storing. After ripening at room temperature for a few days, store in the vegetable bin of the refrigerator about 1 week.
Freezing. Freeze whole in airtight plastic bags. Extracted pulp can be scooped out, a little sugar added, frozen in ice-cube trays, then placed in airtight plastic bags. Freezing the fruit breaks down the fruit pulp, making it easier to use in sauces.

Pato Duck.

Perejil Parsley.

Pimiento rojo Sweet red bell pepper and pimiento.

Piña Pineapple.

Plantain (*Musa* hybrids, *pardisiaca*) Known as *plátano* in Spanish, this versatile banana is a staple in the Cuban diet. It possesses a different taste at its various stages of development. When the peel is green to yellow, the fruit tastes slightly nutty and starchy, much like a potato, and is most often used to make *tostones,* which function as bread or rolls at a meal. When yellow to black, it has a sweet banana flavor and is often served as a vegetable or dessert. It is always cooked before being eaten.
Buying. Avoid cracked skin and mold, cuts in fruit or ends.
Availability. Year-round.
Storing. Keep at room temperature until they have ripened to the stage desired; then refrigerate. Once ripened, plantains are extremely perishable.
Freezing. When overripe, peel and freeze each plantain in a plastic freezer bag.

Pollo Chicken.

Q

Queso Blanco A white farmer's-style cheese, available at most Hispanic markets and many supermarkets.

R

Rabirrubia Yellowtail, a delicious variety of red snapper.

Ron Rum, the distilled spirit made from the molasses that comes from sugarcane. There are many styles, including light, dark, and black.

Scotch Bonnet Peppers

Saffron (*Crocus sativus*) The most costly spice, it is the dried, orange-colored stigmas of purple crocus, and it takes 40,000 flowers to produce 1 pound. Crush strands and soak in warm water or hot mixtures. Other yellow food colorings that are used in place of saffron are *bijol* and *teresita espiga,* found in most Hispanic markets.

Good saffron comes from Portugal and Spain. Transfer to a clean, airtight glass jar and keep in a dark cabinet. Its flavor and coloring diminishes substantially when exposed to light.

Salsa Sauce.

Salt-dried Cod (Bacalao) Popular because of its superb storage capabilities and unique flavor, this cured fish is an imported staple in many Caribbean and tropical regions. Look for pieces with white flesh; yellowing indicates that it has been poorly kept. Can be purchased with or without bones. Although more expensive, the boneless is much easier to work with. Available packaged in many fish stores and in the freezer section of Hispanic markets. (See page 25 for how to prepare salted cod.)

Salted Beef See Tasajo.

Sangria A delicious, refreshing drink that consists of red or white wine, fruits, sugar, and sometimes brandy. It is usually prepared and served in large glass pitchers.

Sapodilla (*Manilkara zapota*) When ripe, this fruit is sweet and can be peeled like a tomato. It has a yellowish brown pulp with black seeds and is used mostly in salads or eaten raw.

Scotch Bonnet Pepper (*Capsicum annum*) Shaped like a Scotman's bonnet and a close relative of the *habanero*, this hottest pepper on the capsicum scale adds heat and flavor to the new style of Cuban cooking.

Serrano Chile Pepper (*Capsicum annum*) A small, medium-green, intensely potent chile pepper that is sometimes used by talented chefs in the evolving Cuban cuisine. It is found in most Mexican markets and some supermarkets and is especially delicious in guacamole.

Serrucho Swordfish.

Seviche or Ceviche Raw fish "cooked" in citrus juices, usually lime or lemon, and seasoned with herbs and spices.

Sherry. A fortified nonvintage wine made around Jerez, Spain, in the Andalusian region. There is a wide range of colors and flavors.

Side Pork Uncured bacon with a nice flavor that is often used to season meat dishes. It's important to trim off the thick outer skin.

Sofrito A vegetable sauté that is the basis of many Cuban dishes. This sauce is made of onions, garlic, and green peppers, with a multitude of variations to include tomatoes, ham, bacon, side pork, and Spanish sausages. The mixture is usually prepared ahead and stored, then used to season stews, soups, rice, braised dishes, and many Cuban favorites.

Sour Orange or Bitter Orange (*Citrus aurantium*) A rough looking orange with a variegated, thick orange and yellow skin. The tart juice is often used to marinate meats and in marmalades. Available year-round at most Hispanic markets. A good substitute is a combination of orange and lime or lemon juice.

Soursop (*Annona muricata*) A bright green, spiny skinned, cigar-shaped fruit with a tart, delicately flavored edible pulp. You will often find it under the Spanish name *guanábana*. The taste is sour-sweet and refreshing with a distinct aroma.

Buying. The fruit is ripe when soft to the touch.
Availability. Year-round.
Storing. Two or three days at room temperature.
Freezing. The pulp can be frozen and is sometimes available in Latin American markets.

Star Anise (*Pimpinellas anisum*) This fruit, native to China, contains an oil similar to that found in anise. The dried fruits are sometimes used in Cuban cookery to flavor eggs, cheese, certain vegetables, and soups and stews. Combined with cinnamon and bay leaves, it admirably enriches poultry, fish, and game.

Star Fruit (*Averrhoa carambola*) See Carambola.

Tamales The word comes from the Nahuatl word *tamalii.* Corn husks are filled with young corn, pork, chicken, or beef and combined with a *sofrito,* or other vegetables and spices. They are then tied and steamed until the ingredients are cooked through.

Tamarind (*Tamarindus indica*) A fruit extracted from skinny brown pods that tastes somewhat like a plum, yet more sour. It is often used as an ingredient in chutney and is mixed with sugar and ice for a popular summer beverage. The unusual flavor is that which you taste in Worcestershire sauce.

Blocks of tamarind pulp can be purchased in Asian and Indian groceries and are easier to use than the whole fruit, which needs to soak in water in order to remove the pulp from the seeds within the pod.

To make tamarind juice, see page 131.

Tasajo Beef that has been preserved with salt. Often used in *ajiaco,* the popular Cuban stew.

Tocino or Slab Bacon Smoked bacon that is packaged unsliced and used for seasoning many dishes.

Water Coconut (*Cocos nucifera*) With the tropical green husk still together, this young fruit has a flavor and aroma like the ripe coconut. Its meat is jellylike. On the island and in subtropical places, it is the norm to puncture a hole in the shell and insert a straw for drinking.

Yuca (*Manihot escuelenta*) Also known as *cassava,* a sweet, buttery, starchy tuber shaped like an elongated sweet potato with a barklike skin and hard white flesh. It is used much like the Irish potato and is especially good when boiled and covered with *mojo* or fried and served with a cilantro dipping sauce.

Buying. Many Hispanic markets will allow you to cut the tuber to check for freshness. When cut, the interior should be very white with few brown spots. The exterior should be free of mold and cracks.

Availability. Year-round in most Hispanic markets and many supermarkets.

Storing. Keep in a cool place or in the refrigerator. When peeled, it should be covered with water and will keep 1 to 2 days this way.

Freezing. Peel, cut into chunks, and wrap tightly. Yuca keeps well frozen.

Z

Zarzuela A stew or soup of assorted shellfish and finfish.

Cuban Cooking Shopping List

Cuban cuisine owes its distinctive flavor to a wide variety of ingredients that range from the everyday—tomatoes, rice, and beans—to the more unusual—yuca, chorizo, mangoes, and plantains. All of these food items are obtainable in major grocery stores and specialty markets across the United States.

This section serves as a preliminary shopping list as well as a handy reference guide to the English and Spanish names of food items used in the recipes in this book.

ENGLISH	SPANISH
Inglés	Español
allspice	pimienta dulce de Jamaica
almonds	almendras
anchovies	anchoas
angel's hair pasta	cabello de ángel
anise seed	semillas (granos) de anís
apples	manzanas
avocados	aguacates
bacon	tocino
baking powder	polvos de hornear
baking soda	bicarbonato
bananas	bananas, plátanos
basil	albahaca
bay (laurel leaf)	hoja de laurel
beans (string, green)	habichuelas
black turtle	frijoles negros
Great Northern	judías blancas
beef	carne
breaded steak	empanizado
dry salted	tasajo
ground	carne molida de res
top sirloin (very thin)	palomilla
beefsteak	bistec
beer	cerveza
beer (with lemon juice and sugar)	bul
bottled water	agua embotellada
bread	pan
bread crumbs	pan rallado
brisket (beef)	pecho de res
brisket (pork)	pecho de cerdo
butter	mantequilla
cabbage	col, repollo
cake	cake, tarta
sponge, pound cake	panetela
Canadian bacon	tocino, jamón de cocina
capers (small)	alcaparras
caraway seed	alcaravea
cardamom	cardamono
carrot	zanahoria
cashews	semillas de marañón
cassava	yuca, manioc
catsup	salsa de tomate
cayenne pepper	chile, pimienta de cayena
celery	apio
cheese	queso
Cheddar cheese	queso Cheddar
cream cheese	queso crema
cherries	cerezas
chervil	perifollo
chick-peas	garbanzos
chicken	pollo
breasts	pechugas de pollo
leg quarters	muslo y encuentro
other parts	presas de pollo

chile peppers	ajies picantes	grapes	uvas
chives	cebollinos	grouper	cherna
chocolate	chocolate	ham	jamón
chocolate chips	trocitos de chocolate	ham hock	lacón, nudillos de jamón
chorizo	chorizo	horseradish	rábano picante
cinnamon	canela	lemon	limón
clams	almejas	lemon juice	jugo de limón
cloves	clavos de olor	lettuce	lechuga
coconut	coco	lime	limón verde
coffee	café	liver	hígado
condensed milk	leche condensada	lobster	langosta
coriander leaf	cilantro, culantro	mace	macis, macia
seeds	semillas de cilantro	mangoes	mangos
cornstarch	maizena	margarine	margarina
cracker meal	galleta molida	marjoram	mejorana
cream	crema	mayonnaise	mayonesa
cucumber	pepino	meat	carne
cumin (ground)	comino (molido)	stew meat	carne de guisar
curry powder	polvo de curry	milk	leche
dates	dátiles	mint leaves	hierbabuena, menta
dill	eneldo	mushrooms	champiñónes
distilled water	agua destilada	mustard seed	semilla de mostaza
eggs	huevos	nutmeg	nuez moscada
yolks	yemas	nut(s)	nuez (nueces)
whites	claras	oil, olive	aceite de oliva
fennel seed	hinojo	oil, salad	aceite vegetal, aceite de ensalada
fenugreek	aljolva		
fish	pescado	okra	quimbombo
flank steak	falda	olive	oliva, aceituna
flour	harina	onion	cebolla
fritters	frituras	green	cebollinos de verdes
garlic	ajo	orange	naranja
garlic powder	polvo de ajo	sour orange	naranja agría
ginger	jengibre	oregano (ground)	oregano (molido)

oysters	ostras	sardines	sardinas
papaya	papaya	savory	ajedrea
paprika	pimentón	shallot	escalonia, chalotas
parsley	perejil	shrimp	camarón
passion fruit	maracuya, parchita	snapper	pargo
peaches	melocotónes	soda water	agua de seltz
pears	peras	sorrel	acedera, vinagrera
peas	guisantes, chícharos	soup	sopa
baby green	petit pois	sour cream	crema agria
pepper, black	pimienta negra	spearmint	hierbabuena
pepper, green (sweet)	ají verde (pimiento verde)	spinach	espinacas
		star anise	anís estrellado
pepper, hot red	ají picante	sugar	azúcar
pepper, pimientos, morrones	pimiento	Swiss chard	acelgar
		tarragon	estragón
pepper, red (sweet) (not processed)	pimiento colorado, ají rojo	tea	té
		thyme	tomillo
peppermint	menta	tomato	tomate
pineapples	piñas	tomato paste	pasta de tomate
plantain	plátano	tomato sauce	salsa de tomate
green	plátanos verdes	turmeric	cúrcuma
ripe	plátanos maduros	turnip	nabo
plums	ciruelas	vanilla	vainilla
poppyseed	adormidera	veal	ternera
pork	carne de cerdo, puerco, lechón	vegetables	verduras, vegetales, legumbres
chops	chuletas de cerdo	fusilli	fideos
potatoes	papas, patatas	vinegar	vinagre
rice	arroz	walnuts	nueces
rice with chicken (made with beer)	arroz con pollo a la chorrera	wine	vino
		dry white	vino seco, vino blanco
rosemary	romero	dry red	tinto, vino rojo
saffron	azafrán	yuca	cassava, manioc
sage	salvia	zucchini	calabacines
salt	sal		

Substitutions Although you should try to use the ingredients called for in the recipes, there may be times when certain ingredients may be difficult to find. Here's a list of substitutions that you may find helpful.

INGREDIENT	SUBSTITUTION
boniato	white potato
calabaza	summer squash
cilantro	culantro
coconut (fresh)	canned unsweetened coconut
coconut (grated)	1 cup grated = 1⅓ cups flaked
coconut milk (fresh)	1 cup fresh = 3 tablespoons cream of coconut plus ⅞ cup lowfat milk
conch	clams, whelk
garlic	1 clove = ⅛ teaspoon garlic powder
honey	1 cup = 1¼ cups granulated sugar plus ¼ cup additional liquid called for in the recipe
Key lime	1 Persian lime = 3 Key limes
lemon (fresh)	1 lemon = 2 to 3 tablespoons bottled lemon juice
lemon juice (fresh or bottled)	1 teaspoon = ½ teaspoon vinegar
lime (fresh)	1 lime = 2 to 3 tablespoons bottled lime juice
mango (fresh)	peaches
orange (fresh)	1 orange = 6 to 8 tablespoons frozen reconstituted orange juice
orange, sour	equal parts lime or lemon juice and orange juice
red pepper (fresh)	canned whole pimientos
saffron	*bijol* or *bija-bekal* (annatto)
soursop (*guanábana*) (fresh)	canned nectar

Cuban Menus

Here's a selection of menus that will make your meal planning easier and lots of fun.

Grapefruit Varadero
Garden Eggs
Basque Tossed Salad
Fruit Compote with Sparkling Wine

Moro Crab Cocktail
Pork Tenderloin with Mango-Ginger Sauce
Avocado, Tomato, and Onion Salad
Fried Sweet Potatoes
Stewed Guava Shells with Cream Cheese

Picadillo Meat Pies
Boniato Croquettes
Shrimp in Garlic-Wine Sauce
Potato Plantains
Fresh Mango Ice Cream

Grilled Pineapple Rings
Cuban-Style Lobster
Papaya Salad
Natilla

1905 Tossed Salad
Picadillo
Yellow Rice
Minute Fish
Baked Mango Treats

Spiced Marinated Shrimp
Cuban Meatballs
Yellow Rice
Fresh Mango-Almond Bake

Marinated Olives
Sherried Consommé
Fresh Conch and Lobster Seviche
Fried Chicken, Cuban Style
Chayotes in Cheese Sauce with Nutmeg
Soursop Star Mousse

Mojito Cocktails
Braised Meat Soup
Red Snapper, Alicante Style
Baked Yuca
Snow Peas in Olive Oil Sauce
Kisses

Avocado Salsa
Gazpacho
Shredded Beef in Tomato Sauce
White Rice
Fried Sweet Plantains
Diplomatic Pudding

Fried Almonds
Yuca Puffs
Pasta-Style Seafood Paella
Stuffed Eggplant
Gypsy's Arm

Cuban Antipasto: olives, sardines, radishes,
   pickled shrimp
Cuban Creole Stew
White Rice
Fried Yuca-Malanga Puffs

Marinated Conch, Cuban Style
Chicken in Tomato Cups
Easy Corn Salsa
Coconut Bars

Fresh Papaya
Guacamole with Fresh Cilantro and Chips
Chicken and Yuca Bocaditos
Mango Yogurt Ice

Rum Cooler
Gazpacho Festival
Saffron Rice Salad
Tropical Fruit Salad with Avocado Dressing
Banana Flan with Coconut Rum Sauce

Daiquiri Cocktails
Chilled Avocado Soup
Lobster Salad Calle Ocho
Rice Pudding with Raspberries and Toasted
   Almonds

Yucassoise
Beef Bayamo Casserole
Mixed Greens with Sherry Vinegar Dressing
Fried Milk with Pineapple Sauce

Cuban Black Bean Soup
Cuban Special Sandwich
Caramel, Chocolate, and Almond Squares
Mamey Sapote Ice Cream

Techniques

How to Prepare an Avocado

Using a sharp knife, cut the fruit lengthwise around the large seed. Place one hand on each side and twist gently to separate into two halves. Remove the seed by cutting into the fruit, then thrust the tip of the knife gently under the seed to lift it out. Peel and slice, or use whole as a natural container for salads, fillings, or party dips.

How to Cut a Mango

Be careful when handling the mango as some people have an allergic reaction that causes a nasty rash. The risk is in getting the juices on the face or in the eyes, not in eating the fruit. As a general precaution, I recommend wearing gloves when preparing mangoes and, after handling them, washing your hands thoroughly with warm soapy water. Papayas should be handled in the same manner, as they can cause a similar reaction.

Because the flesh of the mango is very slippery, it adheres fiercely to the large flat pit in the center. The best way to slice the mango away from the pit is to lay it on its side and, using a very sharp knife, cut a piece from the top, just above the pit. Cut another slice from the bottom. Set mango upright and slice it lengthwise close to the pit all the way around. Using a paring knife, carefully cut the flesh out of the peel, trying to keep the piece intact. Then slice into sizes you need. To dice the flesh while still in the sections, carefully cut the flesh lengthwise and then crosswise (like a tic-tac-toe board) just to the skin. Turn the skin inside-out and slice the small squares away from the skin into a nonreactive bowl.

You can also peel the whole mango first, then cut off the slices while holding the fruit in one hand. But remember to be careful, as this is a slippery critter.

How to Cut and Peel a Plantain

Plantains can be difficult to peel because the tough skin clings firmly to the fruit. First slice off ¾ inch from each end of the plantain and discard. Next cut the fruit in half lengthwise. Make four evenly spaced slits lengthwise, cutting through the peel from the top to the bottom. Beginning at the corner of each slit and using a sharp paring knife, pull the skin away lengthwise, one strip at a time.

Depending on the recipe, slice the fruit lengthwise or diagonally.

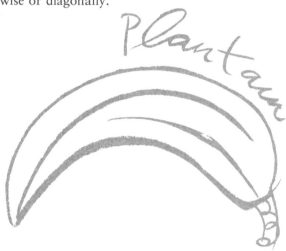

How to Slice a Pineapple

Place the whole pineapple on a cutting board with the leafy stem toward you. Place the knife at the end farther from you and using a firm stroke, pull the knife toward you to cut the pineapple in half. Cut each of the two pieces in half lengthwise.

Cut off the base tip of each piece. Hold the fruit straight up and slice off the fibrous center core with a downward stroke. Stand it up again and cut away the fruit close to the skin. Place the fruit back into the rind and cut into slices about 1 inch apart. Divide those slices in half by cutting down the center of each of the four pieces. Cut chunks in sizes specified by recipes or serve out of the "boat."

How to Open a Coconut

Shake coconut to see that it is mature. It should contain a lot of juice (coconut water) that you will hear sloshing around.

Puncture the coconut with an ice pick by driving the pick into the eyes. Drain the coconut water into a bowl and reserve. Preheat the oven to 350° F.

Place the coconut on the oven rack and heat for about 20 minutes. Remove from oven and tap the shell with a hammer in several places until it cracks into a number of pieces. Insert a sharp paring knife between the shell and the meat to separate the meat from the shell. Trim off the outer brown layer if you wish, but there is really no need to. Slice or grate the fruit, or just eat it raw.

How to Cut a Lime to Retain More Juice

Stand a lime on its stem end and slice in half lengthwise, just slightly off center. Fold and twist the fruit to extract juice. You will be surprised by how much more juice you get out of the lime.

How to Peel Peppers

Roasting Method: Wash and dry bell peppers. Preheat broiler and line the rack with aluminum foil. Place peppers on rack and broil about 2 inches from the heat source, watching carefully and turning constantly until nearly all parts of peppers are charred.

Transfer peppers to a brown grocery bag, or put in a heavy glass bowl. Close bag tightly or cover the bowl with plastic wrap. Allow at least 15 minutes for steam to penetrate and for peppers to cool, then pull off charred skin with a sharp knife.

Cut around the stem with the knife and pull out stem with core. Trim tops, slice peppers in half, and scrape away seeds and white pith. Halve, quarter, or cut into strips, depending on the recipe. To keep, place in a shallow glass dish, cover with olive oil, and refrigerate. Add a few whole peeled garlic cloves for flavor.

Grilling Method: To peel 1 or 2 peppers easily, use a long-handled fork and hold peppers over an open flame. Turn carefully and slowly until skins are thoroughly charred. Then proceed to steam peppers and prepare as outlined in the roasting method.

How to Cook Yuca

Halve yuca lengthwise and remove the fibrous cord running down the center. Insert a paring knife under the peel and pale rose-colored underlayer and pull off both. Cut tubers into small pieces. Place peeled yuca in a large saucepan and cover with cold water. Add a teaspoon of salt and a tablespoon of vinegar to the water. Bring to a simmer over medium-high heat. Each time liquid begins to boil, "shock" it by adding cold water to keep it at a simmer. Simmer about 30 minutes, or until tender. Test for doneness by piercing with the tines of a fork. Pieces will not be tender at the same time, so remove individual pieces when cooked. Drain and serve steaming hot. Yuca will keep in the hot water for about an hour.

How to Prepare Salted Cod (Bacalao)

Cover with cold water and allow to soak for at least 24 hours, changing the water two or three times to remove excess salt.

Drain well and cover once again with fresh water. Bring to a boil and simmer, covered, for 5 to 10 minutes. Drain and cool. When cool, remove bones and dark skin, then proceed with recipe.

How to Extract and Tenderize Conch

To extract conch from its shell, first wash the shell containing the conch under cold running water. Carefully drop 1 to 3 whole shells into 6 quarts of boiling water, adding in 1 tablespoon of salt. Boil for about 40 minutes. Using a fork or other tined instrument, extract the conch meat from the shells, discarding the green matter and shell attached to the meat. You may want to save the shell for decoration. Rinse conch meat in cold water.

Another method of extraction is to knock the bulging side of the shell with a heavy mallet or hammer to help break it. Insert a knife, then twist it around until you feel the muscle being severed from the shell. Grab the piece sticking out and pull hard, then cut away the stomach and tail.

Peel or cut off the tough leathery skin. Pound each piece with the pointed side of a metal mallet until it doubles in size. The resulting piece will be riddled with holes. Drop pieces into boiling water to which salt has been added (¼ cup salt to each 5 pounds of conch). Cover and boil on low heat for 40 minutes.

Another method of tenderizing, especially quick for making conch soups and fritters, is to place the conch in the container of a food processor or blender and process until meat is chopped into tiny pieces.

How to Caramel-line a Mold

Caramelized sugar, also called "burnt sugar," is sugar that is heated and stirred until it melts and turns brown. It is important to work fast when lining a dessert mold since the sugar sets very fast. Some Cuban cooks add a little water to the hot sugar syrup to thin the sauce, but if you do this be certain to add the water carefully to avoid steam burns.

Top-of-Stove Method:
½ cup granulated sugar

Sprinkle the granulated sugar evenly over the bottom of a heavy skillet or saucepan. Cook over medium heat, stirring constantly with a wooden spoon after it begins to bubble and until sugar melts into a syrup. Be cautious not to cook sugar at too high a temperature, or for too long, as it will rapidly turn too dark and/or burn. When melted and syrupy, quickly pour into the bottom of the mold or custard cups to be used. Tilt the mold while syrup is still warm and liquid to coat the bottom and sides. When using a ring mold, it may be necessary to help spread the caramel over the inner sides with a spatula. Allow to cool, then proceed with directions for preparing custard. To clean up syrup that has dried in the skillet, fill the skillet with water and heat it for a few minutes until the hardened syrup dissolves, then wash.

Oven Method:
½ cup granulated sugar

Preheat the oven to 475° F. Evenly cover the bottom of an ovenproof mold or Pyrex custard cups with granulated sugar, about ½ inch deep. Place mold or cups in the oven for about 15 minutes. If sugar is still white in some areas, stir with a wooden spoon to mix together with the browning areas. When all becomes golden brown in color and starts to foam, 3 to 4 minutes, remove from the oven. Grasping mold or cups with both hands, tilt in all directions to allow caramel to coat the sides and bottom.

Basic Recipes

Recetas Básicas

Many Cuban recipes call for seasoning oils and sauces that can be prepared in advance and kept on hand in your kitchen. The most commonly used are annatto oil, *sofrito,* and *mojo.*

Sofrito, the traditional Spanish sauce and the basis for many classic dishes, is a sauté of fresh vegetables in annatto oil, a bright orange coloring agent. *Mojo* is perhaps Cuba's favorite sauce, with citrus as its base, and each cook has a slight personal variation that makes a *mojo* one's own. (All sauces are called *salsas* in Spanish, but the more familiar relish type of salsas are covered in a separate chapter.)

Annatto Oil

Aceite de Achiote

Annatto oil is prepared from olive oil and the seeds of the annatto tree. It is used extensively in Cuban cooking as a seasoning and coloring agent, often in place of saffron. The red clay-colored seeds, also called *achiote* seeds, give a bright orange hue to the oil.

Be sure to prepare this annatto oil over medium-low heat and watch the pan carefully to ensure that the oil does not overcook. This versatile seasoning, used in many *sofrito* recipes in this cookbook, will keep for a month in a tightly closed glass jar in the refrigerator.

Makes about 1 cup

1 cup olive oil
½ cup annatto seeds*

Pour olive oil and seeds in a small heavy saucepan. Cook over medium-low heat for 5 to 6 minutes, stirring until a rich reddish-orange color is achieved. Cool. Strain, discard seeds, and store oil in a covered jar in the refrigerator. Use as directed in recipes.

*Available in most Hispanic specialty markets.

Annatto Paste

Achiote

This paste can be used to season anything from fish to fowl and is often used by cooks of the *nuevo Cubano* persuasion. Different from the classic annatto oil, this paste contains other seasonings, which makes it spicier.

Makes scant 1 cup

½ cup annatto seeds*
¾ cup olive or vegetable oil
2 tablespoons fresh lime juice
2 tablespoons dried oregano
½ teaspoon ground cumin
3 garlic cloves, peeled and mashed
½ teaspoon salt

In a medium saucepan, cover annatto seeds with olive oil and bring to a boil. Reduce heat to medium-low and cook about 5 to 6 minutes. Remove from heat and allow to cool.

Strain annatto seeds from oil and discard, then add lime juice, oregano, cumin, garlic, and salt. Process mixture in the container of a food processor or blender to produce a smooth paste. Add more oil if necessary. Pour into a glass jar and refrigerate.

*Available in most Hispanic specialty markets.

Spanish Sauce

Sofrito Español

There are almost as many variations of *sofrito* as there are Cuban Americans, and it is always kept on hand as an essential ingredient in many classic dishes. The word *sofrito* means "lightly fried," the basic technique used here to make the sauce.

Find the freshest vegetables possible; it will make a difference. A quality smoked ham or baked pork is also important because it adds a distinctive flavor and aroma to the sauce.

Makes about 2 cups

1 tablespoon annatto oil (page 28)
¼ pound smoked ham or pork, chopped
½ cup chopped celery
½ cup chopped onion
½ cup chopped carrot
1 cup chopped very ripe tomatoes
1 tablespoon chopped fresh parsley
1 cup chicken stock (page 36) or defatted
  chicken broth*
2 tablespoons cornstarch, mixed with
  1 cup water
1 tablespoon chopped fresh thyme, or
  1 teaspoon dried
2 bay leaves, crushed
½ teaspoon salt, or to taste
¼ cup dry white wine

Heat a large sauté pan and add annatto oil. When oil is heated and begins to smell fragrant, add the ham or pork, celery, onion, carrot, tomatoes, and chopped parsley.

Cook for about 5 minutes, then slowly add the chicken broth and bring to a boil. Add the cornstarch mixed with water, thyme, and bay leaves and allow to simmer for about 1 hour. Strain. Add salt and wine. Cook another 5 minutes, or until mixture is thick. Cool. Store in a tightly covered glass container. The sauce will keep for several days or longer.

*To defat canned broth, place can in refrigerator. When chilled, open can, skim fat from the surface, and discard fat.

Easy-Does-It Spanish Sauce

Salsa Sofrito para Sazonar

Here's a light and easy variation of *sofrito* that is delicious with eggs, meat, poultry, and fish. **Makes 1 cup**

¼ cup olive oil
  3 garlic cloves, peeled and minced
  1 white onion, finely chopped
  ½ green bell pepper, seeded and finely
    chopped
  ½ cup tomato sauce
  ¼ cup water
  ½ teaspoon ground cumin
  Salt, to taste
  2 teaspoons white vinegar

Heat a medium sauté pan and add olive oil. When oil is heated and begins to smell fragrant, add garlic, onion, and green pepper. Cook until translucent, then add the remaining ingredients. Cook over medium-low heat for 8 to 10 minutes.

Spanish Sauce with Sherry

Sofrito con Vino

There are endless variations of *sofrito*. Some include no wine, others insist that it is essential. Some use canned tomatoes, others insist on fresh. Some use large quantities of bell peppers, others use very little. Many versions include annatto oil for flavoring the olive oil, others do not.

In this recipe, tomato sauce is used instead of fresh or canned tomatoes and sherry is considered an important element for success.

Makes about 2 cups

½ cup annatto oil (page 28)
1 cup minced white onion
1 cup minced green bell pepper
4 garlic cloves, peeled and crushed
1 (8-ounce) can tomato sauce
¾ cup dry sherry
Salt, to taste

Heat a heavy skillet and add annatto oil. When oil is heated and begins to smell fragrant, add onion, green pepper, and garlic. Cook until lightly browned. Add tomato sauce and sherry. Season to taste. Cook over low heat for about 30 minutes.

Creole Seasoning Sauce

Mojo Criollo

Mojo criollo means a Creole salsa, or seasoning sauce. Combinations vary from family to family, while basic ingredients in most consist of parsley, citrus juice, and onion. This very distinctive sauce, an essential in Cuban cooking, is often served over boiled tubers such as yuca or malanga.

This recipe is a favorite of mine because of the tangy sour orange juice, which Cubans use frequently. This cooked version also makes a sublime marinade for chicken, whether baked or grilled.

Makes 1¾ cups

¼ cup olive or vegetable oil
1 medium onion, thinly sliced
8 garlic cloves, peeled and minced
Juice of 8 sour oranges*
2 tablespoons chopped fresh parsley
1 tablespoon chopped fresh oregano
Salt and coarsely ground pepper, to taste

Heat a large skillet or sauté pan and add the olive oil. When oil begins to smell fragrant, add the onion and sauté over medium heat until translucent; be careful not to burn. Add garlic, orange juice, herbs, and salt and pepper. Continue to cook over medium-high heat for about 12 minutes, stirring constantly to blend the ingredients thoroughly. Pour over boiled vegetables and serve steaming hot, or use as a marinade for poultry or meats.

*Substitute 1 cup orange juice mixed with ½ cup lime juice if sour oranges or sour orange juice is not available.

Hot Garlic Seasoning Sauce

Mojo Agrio

Here's another variation of hot *mojo* that my friend Gustavo Herrara in Havana taught me how to make. For many years he was a choreographer for the National Ballet of Cuba, but today he duplicates these skills by orchestrating great meals in his home. When he makes this sauce, he does it over an outdoor fire with red mangrove wood as fuel.

Gustavo strongly emphasized the importance of adding the hot oil at the last minute, combining it with tubers such as organically grown malangas, and serving immediately. The combination was divine. **Makes about 1 cup**

1 whole head garlic, cloves separated
  and peeled
Salt, to taste
¼ pound butter or margarine
1 onion, minced
½ cup sour orange juice*
½ cup olive or vegetable oil, heated

Using a mortar and pestle, crush the garlic well with the salt. Heat the butter in a large sauté pan and add the onion. Cook until translucent, then add the garlic-salt mixture and sour orange juice. In a separate pan, heat the olive oil until almost sizzling. When ready to serve, very carefully pour hot olive oil into the garlic mixture. Stir and pour over vegetables or other foods.

*Substitute ¼ cup lime juice mixed with ¾ cup orange juice if sour orange juice is unavailable.

Fresh Creole Garnishing Sauce

Mojo Criollo Crudo

Both cooked and uncooked versions of *mojo* are popular. This uncooked version uses sour orange with lime and cumin for extra savoriness. The sauce will keep for several weeks if refrigerated in a tightly sealed glass jar. **Makes about 1½ cups**

1 cup sour orange juice* (about 5 oranges)
4 to 7 garlic cloves, peeled
½ cup olive or vegetable oil
½ teaspoon salt
1 teaspoon dried oregano
1 teaspoon ground cumin

Pour sour orange juice into a nonmetallic bowl. In a mortar with a pestle, mash the garlic and add the olive oil. Add this mixture to the juice. Add salt, oregano, and cumin and combine well.

Bottle this mixture and refrigerate for at least 24 hours.

*Substitute ¼ cup lime juice mixed with ¾ cup orange juice if sour orange juice is unavailable.

Coconut Milk

Leche de Coco

If you have difficulty opening a coconut, turn to page 24 and use my oven method to extract the fruit and liquid easily. A 1-pound coconut will yield approximately 3 cups of shredded coconut meat.

This milk adds a wonderful flavoring to many dishes.   **Makes about 3½ cups**

3½ cups lukewarm water with coconut water*
1 coconut, cracked, fruit removed and diced

Place the coconut water and enough lukewarm tap water to equal 3½ cups in the container of a food processor. With the motor running, slowly add coconut pieces to water until mixture becomes almost a purée. Strain the juice through a wire mesh strainer into a bowl. Discard the strained coconut and pour the juice into a glass jar. Cover and refrigerate until ready to use.

*Coconut water is the liquid saved from the inside cavity of the coconut.

Brown Sauce

Salsa Española

This is a traditional roux prepared with beef stock.

Makes 2 cups

1½ tablespoons butter or margarine
1½ tablespoons all-purpose flour
2 cups beef stock

Melt the butter in a small saucepan. Blend in flour with a whisk and stir over low heat until flour is browned. Add the beef stock, bring to a boil, and whisk for 3 to 4 minutes. Reduce the heat and simmer another 30 minutes, continuing to stir.

Easy Blender Garlic Mayonnaise

Aioli Fácil Hecha en Licuadora

Compound mayonnaise sauces can be flavored with any herbs or spices to impart flavor accents in a number of dishes. This recipe uses garlic as its seasoning base and is ideal with soup, fish, vegetables, and eggs.

Be sure to follow directions carefully, especially when adding the oil, or you may wind up with a blender full of garlic soup.

Makes 1¼ cups

5 garlic cloves, peeled and finely chopped
2 egg yolks
Juice of 1 lime
½ teaspoon Tabasco sauce
½ teaspoon salt
1 cup extra-virgin olive oil
1 teaspoon white wine vinegar, mixed with
1 teaspoon cold water

Put the garlic cloves, egg yolks, lime juice, Tabasco, and salt in the container of a food processor or blender. Process for about 5 seconds, until sauce thickens, then slowly add the oil in a thin steady stream while the motor is running. Add the vinegar mixture and blend for a few more seconds, but be careful not to overprocess. Store refrigerated in a glass container that is tightly closed.

Cilantro Mayonnaise

Mayonesa de Cilantro

Cilantro mayonnaise differs considerably from other mayonnaise preparations because it uses milk as the emulsion agent to bind together the ingredients. This sauce enlivens fish or egg dishes and is a hands-down winner when served as a dressing for the deep-fried yuca on page 50. **Makes about 1½ cups**

1 cup light mayonnaise
1 garlic clove, peeled and crushed
1 teaspoon chopped fresh cilantro
¼ teaspoon chopped fresh thyme
¼ cup chopped fresh parsley
¼ cup milk

Put all ingredients except the milk in a glass mixing bowl and blend well. Slowly add milk and mix until smooth. Serve on the side with whole fish, shellfish, or meats.

Island Tartar Sauce

Salsa Tártara Isleña

Here's a contemporary version of tartar where capers, which have been pickled in vinegar, add a lovely pungency to the sauce. **Makes about 1¼ cups**

1 cup light mayonnaise
1 teaspoon lime juice
1 teaspoon lemon juice
1 tablespoon chopped fresh parsley
1 tablespoon grated red Spanish onion
¼ cup drained sweet pickle relish
1 tablespoon drained capers in brine
Salt and pepper, to taste
Fresh parsley sprigs, for garnish

In a medium-size glass bowl, combine the mayonnaise with the lime and lemon juices, parsley, onion, relish, and capers. Season with salt and pepper. Refrigerate, covered, until tartar sauce is chilled and flavors meld, 3 to 4 hours.

Serve in a separate small bowl, garnished with fresh parsley sprigs.

Cilantro-Garlic Sauce

Salsa de Ajo y Cilantro

Cilantro, also called leaf coriander or Chinese parsley, possesses slightly fringed, very delicate leaves that have a distinctive and pungent flavor. You can use the dried version of the herb, but you will never have the same robust flavor.   **Makes about 2 cups**

1 cup (8 ounces) nonfat plain yogurt
½ cup light sour cream
½ cup chopped fresh cilantro
1½ tablespoons chopped fresh parsley
1 teaspoon minced red onion
2 garlic cloves, peeled and pressed
1 teaspoon fresh lime juice
1 tablespoon Dijon mustard
1 tablespoon light corn syrup
2 dashes of Tabasco sauce

In the container of a food processor, blend together the yogurt, sour cream, cilantro, parsley, onion, garlic, lime juice, mustard, corn syrup, and Tabasco for 8 to 10 seconds or more, until dressing is creamy and void of lumps. Refrigerate until slightly chilled. Serve with fish, sandwiches, or salads, or as a dip for crudités.

Cilantro-Lime Sauce

Salsa de Cilantro y Limón Verde

This sauce imparts a tangy flavor to oven-broiled fish fillets, beef, poultry, or nearly any grilled meats.   **Makes about 1 cup**

¼ pound butter or margarine
1 cup chopped onion
3 tablespoons fresh lime juice
¼ cup Worcestershire sauce
Dash of Tabasco sauce
2 tablespoons chopped fresh cilantro
Salt, to taste

Melt butter and add the onion, lime juice, Worcestershire, Tabasco, cilantro, and salt. Simmer for a few minutes over medium-low heat. Remove to a food processor and blend until smooth. Serve hot.

Old Sour

Mojo Agrio Antiguo

This is a favorite hot seasoning sauce of Cubans living in Key West and a staple on nearly every table in town. When bottled, it's so hot that it should probably come with fire extinguisher instructions.

Prepared correctly it enhances seafoods and meats, especially pork. Some say to keep the salted juice at room temperature for 3 to 4 weeks before using it, then store it in a cool dark place. Others use the condiment as soon as it is made and refrigerate the remainder.

Makes 1 pint

    2 cups fresh lime juice, preferably Key limes*
    1½ teaspoons salt
    5 to 6 hot red bird peppers,† sliced

Thoroughly combine the lime juice and salt in a large quart measure with pouring spout. Strain liquid through fine cheesecloth 3 to 4 times. Pour liquid into a large bottle, add the peppers, and allow to age in the refrigerator for 2 to 3 weeks. Covered tightly, it will keep for about 2 months.

*If you have access to Key limes, the flavor will be much more tart.
†Small, very hot peppers. Substitute any hot fresh pepper.

Orange Sauce

Salsa de Naranja

Here's a classic sauce that works especially well with roast pork. The rum adds a grand spray of flavor.

Makes about 1¼ quarts

¼ cup granulated sugar
1¼ cups water
¾ cup chopped fresh ripe pineapple
3 large Valencia oranges, sliced and seeded, rind intact
1¼ cups fresh orange juice
¼ cup fresh lime juice
2 tablespoons plus 1 teaspoon dark rum
2 teaspoons cornstarch, dissolved in 2 tablespoons water

In a medium saucepan, combine the sugar and water and simmer over low heat, whisking constantly to combine. When it begins to thicken and get syrupy, add the pineapple, oranges, orange juice, lime juice, and dark rum and simmer over low heat for about 25 minutes, or until the rinds become softened.

Strain sauce through cheesecloth or a wire mesh strainer. Discard the fruit and pour the sauce back into the pan. Add cornstarch mixture and simmer again, stirring constantly with a wooden spoon until thickened. Serve over roast pork, along with beans, white rice, and plantains.

Chicken Stock

Caldo de Pollo

A corner of my freezer is reserved for plastic bags of various chicken parts and scraps that eventually end up in the stockpot. One can never have enough stock on hand. Canned broths are acceptable in a pinch, but there's nothing like the flavor of homemade. If you have to substitute with a commercial brand, the flavor can be improved by simmering it for a half hour or more with the aromatic vegetables in the following recipe.

When making stock, be sure that it's completely defatted, by placing it in the refrigerator for a few hours or overnight, then removing the solid sheet of fat on the surface. Do not add any salt to the stock. Since it will be used as a base for sauces and soups, often reduced in quantity in the cooking process, any added salt will be greatly emphasized.

Makes about 2½ quarts

- **2 bay leaves**
- **6 basil leaves**
- **6 white peppercorns***
- **6 black peppercorns**
- **1 tablespoon chopped fresh thyme, or**
  1 teaspoon dried
- **8 fresh parsley sprigs**
- **4 whole cloves**
- **5 pounds chicken necks, wings, backs,**
  and feet
- **1½ gallons cold water**
- **1 large onion, diced**
- **2 large carrots, diced**
- **3 celery stalks, diced**
- **1 whole head garlic, cut in half crosswise**
- **2 cups dry white wine**

Make a bouquet garni by tying together the bay leaves, basil, peppercorns, thyme, parsley, and cloves in a cheesecloth bag.

Put chicken pieces in a large stockpot filled with 1½ gallons of cold water, then add bouquet garni and remaining ingredients except the wine. Slowly bring to a boil and reduce to a simmer as soon as boil is reached. Add the white wine and simmer for 2½ to 3 hours, or until reduced by about half and stock has a rich chicken aroma.

Strain stock. Cool uncovered, then refrigerate for a few hours. Remove fat by skimming with a spoon. Will keep in the refrigerator for a few days, but freeze for later use.

*Available at gourmet specialty stores.

Fish Stock

Caldo de Pescado

Here's an easy yet rich fish stock that can be frozen for future use. Although you can substitute bottled clam juice in place of fish stock in many of the dishes, clam juice will not have the same flavor complexity.

You can make your own bouillon cubes by carefully simmering a quart of stock over low heat until it reduces and thickens. Pour the reduced stock into an ice cube tray and freeze. The cubes can be stored in a plastic bag and retrieved as needed. **Makes about 3 quarts**

2 quarts water
1 quart (4 cups) dry white wine
2 whole garlic cloves, peeled
2 onions, chopped
3 celery ribs with leaves
3 bay leaves, cracked
½ teaspoon dried thyme
6 peppercorns, cracked
3 tablespoons chopped fresh parsley
3 carrots, halved
2 medium white onions, halved
1½ pound fish trimmings, heads split
   lengthwise, gills removed

Combine all ingredients except fish trimmings in a large stockpot. Bring to a boil, reduce heat, and simmer for 35 to 40 minutes.

Strain the broth by pressing the vegetables through a sieve to extract all the juices. Add fish trimmings and cook 15 to 20 minutes. Strain out bones and reserve liquid. Freeze in pint-size, quart-size, or cup-size plastic containers.

Easy Fish Stock

Caldo de Pescado Rápido

The best stock is always made from scratch, using fresh fish trimmings. But when I don't have those on hand, this is a good substitute. **Makes 2 pints**

1 tablespoon butter or margarine
1 medium onion, sliced
2 cups water
2 cups bottled clam juice
1 bouquet garni (bay leaf, parsley,
   peppercorns, thyme, and celery)
1 cup dry white wine

Melt butter in a large saucepan. Add onion and sauté until soft but not brown. Pour in water, clam juice, bouquet garni, and white wine. Bring slowly to a boil, skimming off any residue that forms on the surface. Simmer uncovered for 20 to 25 minutes. Remove from heat and allow to cool. Strain through cheesecloth and season to taste. Refrigerate until ready to use.

Appetizers, Dips, and Snacks

Aperitivos, Salseos, y Bocadillos

The selection of Cuban-style appetizers at Cuban cafés across the United States is growing. They can be as simple as fried almonds or a mélange of luscious tropical fruits.

Many appetizers are prepared *en escabeche*, pickled with herb-flavored vinegars and special spices. Some appetizers consist of a small plate with thin slices of meats, cheeses, and pickles, known to Cubans as *entremés*. Some are salsas and dips, often made with avocados or black beans, served with tortilla chips. And there are many other choices—fritters, fried vegetables, and the always popular tamales.

Much like Spanish *tapas*, those little dishes served in Spanish restaurants, Cuban appetizers are often accompanied by fruity rum cocktails or frosty cold beer, called *cerveza*.

Fried Almonds

Almendras Fritas

Almendras fritas, or fried almonds, are a tantalizing way to tune the palate for the feast that follows. Almonds are a favorite of Cuban children and highly valued for their oil, held by many to be as medicinal as chicken soup.

In this easy recipe, slivered almonds are combined with olive oil and just a little hot sauce to enhance the luscious nuttiness. It's important to use fresh almonds and to watch them carefully so as not to overcook. Also, the better the quality of the olive oil, the more fragrant and better the taste. **Serves 8 to 10**

    ¾ cup olive oil
    1 (8-ounce) package raw blanched slivered
      almonds
    ½ teaspoon Tabasco sauce
    Salt, to taste

Place olive oil, almonds, and Tabasco in a large skillet. Turn heat on low and slowly bring up to high heat until the oil is very hot. When almonds start to brown, remove from oil with a large slotted spoon and drain in a large strainer or colander over paper towels. Be careful not to overcook. Sprinkle with salt. Cool slightly and serve.

Marinated Olives

Aceitunas Adobadas

It began as a Spanish tradition, but today, serving olives with cocktails, both in homes and at restaurants, is a daily occurrence. As an appetizer, they are often accompanied by a small glass of chilled dry sherry.

The longer the olives are marinated, the better the flavor. Once marinated, the olives will keep, refrigerated, for 6 to 8 weeks. Be sure to keep them tightly covered. **Makes 3 cups**

    3 (6¾-ounce) jars small unpitted Spanish
      olives in brine (3 cups)
    ¾ cup red wine vinegar
    2 teaspoons fresh oregano
    4 garlic cloves, peeled
    1 teaspoon coarsely grated black pepper
    1 teaspoon Tabasco sauce
    ½ cup lime juice
    ½ cup extra-virgin olive oil
    1 bay leaf, crushed
    3 fresh thyme sprigs, or 1 teaspoon dried

Drain half the brine from the jars of olives and measure and reserve 1 cup. Pour brine into a large glass mixing bowl. Add the red wine vinegar, stir, add the olives, and set olive mixture aside.

Using a mortar and pestle, crush the oregano together with the garlic cloves to form a smooth paste. Add black pepper, then whisk in the Tabasco sauce and lime juice. Add olive oil and whisk to combine well. Pour this mixture into the bowl with the olives. Add the bay leaf. Using a wooden spoon, gently mix together.

Pour olives into a half-gallon glass jar with lid, or separate olives into the three 8-ounce jars in which olives were packed. Add thyme sprigs. Pour liquid to cover to top of olives. Shake well. Store refrigerated, continuing to turn olives several times a week. Use a wooden spoon to remove the olives.

Cuban Meatballs

Albóndigas

A favorite Cuban dish, often served on special occasions but also as an every-day main course, are *albóndigas,* or small meatballs. As an aperitivo, they are a curtain raiser for any special occasion.

This dish has a special zing when made with Pecorino, an Italian cheese with a zestful bite, but any hard grating cheese will work as well. Pickapeppa Sauce, rich with a luxurious tamarind flavor, is available at most supermarkets.

Serves 4 to 6

1 pound very lean ground sirloin
¼ pound smoked baked ham
1 tablespoon minced onion
¼ cup chopped toasted almonds
1 tablespoon chopped fresh parsley
1 teaspoon chopped fresh cilantro
1 large slice day–old Cuban or French bread
¼ cup plus 3 tablespoons dry sherry
2 tablespoons light cream
¼ cup grated Pecorino or Romano cheese
1 teaspoon chopped fresh thyme, or
  ½ teaspoon dried
1 teaspoon chopped fresh oregano, or
  ½ teaspoon dried
1 teaspoon salt
2 dashes of Tabasco Sauce
1 teaspoon Pickapeppa Sauce
3 whole eggs, slightly beaten
¼ cup or less olive oil
1 red bell pepper, seeded and sliced into
  rings, for garnish
Fresh cilantro sprigs, for garnish

In the container of a food processor or blender, combine sirloin, ham, onion, almonds, parsley, and cilantro. Blend well for 10 to 15 seconds, or until a smooth consistency is achieved.

Place bread in a small bowl. Pour ¼ cup of the sherry and the light cream over bread. When liquids are absorbed, crush bread with your fingers into small bits.

Add cheese, thyme, oregano, salt, Tabasco, and Pickapeppa sauces to the meat mixture. Add soaked bread and beaten eggs. Mix thoroughly. Place in refrigerator for 1 to 2 hours. When mixture is chilled, use your hands to form into tiny meatballs, about the size of a quarter.

Heat a large skillet and add olive oil. When oil begins to smell fragrant, add meatballs and brown over a low-medium flame, being careful not to break meatballs. Add the remaining 3 tablespoons sherry, cover the pan, and simmer for 20 to 25 minutes, or until meat is thoroughly cooked.

Serve on a colorful platter garnished with red pepper rings and sprigs of cilantro. Serve with white rice and a fruit salad.

Heat vegetable oil in a deep-fryer to 375° F.

In a large glass bowl, combine the grated cheese, olives, almonds, flour, salt, Tabasco, and paprika. In another mixing bowl, beat egg whites until stiff, then fold in sherry and the cheese-olive mixture. Using the palms of your hands, form small balls, about the size of a quarter, and roll in the cracker meal to coat. These may be refrigerated at this point until ready to serve.

Deep-fry balls until golden. Remove to brown paper bags or paper towels to drain. Sprinkle with fresh lime juice. Serve piping hot.

*Available at most supermarkets, or make your own by processing saltine crackers in a food processor until finely ground—36 saltines make about 1 cup crumbs.

Miniature Cheese Balls

Bolitas de Queso Fritas

I have often noticed that Cuban cooks rarely throw anything away. These cheese balls are good vehicles for using any leftover cheese, and a combination of cheeses makes for even more flavorful *bolitas*. The smoothness of the appetizer is key here—it should be so silky smooth that guests can't help but compliment you.

Use Spanish manzanilla olives for this recipe; it will make a difference. Add a quality sherry and serve with an extra glass for a toast; Tio Pepe from Jerez, Spain, goes well served in a traditional frosted glass.

Keep a bottle of Tabasco handy for those who like an even spicier surge. **Makes about 2 dozen**

Vegetable oil, for deep-frying
**2 cups grated Monterey Jack, Gruyère, or
    combination of other firm cheeses**
**2 tablespoons chopped pimiento-stuffed
    manzanilla olives**
3 tablespoons chopped toasted almonds
3 tablespoons all-purpose flour
½ teaspoon salt
2 dashes of Tabasco sauce
1 teaspoon Spanish paprika
2 egg whites, at room temperature
1 tablespoon dry sherry
1 cup cracker meal*
Fresh lime juice

Chorizo Sausage Cooked in Wine

Chorizo al Vino

Some Cuban cooks still prepare their own chorizo, but most purchase them fresh from a nearby Hispanic market, or in a 3-ounce plastic pressurized bag found today at the deli counter of most supermarkets. The chorizo, a tradition in families of Spanish ancestry, consists of ground pork, Spanish paprika, red wine, sugar, garlic, and vegetable oil or lard. Since the packaged brand is sometimes preserved in lard, it's important to cook off excess fat into the water.

Makes 18 to 22 pieces

1 pound chorizo sausage
1 white onion, cut into small chunks
2 bay leaves
2 cups dry red wine
1 red bell pepper, roasted, peeled, and seeded, cut into 1-inch squares*
1 yellow bell pepper, roasted, peeled, seeded, and cut into 1-inch squares*
1 cup salsa (see salsa recipes on pages 200–205 or use a commercial brand)
Fresh parsley sprigs, for garnish

With a fork, pierce sides of the chorizo sausages to release flavor and juices. Heat a heavy skillet, add sausage, cover, and cook over low heat, turning the sausages frequently until they are plump and quite a bit of the fat has been cooked off. Remove sausages and place them in a large saucepan. Add onion, bay leaves, and wine. Bring to a boil. Reduce the heat, cover, and cook until the sauce is reduced by half, 10 to 15 minutes.

Remove the onion and bay leaves. Cool, then cut into small 1-inch rounds. Place 1 square of each colored roasted pepper on each side of the round and pierce each with an extra long party toothpick. Place on a platter with a small bowl of your favorite salsa in the middle. Garnish with fresh parsley sprigs.

*See page 24 for how to peel peppers.

Pickled Chicken, Havana Style

Escabeche de Pollo Habana

In Spain and the island of Cuba, pickling was originally done because of lack of refrigeration. Some of the recipes developed then became favorites and remain in cooking repertoires today. *Escabeche* usually refers to pickled fish dishes, but the method works equally well with chicken.

Native to Asia, ginger wasn't cultivated in the islands until the Europeans brought it to the New World. Today, white ginger is grown abundantly on the beautiful island of Jamaica, which borders Cuba.

Serves 24 to 30

6 skinless boneless chicken breasts, slightly pounded
1 (3-inch) piece of peeled fresh ginger
2 garlic cloves, peeled and minced
2 bay leaves
¾ cup olive oil
¾ cup white vinegar
2 cups chopped white onion
Salt, to taste
8 to 10 whole black peppercorns
Fresh rosemary and basil sprigs, for garnish

Put chicken breasts in a large kettle of hot water with the ginger. Bring to a boil and cook until chicken is done. Drain and shred the breasts into thin strips.

In a medium glass bowl, combine chicken strips, garlic, bay leaves, olive oil, white vinegar, chopped onion, salt, and pepper. Mix well. Allow to marinate, refrigerated, for 6 to 8 days.

Serve on a colorful platter garnished with sprigs of rosemary and basil.

Pickled Fish, Varadero Style

Escabeche de Pescado Varadero

Fish prepared *en escabeche* is first fried in oil with fresh herbs, spices, and vegetables, then pickled in vinegar. Use a firm slightly fatty fish for this dish since its flavor stands up well to the vinegar and the flesh is not apt to become flaky.

Most Cubans, steeped in tradition, refuse to add spicy peppers to their foods. Yet many have been assimilated into the American craze for peppers of every size and style.

Christopher Columbus had a lot to do with that small bottle of hot sauce sitting next to the chicken croquettes at the local *mercato*. According to past historic records, it was he who also brought the chile pepper, a member of the *Capsicum* genus, back to Spain. Keep in mind when preparing this dish that the heat is centered in the seeds and membrane of the peppers, so remove them if you want flavor but not much heat.

Serves 6

2 pounds red snapper fillets, cut into
  about 12 strips
¼ cup all-purpose flour
1 cup vegetable oil
2 pounds white or yellow Bermuda onions
2 red bell peppers
4 chile peppers, seeds removed (optional)
1 cup water
2 cups white vinegar
Salt, to taste
2 garlic cloves, peeled and chopped
1 teaspoon ground oregano
1 teaspoon ground cumin
3 bay leaves
3 tablespoons Spanish paprika
Fresh cilantro sprigs, for garnish

Heat the oil in a large skillet. Dust fillets with 3 tablespoons of the flour and sauté until fish turns white and flakes. Remove fish from skillet with a slotted spoon and set aside to drain on paper towels. Keep pan with fish drippings on the stove.

Slice onions, red peppers, and chilies into ¾-inch strips and place in a heavy saucepan. Add water, vinegar, and salt and bring to a boil. Remove vegetables from heat while they are still crisp; do not overcook. Remove from heat and stir.

Sauté garlic in the skillet used to cook fillets. Add the oregano, cumin, bay leaves, and paprika. Add the remaining 1 tablespoon flour and combine well using a wire whisk. Slowly add onions, peppers, and chiles with their cooking liquid. The oil may spatter if you work too quickly. Pour this onion mixture over snapper. Cover and refrigerate overnight, or for at least 10 hours. Serve on a beautiful platter garnished with fresh cilantro sprigs.

Marinated Fish with Cilantro

Seviche al Cilantro

Seviche, also spelled *ceviche* and *cebiche*, is a popular appetizer in many Cuban restaurants. Recipes were originally obtained from Latin American countries as well as island neighbors. The dish consists of very fresh raw fish marinated in citrus, usually lime or lemon juice. The acid of the juice "cooks" the fish, firms the flesh, and turns it opaque.

Use a firm fish when preparing *seviche*. Pompano, red snapper, and sole work well. I have used a mild pepper in this dish, but if you prefer fiery peppers, add a small seeded hot pepper, such as a jalapeño. **Serves 4**

1 cup fresh lime juice
½ cup finely chopped onion
4 garlic cloves, peeled and minced
1 green or red bell pepper, seeded
  and minced
½ teaspoon sea salt
1 teaspoon granulated sugar
1 teaspoon chopped fresh basil, or
  ½ teaspoon dried
½ teaspoon chopped fresh parsley
2 fresh cilantro sprigs, chopped
¼ cup extra-virgin olive oil
2½ cups roughly diced raw white fish
Fresh cilantro sprigs, for garnish

Combine all the ingredients except diced fish and blend well. Pour over fish and store in a glass bowl. Cover tightly and allow to marinate in refrigerator overnight, or for at least 8 hours. Turn several times while marinating to distribute juices. Serve garnished with several sprigs of cilantro.

Shrimp in Garlic Wine Sauce

Camarónes al Ajillo

This recipe, Spanish in origin, is a popular dish among Cubans. Fresh lime juice helps to "cook" the shellfish, while olive oil gives added depth. Many cooks sauté the shrimp, but I prefer the golden brown finish broiling affords. Brevity is the key here—don't overcook the shellfish.

Always serve hot and with lots of Cuban bread to dunk in the precious garlic oil.

Makes about 1 dozen

1 pound jumbo shrimp, peeled and butterflied,
  with tails intact
¼ cup olive oil
2 tablespoons clarified butter
6 garlic cloves, peeled and chopped
Juice of 1 lime
Dash of Tabasco sauce
3 tablespoons dry white wine
Spanish paprika
Fresh parsley and lemon or lime slices, for
  garnish

Place shrimp in a medium broiler pan.

Heat a large skillet and add olive oil, then butter. When the butter is melted and oil begins to smell fragrant, add garlic. Sauté over moderately high heat for about 1 minute, or until garlic is translucent but not browned. Add lime juice, Tabasco, and wine. Mix well with a wooden spoon. Pour mixture over the shrimp, saturating all shrimp well.

Preheat the broiler, placing rack about 6 inches from heat. Allow shrimp to marinate for about 20 minutes while broiler is heating.

Sprinkle shrimp with paprika, then broil, turning once or twice until the shellfish turns pink and is cooked through. This will take just a few minutes. Do not overcook. Remove from oven and garnish with fresh parsley and lemon or lime slices. Serve with fancy colored toothpicks.

Spiced Marinated Shrimp

Camarónes Adobados Picantes

L ight green cilantro looks similar to flat-leaf Italian parsley, but possesses a distinct flavor. The herb adds a simple elegance and one-of-a kind flavor to many dishes, and it is readily available in many supermarkets.

The lovely fresh herbs and spices combine with the vinegar to produce a classic dish that can be prepared a few days ahead.   **Serves 8 to 10**

> **5 pounds medium to large shrimp**
> **½ cup pickling spice**
> **1 teaspoon salt, or to taste**
> **2 cups thinly chopped scallions**
> **1 tablespoon chopped fresh cilantro**
> **1 cup vegetable oil**
> **½ cup olive oil**
> **1 cup garlic vinegar, or 1 cup cider vinegar**
>   **with 2 garlic cloves**
> **Juice of 2 limes**
> **1 tablespoon celery seed**
> **Salt and cracked black pepper, to taste**
> **2 dashes of Tabasco sauce**
> **2 onions, thinly sliced**
> **1 lemon, cut into wedges**
> **1 lime, cut into wedges**
> **Fresh cilantro sprigs, for garnish**

To a large heavy kettle, add 4 to 5 quarts water, the pickling spice, and salt. Bring to a boil. Add shrimp and cook until shellfish turns pink. Do not overcook. Drain. Chill. Clean and devein.

In a large Pyrex baking dish, alternate layers of shrimp and scallions. Combine oils, vinegar, lime juice, celery seed, salt, pepper, Tabasco, and onions, then pour mixture over shrimp and scallions. Marinate, covered, in refrigerator for 12 to 15 hours, turning gently three to four times. Serve cold with lemon and lime wedges and garnish with cilantro.

Moro Crab Cocktail

Coctel de Cangrejo Moro

A rmando Gonzalez, who recently came to the United States from Cuba, told me that the best time to catch crabs was late at night with a flashlight and a bag. When the crabs were spotted, hunters would shine the light at them, stunning them sufficiently so they would linger enough to be caught and dumped into the bag.

At night at the beaches of Boca Ciega and Guanabo, he told me, he and his friends would fill a huge bag in just a few hours. After capture, the crabs were placed in wire cages and fed vegetables for a week or more, until they were freed from any harmful toxins from the land or sea.

Fortunately, pasteurized lump crabmeat is easily found at most seafood markets. The simple sauce used here is also excellent when combined with small raw clams or oysters.   **Serves 4**

> **1 pound cooked crabmeat, picked through**
>   **to remove cartilage**
> **8 drops of Tabasco sauce**
> **Juice of 2 limes**
> **3 teaspoons ketchup**
> **Salt, to taste**
> **Fresh parsley, for garnish**
> **1 lime, sliced into 8 wedges**

Mix together the Tabasco sauce, lime juice, ketchup, and salt in a medium bowl. Add the crabmeat and blend well. Serve in small clear glass bowls surrounded by crushed ice. Garnish with parsley and lime wedges.

Marinated Conch, Cuban Style

Cobo Cubana al Estilo Escabeche

O f utmost importance when preparing this dish is the tenderizing of the conch (pronounced "konk"). Whether fresh or frozen, the conch must be beaten well by placing on a solid surface and pounding with a mallet. The process, which takes 15 minutes or more, breaks down the tissue of the muscle and makes it tender and delicious. Frozen conch is readily available at most seafood stores, or it can be ordered for you. Fresh conch is hard to find unless you live near warm waters in which they thrive in abundance, such as Nassau or the Turks and Caicos Islands in the Caribbean.   **Serves 6**

    1½ pounds conch, cleaned
    ½ jalapeño pepper, seeded and diced, or
        ½ Scotch bonnet, seeded
    1 mild cubanella pepper,* or other mild
        pepper
    ½ cup chopped sweet onion
    1 cup chopped green bell peppers
    1 cup blanched, seeded, and diced ripe
        tomatoes
    2 celery stalks, peeled and chopped
    Juice of 6 sour oranges†
    Juice of 4 limes
    Coarsely ground black pepper, to taste
    Radicchio leaves or other attractive salad
        leaves

Tenderize conch by beating it with a heavy metal or wooden mallet for about 15 minutes. Dice conch and place in a large glass bowl. Add peppers, onion, bell pepper, tomatoes, and celery and gently toss with conch pieces. Add sour orange and lime juices. Season with pepper. Allow to marinate for 1 to 2 hours. Drain excess liquid from mixture and serve on glass plates lined with radicchio leaves.

*Available in most Hispanic markets and in many supermarkets.
†If you do not have sour oranges, substitute the juice of 1½ limes and 6 oranges.

Fresh Conch and Lobster Seviche

Seviche de Cobo y Langosta

H ere's a delicious version of *seviche* by Oliver Saucy, chef at the popular Café Max in Pompano Beach, Florida.
   Serves 8 to 10

    2 cups cleaned and diced conch
    2 cups diced poached spiny lobster
    ¼ cup diced Bermuda onion
    ¼ cup diced red bell pepper
    ¼ cup diced yellow bell pepper
    ¼ cup fresh corn kernels
    ¼ cup diced papaya
    2 tablespoons lime juice
    ¼ cup rice wine vinegar
    ½ cup extra-virgin olive oil
    1 teaspoon chopped jalapeño pepper
    1 tablespoon honey
    2 tablespoons chopped fresh cilantro
    2 tablespoons chopped fresh basil
    2 tablespoons chopped fresh mint leaves
    ¼ cup sliced scallions
    1 tablespoon grated fresh ginger
    Salt and pepper, to taste

Prepare the seafood, being certain to wash well. In a medium bowl, combine all ingredients and mix well. Season to taste. Marinate for about 3 hours in the refrigerator, tossing occasionally to mix. Just before serving, check seasonings again.

Shrimp-Buttered Tea Sandwiches

Bocaditos de Mantequilla de Camarónes

A *bocadito* is a miniature sandwich or canapé. These tea-style sandwiches, so popular in the United States in the fifties, made their way to the Caribbean island and were prepared with just about every filling imaginable.

The *bocadito* consists of a thin filling between two slices of bread. Crusts are carefully trimmed with a very sharp knife, and the bread is formed into different shapes. Here's one of my favorite fillings.

Makes 36 canapés

    2 cups cooked fresh shrimp
    ¼ pound butter or margarine, softened
    2 tablespoons light cream
    2 teaspoons fresh lime juice
    ½ teaspoon prepared mustard
    1 tablespoon dry vermouth
    ½ teaspoon chopped fresh parsley
    1 teaspoon salt
    ½ teaspoon Tabasco sauce
    1 loaf unsliced white bread

Combine all the ingredients except bread in a medium bowl and mix together well, or coarsely combine in a blender or food processor.

Remove crusts and cut bread lengthwise into ⅜-inch-thick slices. Spread ¼ cup of the shrimp butter filling on each slice, then roll up and wrap in foil. Repeat with each slice. Chill for 1 to 2 hours. Using a sharp knife, slice into pinwheels about ¾ inch thick.

Chicken and Yuca Tea Sandwiches

Bocaditos de Pollo y Yuca

T his chicken filling has the subtle taste of the yuca tuber, yet is saturated with the lively flavor of ginger. I often serve this spread in pinwheels, but small tea sandwiches prepared with a variety of breads such as pumpernickel and whole wheat are always a big hit, too. For convenience, canned chicken and frozen yuca will save time without sacrificing much flavor.

Makes 36 canapés

    3 skinless boneless chicken breasts
       (about 1 pound)
    1 (2-inch) piece of ginger, peeled
    3 eggs, hard-boiled and finely chopped
    1 cup diced cooked yuca*
    1 tablespoon minced white onion
    ½ cup mayonnaise
    1 teaspoon chopped fresh parsley
    1 tablespoon chopped red pimiento
    ½ teaspoon Tabasco sauce (optional)
    ¼ cup sour cream
    Salt and coarsely ground pepper, to taste

Boil the chicken breasts in water to which ginger has been added. Cook until just done. Do not overcook. Drain and cool chicken. Discard ginger. Put in a food processor and process until chicken is ground. You should have about 2 cups.

In a medium bowl, combine chicken with remaining ingredients and mix together well. Spread on bread rounds, triangles, or squares. Serve immediately or refrigerate spread until ready to use, then bring to room temperature.

*See page 24 for how to cook yuca.

Black-eyed Pea Fritters

Bollitos de Carita

Those Cubans who settled in the Tampa area before the turn of the century were called *Tampeños*. This group, anxious to begin their new life in America, founded quaint Ybor City and began the once very profitable cigar industry there. Today, locals still roll a few cigars, but the focus is on the classic Cuban food served in their restaurants.

One traditional appetizer served at many of the celebrations, particularly at Gasparilla Fest, a huge Hispanic fest held in Tampa in February, are *bollitos,* luscious fritter-style hors d'oeuvres prepared from dried black-eyed peas.

Today many Cubans purchase a *bollito* mix to which you simply add water and drop by teaspoonfuls to fry. They are also good, but don't compare to the flavor of the peas when prepared in the following traditional manner. Of course, skinning the peas takes patience and effort, so ask the kids to help.   **Makes about 5 dozen**

2 cups (1 pound) dried black-eyed peas, soaked in cold water overnight
4 garlic cloves, peeled
½ teaspoon salt, or to taste
Coarsely ground black pepper
1 teaspoon Louisiana Hot Sauce, or a few drops of Tabasco sauce
Pinch of baking soda
Vegetable oil, for deep-frying

Drain the peas, then skin them by rubbing them vigorously, a few at a time, between the palms of your hands. If the skin does not come off easily, use your fingernail or a very sharp paring knife. Don't get discouraged—skinning the peas can take nearly an hour. Put them in a glass bowl.

Add garlic, salt, pepper, hot sauce, and baking soda to the bowl of skinned peas. Pour mixture into the container of a food processor or blender, or you can use a meat grinder. Process several times until mixture is combined well. Transfer to a mixing bowl and beat with an electric mixer at high speed for about 15 minutes, until it has reached the consistency of a smooth cake batter.

Cover and chill for about 2 hours.

Heat vegetable oil in a deep-fryer equipped with a wire basket to 375° F. Preheat oven to 150° F.

Remove mixture from the refrigerator and beat briskly by hand. Drop by teaspoonfuls into the heated oil and fry until balls turn a medium brown, 3 to 4 minutes. Drain on paper towels and then transfer to the oven to keep warm while you finish frying the fritters. Serve the fritters with a glass of dry sherry or beer.

Fried Yuca

Yuca Frita

Yuca, also called *cassava* or *manioc,* looks much like a slim yam and has a rather bland buttery taste. Choose tubers with no soft spots and be sure to keep uncovered at room temperature in a cool dark area that is well ventilated. Using a vegetable scrubber, clean the fresh tubers well before cooking. To prepare, slit the waxed bark (yuca is waxed to preserve it during shipping) lengthwise. Slip a sharp paring knife under the bark and cut away both the bark and the pinkish layer underneath.

Yuca will keep well for a day or two by placing the whole peeled tuber in cold water and refrigerating. It also freezes extremely well.

Yuca is frequently enjoyed at the Cuban table served boiled with a *mojo criollo* (page 30). When there are leftovers, the yuca is often saved and fried in this manner and served as an aperitivo or snack.

Serves 4 to 6

**2 pounds fresh or frozen yuca*, peeled and
   cut into finger–size pieces
½ gallon vegetable oil
Garlic or salt, to taste**

Place peeled yuca in a large kettle of cold water. Bring water to a rolling boil, then add a quart of cold water. Return to the boil and cook until yuca is fork-tender. Drain and blanch in cold water. Place yuca sticks on a tray covered with wax paper, cover with wax paper, and refrigerate overnight.

Drain off any excess water from tray and dry sticks with paper towels. When ready to serve, heat oil to 325° F. Deep-fry yuca until golden brown. Drain on brown paper bags or paper towels. Sprinkle with garlic salt. Serve with cilantro dipping sauce (page 34).

Yuca Puffs

Bollitos de Yuca

Yuca puffs have been prepared by many cooks and chefs throughout the country, but few have perfected them as has my friend Carole Kotkin. For many years, she owned a popular cooking school in Miami and, on many occasions, taught the necessary techniques for cooking tubers to Cubans and Americans alike.

The flavor of this nontraditional recipe is mild and nutlike, capturing the essence of this extremely popular vegetable.

Makes about 35 puffs

**1 pound fresh yuca, peeled and cooked*
2 eggs, well beaten
1 teaspoon baking powder
1 small onion, finely minced
½ red bell pepper, seeded and minced
½ green bell pepper, seeded and minced
1 garlic clove, peeled and minced
Salt and pepper, to taste
1 cup toasted bread crumbs**

Preheat the oven to 400° F.

Place cooked yuca in a mixing bowl and mash, using a potato ricer or food mill. Add eggs, baking powder, onion, peppers, garlic, and salt and pepper and mix thoroughly.

Using your hands, shape mixture into 1½-inch balls and roll each one in bread crumbs, coating evenly.

Place puffs on a well-greased baking pan and bake until golden brown, about 15 minutes. Serve as an hors d'oeuvre or as an accompaniment to a main dish.

*See page 24 for how to cook yuca.

Grilled Pineapple Rings

Ruedas de Piña Asadas à la Parrilla

Cuban families often serve pineapple at the beginning of a meal—a centuries-old sign of hospitality and a harbinger of the fragrant feast to follow. Buy the ripest pineapple available, since it will not ripen once harvested. You can test for ripeness by sniffing at the bottom end of the fruit for a full fruity aroma; also a slight give indicates it is ripe.

This recipe also works well under the broiler, but be careful to place 3 to 4 inches from the flame.   **Serves 4**

    1 fresh pineapple, peeled, cored, and
      cut into 8 equal rings
    ½ cup plus 1 tablespoon brown sugar
    2 tablespoons butter or margarine
    1 tablespoon olive oil
    ½ cup light sour cream

Dip pineapple rings into the ½ cup brown sugar to coat evenly. Heat a large skillet and add the oil and butter. When butter has melted and oil is fragrant, sauté the rings until golden brown. Using tongs, place on a hot grill for a few minutes to finish. Remove from the grill and place a dab of sour cream in the hole of the pineapple and a pinch of brown sugar on top of the cream. Serve hot.

Unripe Plantain Chips

Mariquitas de Plátanos

Plantain chips are popular today throughout the United States and the Caribbean. I have enjoyed them at a myriad of eateries, from La Esquina de Tejas in Little Havana, Miami, to Lola in New York City. There are many packaged varieties available today, but they don't compare to the fresh crisp taste of just-cooked chips.   **Makes 4 to 5 cups**

    4 green plantains, peeled and cut lengthwise
      into paper-thin slices*
    4 to 5 quarts fresh vegetable oil,
      for deep-frying
    Salt, to taste

Soak peeled and sliced plantains in cold water with ice for about 30 minutes so that plantains are very crisp.

Preheat a deep-fryer filled with vegetable oil to 375° F.

Drain plantain slices and place on paper toweling and blot to absorb any excess moisture.

Place a few slices into fryer basket and fry until golden brown. Drain on paper toweling and keep warm in oven until the rest of the batch is done.

Serve in a bowl lined with absorbent paper. Season with salt and serve sour cream or cilantro dipping sauce (page 34) on the side.

*See page 23 for how to peel plantains.

Cottage-Fried Boniato Chips

Hojuelas de Boniato Fritas

One of my extraordinary discoveries while living in Miami was the sweet boniato, a thin-skinned tuber that looks much like the common sweet potato, although the skin is reddish and always mottled. But looks deceive. The white flesh is fluffy, smooth, and dry, a little less sweet than our sweet potato, with a heavenly one-of-a-kind smoothness.

After boniatos are peeled, it's important to put them immediately in a bowl of cold water; otherwise the flesh will discolor very rapidly. Place them in the refrigerator if you aren't going to prepare them immediately.   **Serves 4**

**4 boniatos, peeled and cut into the thinnest
  possible slices
1 quart vegetable oil, for frying
Salt, to taste**

Soak boniato slices in ice water until ready to serve.

Heat the vegetable oil in a deep-fryer to about 400° F. Blot the boniato slices on paper towels, then fry until crisp and golden brown, 1 to 2 minutes. Watch carefully; do not allow to brown. Remove with a slotted spoon and drain on paper towels. Sprinkle with salt and serve hot.

Easy Cheese Croquettes

Croquetas de Queso Faciles

Here's another croquette that makes entertaining uncomplicated, since croquettes can be prepared ahead and simply warmed before serving.

Many Cuban Americans use *queso blanco,* a lovely smooth mild white cheese, or the Spanish-style *manchego,* which has a distinctly sharp bite (the cured is best), but a sharp New York Cheddar also works favorably.   **Serves 8 to 10**

**2 tablespoons Spanish paprika
1 teaspoon salt, or to taste
1 teaspoon ground cumin
2 tablespoons all-purpose flour
2 eggs, beaten with 2 teaspoons oil
¼ cup cracker meal***
**1 pound queso blanco or other semisoft white
  cheese, cut into 1-inch cubes
1 cup olive oil, for frying**

You will need four small bowls for dredging. Place paprika mixed with salt and cumin in one; the flour in the second; the egg mixture in the third; and the cracker meal in the fourth.

Using your hands, roll cheese cubes into small balls. Dip cheese balls into the bowls, starting with paprika mixture, then flour, eggs, and cracker meal.

Chill the cheese balls for a few minutes. Heat olive oil in a small deep saucepan. Fry cheese balls, carefully turning so that croquettes do not break up. Drain on brown paper bags or paper towels and serve piping hot.

*Available at most supermarkets, or make your own by processing saltine crackers in a food processor until finely ground—36 saltines make about 1 cup crumbs.

Mash boniatos by hand or with an electric mixer, then place in a large glass bowl. Add the butter, 2 of the eggs, cinnamon, and granulated sugar and mix well. Using your hands, shape the dough into croquettes by rolling into small logs, about 1½ inches long by ¾ inch wide. Roll the croquettes in the bread crumbs, dip in the 3 beaten eggs, then roll in bread crumbs once more. If you wish to serve the next day, refrigerate at this time, being careful to cover well.

Heat vegetable oil in a deep-fryer or very heavy deep skillet to 375° F. Preheat the oven to 275° F. Fry croquettes until golden brown, 4 to 5 at a time. Drain on paper towels and keep warm on a Pyrex dish in the oven until ready to serve. Sprinkle with fresh lime juice. For a special occasion, serve on a bed of parsley with several sweet sauces, such as an orange marmalade, for dipping.

*Bake boniatos at 400° F for about an hour, as you would a potato.

Boniato Croquettes

Croquetas de Boniato

Croquettes are almost always served on special occasions, yet they are a mainstay at most Cuban cafés and are eaten as a snack, often served with the Cuban coffee. If Mama isn't making them at home, they can be collected at the local grocery, the bakery, or many cafés for under a dollar. All types of fillings are used, ham being the most popular. They're prepared with fish, beef, and cheese, but I prefer those made with boniato, a popular Cuban tuber and one of my favorite vegetables.

Makes about 12 croquettes

3 cups cooked mashed boniatos,* about
  4 pounds
2 tablespoons butter or margarine
2 eggs, slightly beaten
½ teaspoon ground cinnamon
¼ cup granulated sugar
1½ cups fresh bread crumbs
3 eggs, slightly beaten
Vegetable oil, for deep-frying
Juice of 1 lime

Ham Croquettes

Croquetas de Jamón

If a vote were to be taken among Cubans for their favorite croquette, I guarantee you, ham would be the hands-down winner.

This soul-satisfying *aperitivo*, consumed throughout the day by those smitten with love for Cuban food, demands a quality smoked or baked ham; the better the flavor of the ham, the better the croquette.

Making croquettes is a time-consuming although not difficult task. It will take several batches until you become an expert in uniformity. Take your time. Start by making a small round ball, then gently rub it between your hands and smooth into a cylindrical shape. Also, when rolling in the bread crumbs, be sure to coat them evenly so they will brown well.

For a special occasion or party, you can prepare these a day ahead. Cover the uncooked croquettes with plastic wrap until ready to deep-fry.

Makes about 24 croquettes

4 tablespoons butter or margarine

⅓ cup finely minced onion

¼ cup all-purpose flour

1½ cups milk

½ teaspoon ground black pepper

½ teaspoon salt, or to taste

¼ teaspoon grated nutmeg

1 tablespoon chopped fresh parsley

1 tablespoon dry sherry

12 ounces smoked or baked ham, ground* (2 cups)

2 eggs, mixed with 1 tablespoon water

1 cup seasoned fine bread crumbs†

2 tablespoons all-purpose flour

Vegetable oil, for deep-frying

Fresh parsley sprigs

Heat a large skillet and add the butter. When butter is melted, add onion and sauté until translucent and soft. Add flour and whisk to make a roux. Remove skillet from heat. Slowly add milk and whisk to form a smooth sauce. Return to medium heat and cook until sauce is thick and creamy. Add pepper, salt, nutmeg, parsley, sherry, and ham. Combine well and cook for 4 to 5 minutes on low heat.

Pour mixture into an 8 × 8 × ½-inch baking pan and cool in refrigerator so that mixture will be easy to handle. Refrigerate for 2 to 3 hours, or until well chilled.

In a small mixing bowl, beat eggs with water until frothy and pour into a medium bowl. Combine bread crumbs and flour and place in a second bowl. Using your hands, shape ham into logs 1½ inches long and ¾ inch wide. Dip croquettes into beaten eggs, then roll in crumb mixture. Place rolled croquettes on a large jelly roll pan or cookie sheet and cover with plastic wrap. Chill for 2 to 3 hours.

When ready to cook, heat oil in a deep-fryer to 375° F. Fry croquettes until golden brown, 3 to 4 minutes. Drain on paper towels. Sprinkle with fresh lime juice and serve piping hot. Garnish with parsley sprigs.

*Have your butcher grind the ham, or place it in the container of a blender or food processor for 10 to 15 seconds.
†Purchase seasoned crumbs or season your own with salt, pepper, and your favorite herbs and spices.

Heat a large skillet or sauté pan and add the oil. When it is very hot and begins to smell fragrant, add the ham, peppers, onion, and garlic. Sauté until onions are limp. Add ¾ cup of the flour, salt, and pepper. Blend well and add the parsley. Remove from heat and place in the container of a food processor or blender and process until the mixture is pastelike.

Mash the boiled yuca and fold into the vegetable mixture. Refrigerate until firm, 2 hours or a little longer. When firm, roll into small cylindrically shaped croquettes. Roll croquettes in remaining 1 cup flour, then in the egg, and finally in the cracker meal.

Heat oil in a deep-fryer to 375° F. Preheat the oven to 150° F.

Place a few croquettes at a time into the frying basket and carefully lower basket into the oil. When croquettes turn golden brown, after a few minutes, remove and drain on paper towels or brown paper bags. Keep cooked ones warm in the oven while frying the others. Serve with a garnish of fresh parsley sprigs and wedges of fresh lime.

*See page 24 for how to cook yuca.
†Available at most supermarkets, or make your own by processing saltine crackers in a food processor until finely ground—36 saltines about 1 cup crumbs.

Crispy Yuca Ham Croquettes

Croquetas Crujientes de Yuca y Jamón

Along with malanga and calabaza, yuca is one of the most highly revered tubers in the Cuban diet. The rather bland tuber is sweet, buttery, and somewhat chewy; yet it is in perfect harmony with the ham, peppers, onions, and seasonings in these delicious croquettes.

Makes 8 to 10

¼ cup olive oil
½ pound smoked ham, diced
½ cup finely diced green bell pepper
½ cup finely diced red bell pepper
½ cup diced white onion
3 garlic cloves, peeled and mashed
1¾ cups all-purpose flour
Salt and freshly ground pepper, to taste
1 teaspoon finely chopped Italian parsley
1 pound yuca, peeled and cooked*
1 egg, slightly beaten
1 cup cracker meal†
Light vegetable oil, for deep-frying
Fresh parsley sprigs, for garnish
2 juicy limes, sliced into thin wedges

Deviled Crab

Cangrejo Endiablado

Historic Ybor City in Tampa, Florida, is worthy of culinary exploration. In addition to the variety of cuisines stemming from Spanish, Cuban, and Italian pioneers who settled in Ybor around the turn of the century, the culinary pot is touched by Creole, Cajun, and Jamaican influences.

Here's a classic recipe from The Columbia Restaurant, the most famous of the Spanish-Cuban eateries in Ybor City. It's the exact recipe that was sold on the streets of Tampa's Latin Quarter many decades ago, when crab vendors chanted the familiar *"Jaibas calientes, quién las quiere hoy,"* which means, "Hot deviled crab, who wants one today?"

This recipe takes a little work, but it's worth it. For parties, you may wish to make miniature balls.   **Makes 3½ to 4 dozen**

CROQUETTE DOUGH

3 loaves stale white American bread, crusts removed
1 loaf stale Cuban bread, ground very fine and sifted
1 tablespoon Spanish paprika
1 teaspoon salt

FILLING

¼ cup olive or vegetable oil
½ red bell pepper, seeded and minced
4 garlic cloves, mashed
3 white onions, minced
1 teaspoon crushed hot red pepper
½ teaspoon granulated sugar
1 teaspoon salt
One 6-ounce can tomato paste
2 bay leaves, cracked
1 pound fresh crabmeat, picked over and finely shredded

DIP

1 cup cracker meal*
½ cup all-purpose flour
2 eggs, well beaten with ½ cup milk
Salt, to taste
Dash of black pepper
Vegetable oil, for frying

Soak American bread in water for about 15 minutes. Drain off water and squeeze bread until almost dry. Gradually add the ground and sifted Cuban bread until dough is formed. Add in paprika and salt. Mix thoroughly. Form into 1 large ball and place dough in the refrigerator for about 2 hours.

Heat a very large skillet and add the oil. When oil is heated and begins to smell fragrant, add bell pepper, garlic, onions, and crushed hot pepper. Reduce heat and cook slowly 15 to 20 minutes. Add sugar, salt, tomato paste, and cracked bay leaves and combine well. Cover and cook another 15 minutes at a simmer. Add crabmeat and cook for 10 minutes longer. Place crab filling in a bowl and refrigerate, covered, for about 2 hours.

To make the balls, take about 3 tablespoons of the bread dough and press into the palms of your hand. Add a tablespoon of prepared crab filling. Seal as you would a croquette, forming 2 narrow ends. Prepare remaining balls until all dough and crabmeat is used.

Mix together the cracker meal and flour. Combine the eggs and milk with salt and black pepper. First roll croquettes in the cracker mixture, then the egg mixture, then again into the cracker mixture. Place in the refrigerator to chill for about 2 hours.

Heat vegetable oil in a deep-fat fryer to 375° F. Fry the croquettes until golden brown and drain on paper towels.

*Available at most supermarkets, or make your own by processing saltine crackers in a food processor until finely ground—36 saltines make about 1 cup crumbs.

Black Bean Pâté

Pâté de Frijoles Negros

Cuban mothers teach their daughters the techniques of washing, selecting, and cooking black beans in all forms. The emigration of large numbers of Hispanics to our shores has popularized a use of the bean in everything from appetizers to desserts. This recipe, although not traditional, is becoming popular with people of all heritages.   **Makes 4½ cups**

   2 (8-ounce) packages light cream cheese, softened
   3 cups cooked black beans, or 2 (15-ounce) cans, drained
   ½ cup chopped red onion
   2 garlic cloves, peeled
   ½ cup thick and chunky medium salsa*
   1 teaspoon chopped fresh cilantro
   ½ teaspoon coarsely ground pepper
   2 tablespoons Worcestershire sauce
   1 teaspoon Tabasco sauce
   1 tablespoon cold water
   2 (¼-ounce) envelopes unflavored gelatin
   Leafy greens, for lining plate
   1 (8-ounce) container sour cream
   1 tablespoon minced fresh parsley
   1 (4-ounce) jar pimientos, drained and cut into strips

Combine cream cheese, beans, onion, garlic, salsa, cilantro, pepper, Worcestershire sauce, and Tabasco in the container of a food processor or blender and process for about 60 seconds, or until mixture is smooth and well combined.

Place cold water in a small saucepan. Add the gelatin and stir with water to make a smooth paste. Let set about 1 minute and then cook over low heat, stirring constantly with a wooden spoon, until gelatin dissolves. Using a spatula, quickly pour mixture into the bean and cream cheese mixture and process another 40 seconds.

Using a rubber spatula, spoon mixture into a 1½-quart mold, cover, and chill until firm. Unmold (you may need to run warm water over outside of mold) onto a bed of leafy greens. Using a rubber spatula, coat entire mold with sour cream. Sprinkle with chopped parsley and decorate creatively with pimiento.

*Available at most supermarkets, or use the simple salsa on page 202.

Picadillo Meat Pies

Empanadas de Picadillo

Cubans are proud to make their own empanadas for their enjoyment and that of their friends. Empanadas, or fritters, with minced meats and other fillings, are found in many cafés in Hispanic-speaking areas throughout the States. They are always served warm and are snacked on from morning 'til night.

Although many Cubans still prepare these favorite turnovers from scratch, they often purchase frozen dough at the supermarket. Frozen puff pastry and phyllo are a fine substitute if you don't want to take the time to make your own.

There are many variations on this recipe and lard is often used instead of butter or margarine in the dough. Lard does add a special flavor, but it is not a healthful ingredient. I also use fast-rising yeast to hasten the process, although some feel it dilutes the texture; I have never found this to be the case.   **Makes 12 empanadas**

DOUGH

- 1 (¼ ounce package) fast-rising yeast
- 1 tablespoon granulated sugar
- ½ cup lukewarm whole milk
- 1 large egg, slightly beaten
- 1 egg yolk
- ⅓ cup sour cream
- 4 tablespoons unsalted butter or margarine, melted and cooled
- 2½ cups all-purpose flour
- 1¼ cups yellow cornmeal
- Pinch of salt

FILLING

- 2 tablespoons olive or vegetable oil
- 2 tablespoons minced garlic
- 2 jalapeño peppers, drained and finely chopped
- 1 cup finely chopped white onion
- 1 tablespoon minced green bell pepper
- 1 teaspoon ground cumin
- 1 teaspoon ground oregano
- 1 teaspoon cinnamon
- Pinch of allspice
- 1 pound ground round of beef
- ⅓ can tomato paste
- 1 (28-ounce) can plum tomatoes, with juice
- ¼ cup seedless raisins
- ½ cup chopped pimiento-stuffed manzanilla olives
- ¼ cup chopped black olives
- 1 tablespoon small capers, drained and crushed
- ½ teaspoon salt, or to taste
- 1 egg, slightly beaten

To prepare the dough, dissolve the yeast with sugar and ¼ cup lukewarm milk in a large mixing bowl for about 5 minutes. Beat in remaining milk, egg, egg yolk, sour cream, and butter.

Add 2 cups of the flour, the cornmeal, and salt. With the dough hook of a mixer, or by hand if necessary, beat mixture until it forms a ball, then knead until smooth. Add as much of the remaining ½ cup flour as necessary to make a smooth and elastic dough; this kneading usually takes about 6 minutes. Form into a large ball, transfer dough to a large oiled bowl, and turn to coat well with oil. Cover bowl with plastic wrap and let rise in a warm place for about 45 minutes, or longer if you are using regular yeast.

To prepare the picadillo filling, heat a large skillet or sauté pan and add the oil. When it begins to smell fragrant, add garlic, jalapeño, onion, bell pepper, cumin, oregano, cinnamon, and allspice and cook over low heat until onion is translucent. Add ground beef and cook over high heat, breaking any large lumps into small pieces. Cook thoroughly. Add tomato paste, canned tomatoes, raisins, green and black olives, capers, and salt. Simmer for about 20 minutes, or until mixture is thickened. Drain off excess fat.

Preheat the oven to 450° F.

Divide dough into 12 balls and roll each to ⅛-inch thickness. Press each with a 6-inch cutter to make an even circle. With a spoon, place about ¼ cup of the filling onto the bottom of dough rounds. Fold in half, carefully enclosing filling. Seal and carefully crimp edges.

Brush beaten egg atop each dough round. Bake for 10 to 15 minutes, or until golden brown. Transfer to a rack and allow to cool.

Easy Garbanzo Bean Dip

Salseo Rápido de Garbanzo

The smoothness and subtle nutty flavor of chick-peas, also known as garbanzo beans, combine with garlic, olive oil, and fresh lime juice for an uncomplicated yet healthful dip. When you don't have time to soak and cook the dried ones, canned chick-peas are a remarkably good substitute.   **Serves 6 to 8**

> 4 cups dried chick-peas, soaked and cooked (page 88)
> 8 garlic cloves, peeled and chopped
> ½ cup extra-virgin olive oil
> 2 tablespoons fresh lime juice
> ½ teaspoon salt, or to taste
> Chopped black and green olives, for garnish

Combine all ingredients except olives in the container of a food processor or blender. Process until mixture is smooth and creamy. Garnish with black and green olives and serve with crisp crackers or melba toast.

Black Bean Dip

Salseo de Frijoles Negros

Cookbooks are saturated with recipes for good appetizers, although not always economical and healthful. The following recipe has both virtues, with the beans supplying important protein and a most inexpensive main ingredient.

As a base for this dip, you can use any of the black bean recipes in this cookbook (which will add superior flavor) or substitute canned beans. They won't be quite as delicious, but they will be good. Just be sure to rinse the canned beans to remove excess salt.

When choosing dried black beans, buy from a grocer who you know turns over his stock. Contrary to many beliefs, beans do go stale. Be sure to remove the beans from the cellophane bag and store them in an airtight glass container in a cool place. A friend of mine who lives in Cuba stores his in pharmacy jars and swears that by using this method they will keep up to a year or more.

Makes 2½ cups

> 2 cups cooked black beans (page 88), drained and mashed
> 1 teaspoon Worcestershire sauce
> ½ cup minced green bell pepper
> 4 tablespoons plain nonfat yogurt
> 1 teaspoon minced onion
> ½ teaspoon Spanish paprika
> Chopped fresh parsley, for garnish
> 1 teaspoon chopped pimiento, for garnish

Combine black beans, Worcestershire, bell pepper, yogurt, onion, and paprika in a medium saucepan. Cook for about 5 minutes. Serve hot with fresh tortilla chips. Garnish with parsley and pimiento.

Black Bean Dip with Simple Salsa

Salseo de Frijoles Negros

con Salsa Simple

Allow a few hours for this *salsa cruda,* or uncooked sauce, to marinate before preparing; the flavors will need time to meld. Dip tortillas first in the bean dip and top with salsa.   **Serves 6 to 8**

> 2 cups cooked black beans (page 88), or
>   1 (15-ounce) can, drained and rinsed
> 1 cup pepper salsa (page 202)
> 4 fresh cilantro sprigs, chopped
> ½ cup sour cream
> ½ teaspoon Tabasco sauce

Put 1 cup beans in the container of a food processor or blender. Add 1 cup of the salsa, the cilantro, and sour cream. Cover and process until chunky, not smooth. If too lumpy, add a little water. Stir in the remaining beans. Add Tabasco to taste.

Serve dip and additional pepper salsa in small separate ramekins with an assortment of flavored tortilla chips and crackers.

Guacamole with Fresh Cilantro

Guacamole con Cilantro Fresco

This guacamole doubles as a salad. Serve on a bed of mesclun with julienned red, yellow, and green bell peppers and chopped ripe tomato.   **Makes about 2 cups**

> 1 large ripe avocado, peeled, pit reserved
> ½ cup minced white onion
> 1 scallion, trimmed and minced
> 3 ripe plum tomatoes, seeded and chopped
> 2 tablespoons fresh lime juice
> 1 tablespoon chopped fresh cilantro
> ½ teaspoon Tabasco sauce, or to taste
> Salt, to taste
> Juice of 1 lemon

Mash the avocado with a fork. Add onion, scallion, 2 of the plum tomatoes, lime juice, cilantro, Tabasco, and salt. Mash and mix together well. To prevent the dip from turning brown, sprinkle with lemon juice and put the avocado pit in the center of the guacamole. Cover tightly with plastic wrap. Should the dip begin to turn dark, fold pit into mixture when ready to serve and it will help to keep dip from turning dark. Refrigerate for 1 to 2 hours.

Bring to room temperature when ready to serve and garnish with remaining tomato. Serve with fresh tortilla chips.

Avocado, Cilantro, and Cheese Dip

Salseo de Aguacate, Cilantro, y Queso

A vocado, cilantro, and Roquefort combine in this easy-to-prepare appetizer to make one of the most savory dips you'll ever experience.   **Serves 4 to 6**

2 large ripe avocados
2 fresh cilantro sprigs, finely chopped
2 ounces imported Roquefort cheese
1 cup sour cream
1 tablespoon light mayonnaise
1 tablespoon very dry sherry
3 drops of Tabasco sauce
3 tablespoons chopped scallion tops
1 tablespoon fresh lime juice
½ teaspoon salt, or to taste
3 garlic cloves, peeled and mashed
½ medium-size red ripe tomato, diced
Chopped fresh cilantro, for garnish

Halve the avocados and remove pits. Carefully scoop out avocado flesh, taking care not to disturb the skin. Place removed avocado flesh in a non-metallic bowl, reserving avocado skin for use as serving bowls. To the bowl, add chopped cilantro, Roquefort cheese, sour cream, and mayonnaise and blend well with a fork, leaving mixture somewhat chunky. Add sherry, Tabasco, scallions, lime juice, salt, and garlic. Blend well. Pour mixture into avocado skins and garnish with tomatoes and chopped cilantro. Serve with freshly fried or baked tortilla chips.

Lime Avocado Dip

Salseo de Aguacate y Limón Verde

W hen Cubans arrived in the United States, they were not accustomed to hot peppers in their food. But many have grown to savor our large assortment of chili peppers—from the datil pepper of northern Florida to the fiery Scotch bonnet (*habanero*) brought here from Jamaica to the wide array of Southwest chiles.

The lime and chile pepper in this guacamole provide a nice counterpoint to the nutty butteriness of the avocado.

Serves 4 to 6

2 large ripe avocados, pits reserved
3 tablespoons fresh lime juice
1 teaspoon chopped hot chile peppers
2 dashes of Tabasco sauce
½ teaspoon salt, or to taste
1 tablespoon minced red onion
1 teaspoon mashed garlic
½ medium-size ripe tomato, diced

Prepare dip about 1 hour before you intend to serve it. Peel and mash avocados with a fork or in a food processor; do not purée. Add remaining ingredients and blend well. Sprinkle with lemon juice and put the avocado pits in the dip to prevent browning. Chill. Serve with freshly fried tortilla chips or garlic-flavored melba crackers.

Tamales with Pork and Chorizo

Tamales de Puerco y Chorizo

When preparing tamales, it is important to be flexible in adjusting the recipe for the corn's consistency. If the corn is not young enough, the mixture will not hold up while being boiled. Adding a little cornmeal to the mixture works well for me. It makes the mixture stay together during the boiling process.

Here's a modern version of the classic recipe. Instead of tomato sauce I have used tomato paste for a more piquant flavor, framing the richness of the chorizo, the popular smoked spiced sausage.

Makes about 2 dozen

2 tablespoons olive oil
2 green bell peppers, seeded and chopped
1 white onion, chopped
3 garlic cloves, peeled and chopped
1 (6-ounce) can tomato paste
1 pound chorizo sausage, ground
1 pound lean pork, chopped and sautéed
Salt and cracked black pepper, to taste
25 ears young fresh corn
Cornmeal (optional)

Heat olive oil in a large skillet. When oil smells fragrant, add peppers, onion, and garlic and cook until onion becomes translucent. Add tomato paste and blend well. Add chorizo and pork and cook for 5 to 7 minutes. Season with salt and pepper and cook until done. Heat for about 2 minutes, then remove from stove and allow to cool.

Husk corn and reserve husks for making tamales. Grate kernels into a large bowl, then transfer to the container of a food processor and process 5 seconds. (If corn is not young enough it will be dry, so add a little milk and cornmeal.) Add to pork mixture.

To prepare tamales, place 2 corn husks on a work surface, overlapping lengthwise. Spoon a heaping tablespoon of the tamale mixture in the center. Roll the husks over loosely, then fold ends inward and tie crisscross with string.

When tamales are made, place in the top of a steamer. Cover husks with a thin cloth towel and steam for about 2 hours.

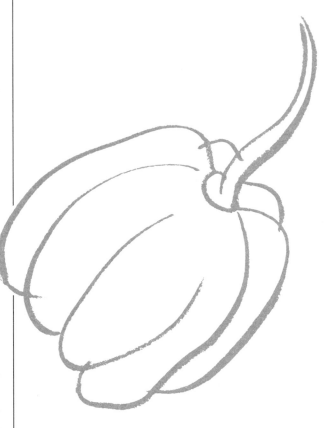

Tamale in Leaf

Tamal en Hoja

Corn, a very important element in Cuba's early days, still has a dominant position in the diet, the tamale being one of its most prideful dishes. *Tamal en hoja,* meaning "wrapped in a leaf," is most frequently served as an appetizer or snack, but is also enjoyed by many Cubans as a principal dish. Since preparing the dish is time-consuming, busy Cubans often purchase tamales already prepared at a local market and simply reheat them. Or they purchase frozen tamales, such as those manufactured at Catalina Finer Foods in Tampa, a national distributor of Hispanic corn-based products. Its "boil-in-bag-style tamales" are extremely popular and are served without the traditional leaves.

Learning to roll the tamale and secure the leaves is by far the most difficult skill to master in preparing this dish. It will take time.

At Bodequita del Medio, a famous restaurant in Cuba, and in many family-operated restaurants, workers still secure bundles with thin strands of the leaves, but today many are tied with white kitchen string.   **Makes about 8 tamales**

6 medium ears of fresh young corn
¾ cup water
2 tablespoons olive or vegetable oil
1 pound chopped lean pork
4 garlic cloves, peeled and finely chopped
1 onion, finely chopped
1 green bell pepper, seeded and finely
  chopped
½ cup tomato sauce
⅓ cup dry white wine
Salt and pepper, to taste
Cornmeal

To remove husks, first cut around the leaf base with a very sharp knife. This will permit you to unroll the leaves with the curved bases unharmed. Rinse, dry and place in an even pile ready for use. Ties can be formed by stripping the leaves into very thin strands and soaking in water for 8 to 10 minutes so they can gain strength. (You may prefer to tie tamales with kitchen string, an easier and time-saving method.)

Husk corn and reserve husks for making tamales. Grate corn into a large glass bowl. Add water and combine well. If corn is not young enough it will be dry, so you may need to add a little more water or milk and cornmeal.

Heat a large skillet and add the oil. When oil begins to smell fragrant, add pork and cook until done. Then, make a *sofrito* by adding garlic, onion, green pepper, tomato sauce, and wine. Cook until vegetables become translucent. Season with salt and pepper. Remove from stove and allow to cool. Add corn to mixture and blend well. If mixture is too thin, add some cornmeal.

To prepare tamales, place 2 corn husks on a work surface, overlapping lengthwise. Spoon a heaping tablespoon of the tamale mixture in the center. Roll the husks over loosely, then fold ends inward and tie crisscross with strands of husk or kitchen string.

When tamales are made, place in the top of a steamer. Cover husks with a thin cloth towel and steam for about 2 hours.

Pork-Stuffed Plantains

Plátanos Rellenos con Puerco

Plantains are usually eaten fried and served as an accompaniment to main dishes. Yet they are often served for a change of pace as an appetizer.

In this recipe it serves as an alternative to the dough used in empanadas. I have combined traditionally popular plantains in a nontypical *nuevo Cubano* style. Flavors meld more agreeably than you may ever imagine.

Use a lean pork sausage and be sure to drain off the excess fat. It will take some practice to get used to working with the plantain dough; work fast while the dough is still warm. I suggest using the small manzanilla olives because I consider them to be the most flavorful, but you can successfully substitute the larger Queens.

Keeping the peel on the plantain while cooking helps to retain the splendid color of the fruit. If beef is preferred, use tenderloin for the ultimate gourmet treat. The look of this appetizer is similar to a croquette, but since they are large, one per person will suffice. **Serves 8 to 10**

6 yellow plantains, washed, tips cut off
1 teaspoon salt
1 teaspoon granulated sugar
2 tablespoons olive oil
1 pound low-fat pork sausage
½ cup finely chopped sweet onion
2 scallions, finely chopped
½ teaspoon grated nutmeg
1 teaspoon ground allspice
½ teaspoon ground cinnamon
½ cup toasted pine nuts
½ cup all-purpose flour
½ cup pimiento-stuffed manzanilla olives, drained and finely chopped
1 cup seedless raisins

2 tablespoons orange juice
2 tablespoons lime juice
All-purpose flour, for rolling dough
Vegetable oil, for deep-frying

Make a lengthwise cut in the peel of the plantain. Cut the plantain flesh diagonally in 2-inch pieces without removing the fruit.

Place the plantains, peels intact, in a large Dutch oven. Pour in enough water to cover, add salt and sugar, and cook over medium-high heat until plantains are tender but still firm, 40 minutes or more. Drain the plantains and remove and discard the peel. Cool for a few minutes.

Meanwhile, prepare the filling. Heat a large skillet and add the olive oil. When oil is hot, add pork sausage and brown for a few minutes. Drain off excess fat. Add the onion, scallions, nutmeg, allspice, and cinnamon, stirring occasionally until juices form. Add pine nuts, flour, olives, and raisins, stirring until well blended. Cook for about 5 minutes, or until raisins become soft. Add orange and lime juices and stir well. Set filling aside to cool.

After plantains have cooled but are still warm, mash the flesh until smooth in the container of a food processor, or by hand. You should have about 4 cups. Before stuffing the plantains, flour your hands. Take a small portion of the plantain dough, about the size of a golf ball, and shape into an even ball. Using a rolling pin on wax paper, gently flatten the ball into an even circle about 3 inches in diameter. Repeat with remaining dough. Drop a spoonful of the prepared filling in the center of each circle, then fold over the dough, empanada style, to cover the filling. Using the tines of a fork, gently press down outer edges to seal. Dust lightly with flour, pressing flour to stay on plantain dough. Cover with wax paper and chill for 2 to 3 hours.

Deep-fry in vegetable oil at 375° F until browned. Drain on brown paper bag or paper towels. Serve hot with a fruit sauce on the side.

Soups, Chowders, and Stews

Sopas, Potajes, y Estofados

Soups are basic to every style of cuisine known to man, and Cuban cookery is no different. The two distinct styles of Cuban soups are *sopa* and *potaje*. A *sopa* is usually lighter and more delicate and often used to start the meal. A *potaje*, on the other hand, is often served as a meal in itself.

In summer, relief from the heat of the subtropics is satisfied with cold avocado soup or perhaps a gazpacho, passed down from the Spaniards who first came to the island.

Black bean soup, of course, is a classic soup of national acclaim, but garbanzo bean soup is also a favorite delicacy, with its tender white chickpeas and a meat-embellished broth.

Ajiaco is considered by many to be the national dish, with as many variations as there are towns in Cuba. The basics, however, rarely change—meats, tubers, and seasonings.

Use a heavy pot and be creative!

Braised Meat Soup

Sopa de Jigote

This palate-pleasing bouillon for many is traditional at special receptions or parties. I've revised the original recipe slightly to remove the excess fat. There's an added bonus; you can use the leftover chicken, mixed with cream cheese, as a luscious pâté.

Makes about 3 quarts, serving 12

1 (3½- to 4-pound) chicken or other fowl, skin removed
1 pound lean pork or veal bones, or beef knuckle bone
3 carrots
1 celery stalk
1 large white onion, peeled, stuck with 3 cloves
3 large red ripe tomatoes
2 tablespoons chopped fresh parsley
Salt and pepper, to taste
2 ounces dry sherry
Chopped scallions, for garnish

Wash chicken and remove giblets. Fill a soup kettle with 4 to 5 quarts cold water and add chicken, giblets, and pork bones. Bring to a boil, then skim fat and discard. Cook for 3 to 4 hours.

Add the carrots, celery, onion, tomatoes, parsley, and salt and pepper. Cook for 2 hours longer. Strain chicken parts and vegetables and set aside. Allow to cool. Skim fat from the broth and add sherry.

Remove bones and vegetables from meat mixture. In a blender or the container of a food processor, chop the meat, including the liver and gizzard, until very fine.

To serve, reheat the broth. Put a tablespoon of the meat into each cup along with 1 teaspoon chopped scallions. Add the broth and serve steaming hot.

Navy Bean Soup

Potaje de Judías

Nearly every Cuban family has its favorite white bean soup recipe, but I favor this classic version, which originated in Havana. Bacon, together with smoked ham and the garden-fresh flavors of spinach and calabaza, produce a mélange of flavors that work well together to make a remarkable meal in itself.

Serves 6 to 8

1 pound dried white beans, preferably Great Northern
1 bay leaf
1 tablespoon olive oil
4 strips lean bacon, or 1 (2-inch-square) piece of salt pork
¾ pound boneless smoked ham, cut into 1-inch pieces
1 pound calabaza or pumpkin, peeled and seeded
1 white onion, chopped
2 cups fresh spinach leaves, kale, or Swiss chard
Salt, to taste
Chopped fresh parsley, for garnish

Soak and cook beans according to directions (on page 88). Add 1 bay leaf for flavor. Do not drain off the liquid.

Heat a large heavy pot or kettle, and add the olive oil. When oil begins to smell fragrant and sizzles, add bacon and cook until crumbly. Remove bacon and reserve. (If using salt pork, remove after 5 to 6 minutes and discard.) Add smoked ham, calabaza, onion, and spinach to kettle and cook for about 1½ hours. Remove the mixture from the kettle, crush with a fork to break up large chunks, and add to the beans. Add the reserved crumbled bacon. Season with salt and garnish with parsley.

Cuban Black Bean Soup

Sopa de Frijoles Negros Cubana

Black bean soup could easily be Cuba's most famous dish. When properly made, the blend of spices and beans produces a memorable soup. Be sure to garnish each bowl with liberal amounts of raw white onion. For added flavor, complete the feast with extra-virgin oil and a little splash of vinegar. **Serves 6**

2 cups dried black turtle beans
2 green bell peppers, 1 whole, the other
   seeded and chopped
6 quarts water
3 tablespoons olive oil
2 ham hocks
2 cups thinly sliced onion
6 garlic cloves, peeled and crushed
3 tablespoons tomato paste
1 teaspoon ground cumin
1 tablespoon ground oregano
3 bay leaves, cracked
1 tablespoon salt, or to taste
1 teaspoon freshly ground pepper
3 tablespoons chopped fresh cilantro
   (optional)
½ cup red wine vinegar (optional)
1 cup chopped white onion
Extra-virgin olive oil (optional)

Rinse the dried beans thoroughly and pour off all water. Soak the beans and the whole green pepper overnight in 6 quarts of water. The water will turn purple, but do not discard; use this water to cook and color the beans. Add enough water, if necessary, so that it is ½ inch above beans. Discard the green pepper.

Heat a large sauté pan and add the olive oil, ham hocks, sliced onions, remaining chopped green pepper, and garlic. Cook until vegetables are soft. Add to the black beans. Add tomato paste, cumin, oregano, bay leaves, salt, and pepper.

Bring to a boil, reduce heat to a simmer, and cook over low heat until the beans are tender and liquid has thickened, 1 to 1½ hours. Remove meat from bones and return to beans.

Add cilantro and vinegar, if desired, to the beans a few minutes before serving. Serve over cooked white rice and top with chopped onion. Splash with extra-virgin olive oil, if desired.

Garbanzo Bean Soup

Sopa de Garbanzo

A meal at the Columbia Restaurant in Tampa's Cuban district, Ybor City, would hardly be complete without their world-famous Spanish bean soup. It's a delicious and hearty blend of beans, chorizos, and bits of ham. **Serves 8**

½ pound dried garbanzo beans
1 tablespoon salt
¾ pound lean baked ham, cut into
   1-inch chunks
8 ounces salt pork or lean bacon
2 large yellow onions, chopped
6 medium white potatoes, cut into quarters
4 chorizo sausages (3 ounces each), thinly
   sliced

Rinse the beans and remove any bad ones. In a soup kettle, soak overnight or at least 8 hours in cold water with the salt.

Drain the water and add 4 quarts of fresh water. Add the ham and simmer for about 45 minutes.

In a large sauté pan, cook the salt pork and add the onions, stirring constantly. Add to the cooked beans and ham along with the potatoes. Cook until potatoes are done. Remove from heat. Add the chorizos. Serve with crusty Cuban bread.

Easy Garbanzo Soup

Sopa Rápida de Garbanzos

This is an easy version of garbanzo bean soup, using canned beans, which work just as well as dried and are great in a pinch. The addition of potatoes results in a hearty thick soup, almost a stew. It tastes even better when reheated the next day.   **Serves 8**

1 (10-ounce) can garbanzo beans,
   drained and rinsed
2 cups water
¾ cup chopped onion
1 quart chicken stock (page 36) or defatted
   chicken broth*
1 tablespoon chopped fresh parsley
1 teaspoon chopped fresh thyme, or
   ½ teaspoon dried
5 medium white Irish potatoes, peeled and
   cut into quarters
2 bay leaves, cracked
1 tablespoon salt, or to taste
4 slices lean bacon
¾ pound lean baked ham, cut into 1-inch
   chunks
4 smoked chorizo sausages (3 to 4 ounces
   each), thinly sliced

Put the beans, water, onion, stock, parsley, thyme, potatoes, bay leaves, and salt in a large soup kettle. Cook over low heat for about 15 minutes. Set aside.

In a large sauté pan, sauté the bacon and ham. Add cooked bean mixture to the pan and combine well, then cook for another 10 minutes. Remove from heat. Add the chorizo sausages. Serve with crusty Cuban bread.

*To defat canned broth, place can in refrigerator. When chilled, open can and skim fat from the surface.

Calabaza Soup

Sopa de Calabaza

When sliced, calabaza is bright orange, much like a pumpkin. It is sold whole, in which case it may weigh as much as 10 pounds, but most produce managers will cut it into smaller pieces for purchase. This fragrant, golden soup is creamy and perfect for a light meal. For best results, used freshly grated nutmeg.
          Serves 6

3 pounds calabaza, or 3 cups pumpkin purée
1 medium-size ripe tomato, peeled and
   chopped
½ cup minced red onion
3 tablespoons olive oil
2 cups light cream
½ teaspoon granulated sugar
Salt and white pepper, to taste
2 egg yolks
⅓ cup sour cream
½ teaspoon nutmeg

Seed and peel the calabaza with a sharp paring knife. Cut into 5-inch chunks and steam or boil until tender, 6 to 8 minutes. Drain.

In a separate pan, sauté tomato and onion in olive oil until soft. In two batches, place cooked calabaza and onion and tomato mixture in a blender or food processor and process for about 30 seconds, until puréed. In a large mixing bowl, add light cream to processed mixture and stir to blend well. Add sugar, salt, and white pepper and mix well. Add a small amount of the hot calabaza mixture to the egg yolks, beating quickly. Continue beating, adding the eggs slowly to the hot calabaza mixture.

Serve in large flat soup bowls with a dollop of sour cream and nutmeg.

Soak white beans overnight or for at least 8 hours. Drain but reserve the water.

Pour the beans into a 4-quart pot, then add the ham hock, beef, and salt pork. Add the reserved water; if necessary, add additional water to cover beans by ½ inch. Bring to a boil then reduce to a simmer. Skim off foam several times while cooking. Cook over medium heat until meat and beans are tender, 1½ to 2 hours.

Add greens and nutmeg. Cook uncovered over low heat for about 30 minutes.

Heat a 10-inch skillet and add bacon fat. When medium hot, add the onion, green pepper, and garlic and sauté until limp. Add to the soup mixture, then add potatoes, chorizos, and salt and pepper. Cover and cook 45 to 55 minutes, until potatoes are cooked. Remove hocks. Serve steaming hot.

*Substitute 3 tablespoons olive oil, if desired.

Hearty Galician Soup

Caldo Gallego

This recipe originated in the area of Galicia, Spain, and is a staple soup in most Cuban kitchens. The combination of ham, beef, and pork, together with the greens, potatoes, and lusty chorizos, make for a robust dish.

This is the recipe used at Valencia Garden restaurant, which opened in 1927 in Tampa and is still one of the favorite haunts of the area's Cuban-Spanish population.   **Serves 6**

1 cup dried white beans, preferably Great
   Northern
1 (1½-pound) ham hock
½ pound lean beef, chopped
½ pound salt pork
1 bunch turnip greens, washed well and
   chopped
Dash of ground nutmeg
3 tablespoons bacon fat*
1 medium onion, chopped
1 green bell pepper, seeded and chopped
1 garlic clove, peeled and minced
3 white potatoes, peeled and cubed
2 chorizo sausages
Salt and pepper, to taste

Thick Vegetable Soup

Locro

Cubans love squash in as many different ways as the varieties of the vegetable itself. Locro is a classic thick vegetable soup or stew also popular on other Caribbean islands; it incorporates squash as the prime ingredient.

Since every mother passed down the family recipes to her daughters, often only orally, I sampled dozens of variations. This recipe includes the best of each. Some cooks like to add a bit of salt pork, salted dried beef, or fish for added dimension. Calabaza is used here with tomatoes and peppers and garnished with olives and cream cheese balls.   **Serves 4 to 6**

2 tablespoons plus 2 teaspoons olive oil
4 medium-size ripe tomatoes, finely chopped
1 large white onion, finely chopped
1 garlic clove, peeled and finely chopped
1 green bell pepper, seeded and finely chopped
2 pounds calabaza or other yellow squash, peeled and cut into cubes
2 teaspoons red wine vinegar
Salt and cracked black pepper, to taste
¼ cup sliced pimiento-stuffed manzanilla olives
¼ pound cream cheese, formed into small balls

Heat a large sauté pan and add 2 tablespoons olive oil. When oil is hot and smells fragrant, add the tomatoes, onion, garlic, and green pepper. Sauté until just tender. Add the squash. Cover pot very tightly and allow to simmer until the squash is soft, about 25 minutes, being careful to avoid burning since the squash will be cooking mostly in its own juices.

Add the 2 teaspoons olive oil, the wine vinegar, salt, and pepper and stir well. Serve in a large heated flat bowl. Decorate with green olives and small rounds of cream cheese.

Chilled Avocado Soup

Sopa de Aguacate Fría

This spicy chilled avocado soup is so welcome on a hot day. To ensure the fullest flavor, use the ripest tomatoes you can find.   **Serves 6 to 8**

1½ cups chicken stock (page 36) or defatted chicken broth*
4 cups ripe avocado pulp
2 ripe plum tomatoes, peeled, seeded, and finely chopped
1 tablespoon minced garlic
¼ cup minced red Spanish onion
2½ cups heavy cream
¼ cup mayonnaise
1 teaspoon Tabasco sauce
2 tablespoons lime juice
½ teaspoon ground cumin
Salt and white pepper, to taste
Lemon peel, for garnish

Combine the chicken stock with the avocado purée in the container of a food processor or blender. Process 5 to 7 seconds. Add the tomatoes, garlic, onion, heavy cream, mayonnaise, Tabasco, lime juice, cumin, and salt and pepper, processing until all ingredients are puréed and combined well. Refrigerate for a few hours. Stir. Serve cold in chilled bowls. Garnish with lemon peel.

*To defat canned broth, place can in the refrigerator. When chilled, open can and skim fat from the surface.

Cold Fresh Vegetable Soup

Gazpacho Fresco

This mild version of gazpacho is close to the one found in Andalusia in southern Spain, where it originated. The use of extra-virgin olive oil—the first press of the olive—adds an aroma and taste not to be forgotten.

Serves 4

    4 large red ripe tomatoes, peeled and
        quartered
    1 cucumber, peeled and coarsely chopped
    ½ cup chopped white onion
    4 garlic cloves, peeled and crushed
    1 green bell pepper, seeded and chopped
    4 (2-inch) slices day-old Cuban or other
        crusty bread
    1 quart water
    1 tablespoon red wine vinegar
    1 teaspoon Spanish paprika
    Salt and freshly cracked pepper, to taste
    3 tablespoons extra-virgin olive oil
    1 avocado, peeled and cut into slivers, for
        garnish
    2 tablespoons chopped fresh parsley, for
        garnish
    1 onion, 1 tomato, 1 green pepper, 1
        cucumber, and 6 scallions, separately
        minced

In a large glass bowl, combine the tomatoes, cucumber, onion, garlic, green pepper, and bread. Mix together well to form a thick paste. Add water and vinegar. Pour all into the container of a blender or food processor. Process until smooth, 6 to 8 seconds. Add paprika and process a few seconds longer. Season with salt and pepper. Add olive oil and stir. Cover and refrigerate for about 3 hours.

Prepare each serving by ladling into individually chilled bowls or bouillon cups. Garnish with avocado slices and parsley. Pass separate bowls of minced onions, tomatoes, peppers, cucumbers, and scallions.

Cold Vegetable Soup

Gazpacho

This gazpacho takes on the flavor of Cuba by the addition of cilantro or culantro, the long-leaf version with a similar flavor. It is a bit spicier than the usual Spanish versions brought to the islands many years ago. Be sure to allow sufficient time for the flavors to meld.

Serves 4 to 6

    2 (28-ounce) cans plum tomatoes, drained
        and crushed
    1 tablespoon chopped fresh Italian parsley
    2 cucumbers, peeled and diced
    2 green bell peppers, seeded and diced
    1 cup chopped white onion
    3 garlic cloves, peeled and chopped
    1 jalapeño pepper, diced
    2 tablespoons red wine vinegar
    1 tablespoon chopped fresh thyme
    1 tablespoon chopped fresh oregano
    1 tablespoon chopped fresh cilantro or
        culantro
    1 tablespoon ground cumin, or to taste
    Salt, to taste
    2 scallions, thinly sliced, for garnish

Combine all ingredients in the container of a food processor or blender. Process for about 1 minute, until vegetables are well combined but not puréed. Chill for at least 2 hours, or marinate overnight. When ready to serve, process for 1 minute to stir up the flavors. Ladle into chilled bowls and garnish with scallions.

Gazpacho Festival

Festival de Gaspacho

This chilled "salad" soup is a cooling treat in midsummer's heat, and it's easy to prepare. The freshest herbs, blended with finely chopped Spanish onion and bell peppers, contribute a zesty flavor that's enhanced as the mixture chills for a few hours.

You can process your ingredients in the container of a food processor, but hand chopping retains the juices better and produces a gazpacho with more substance. **Serves 4 to 6**

1 tablespoon finely chopped fresh cilantro
2 tablespoons finely chopped fresh thyme
2 tablespoons finely chopped fresh basil
2 tablespoons finely chopped fresh oregano
1 medium red Spanish onion, finely chopped
1 carrot, finely chopped
2 green bell peppers, seeded and finely chopped
1 tablespoon finely chopped red bell pepper
2 cucumbers, coarsely chopped
1 (46-ounce) can V-8 juice
½ cup dry white wine
1 tablespoon salt, or to taste
1 teaspoon ground black pepper
⅓ cup chopped yellow bell peppers, for garnish
⅓ cup finely chopped scallions, for garnish

Put all the ingredients except the V-8 juice, wine, salt and pepper, and garnish in a large glass pitcher. Mix well. Add the remaining ingredients and chill. Serve garnished with chopped peppers and scallions.

Yucassoise

Here's a *nuevo Cubano* variation of the traditional vichyssoise. Prepared in the same style with yuca, or cassava, instead of potatoes and leeks, it's a downright delicious and surprising beginning to a meal. **Serves 4**

4 white onions, thinly sliced
1 teaspoon butter or margarine
2½ cups peeled and diced yuca (cassava)
2 cups chicken stock (page 36) or defatted chicken broth*
½ teaspoon Spanish paprika
Salt and white pepper, to taste
About 2 cups whole milk
About 1 cup heavy cream
Chopped fresh chives, for garnish
Pimiento slices, for garnish

Sauté onions in butter in a heavy large skillet until translucent. Add the yuca, chicken stock, paprika, and salt and pepper. Cover and simmer for 35 to 40 minutes, or until yuca is cooked. Pour mixture into the container of an electric blender. Process for 20 to 30 seconds, or until yuca is puréed. Cool at room temperature for 15 minutes. Add milk and cream, more or less, depending on consistency of the soup, then process for 5 to 10 seconds more. Chill for 1 to 2 hours. Serve in chilled bowls garnished with chives and pimiento slices.

*To defat canned broth, place can in the refrigerator. When chilled, open can and skim fat from the surface.

La-Te-Da
Black Olive Soup

Sopa de Aceitunas Negras La-Te-Da

This is an unusual cold soup that was a favorite of the Cuban population in Key West for many years. Originally named after José Marti, the famous Cuban liberator, locals dubbed it "La-Te-Da," after *La Terrazza de Marti.*

There are hundreds of varieties of black olives to choose from. If you go to a market that sells olives in bulk, taste several and select one you find pleasing.   **Serves 6**

    2 cups chicken stock (page 36) or defatted
      chicken broth*
    ½ cup sour cream
    ½ cup plain vanilla yogurt
    ½ cucumber, peeled, seeded, and chopped
    ½ red bell pepper, peeled, seeded, and
      chopped†
    ½ green bell pepper, peeled, seeded, and
      chopped†
    ½ cup cured,‡ pitted, and sliced black olives
    ½ cup chopped scallions
    2 tablespoons chopped fresh parsley
    Salt and white pepper, to taste
    Worcestershire sauce, to taste
    Tabasco sauce, to taste
    Chopped fresh parsley, for garnish

With a wire whisk, mix together the chicken stock, sour cream, and yogurt. Add the remaining ingredients except the salt, pepper, Worcestershire, and Tabasco. Add those to suit. Serve chilled. Garnish with chopped parsley.

*To defat canned broth, place can in the refrigerator. When chilled, open can and skim fat from the surface.
†See page 24 for how to peel peppers.
‡Uncured olives may also be used.

Sherried Consommé

Consomé al Jerez

The key to the flavor of this light delicious consommé of Spanish origin is the quality of the chicken stock and sherry. You may substitute canned broth, but be sure to place it in the refrigerator to chill, then skim off the fat that gathers at the top.

                                    Serves 6

    1 quart chicken stock (page 36) or defatted
      chicken broth*
    2 garlic cloves, peeled and crushed
    2 tablespoons chopped fresh parsley
    4 ounces dry sherry

Combine all ingredients except the sherry in a large heavy saucepan. Bring to a boil and simmer for about 15 minutes. Add the sherry and cook an additional 4 to 5 minutes. Serve steaming hot.

*To defat canned broth, place can in the refrigerator. When chilled, open can and skim fat from the surface.

Garlic Soup

Sopa de Ajo

In this garlic soup, the basic essence of garlic is imparted to the fragrant olive oil and onions, then spread on pieces of thick bread placed in the soup bowls.

Use the freshest garlic available; it will make a difference in the tangy flavor.

Serves 4

    2 tablespoons olive oil
    10 garlic cloves, peeled and slightly crushed
    ½ onion, chopped
    1 teaspoon salt
    4 thin slices stale Cuban or French bread
    1 quart chicken stock (page 36) or defatted
      chicken broth*
    1 bay leaf
    4 eggs
    Chopped fresh parsley, for garnish

Heat a large skillet or sauté pan and add the oil. When hot, add the garlic cloves and sauté until golden on all sides. Add the onion and cook 4 to 5 minutes longer. Remove the mixture, mash and season with salt, then spread it on bread pieces.

Add the chicken stock and bay leaf to the pan and combine well. Simmer for about 5 minutes. Beat eggs until frothy. Place 1 slice of the garlic-covered bread in each large soup bowl. Remove soup pot from heat and stir in eggs. Pour over bread and serve piping hot. Garnish with fresh parsley.

*To defat canned broth, place can in the refrigerator. When chilled, open can and skim fat from the surface.

Garlic-Tomato Soup

Sopa de Ajo al Tomate

This is the simplest version of my garlic soup recipes and can be prepared on the spur of the moment for a quick lunch dish. The fresh plum tomatoes add a delirious touch.

Serves 6

    2 tablespoons olive oil
    8 garlic cloves, peeled
    2 cups peeled, chopped ripe plum tomatoes
    1 bay leaf
    1½ quarts (6 cups) chicken stock (page 36)
      or defatted chicken broth*
    1 teaspoon salt
    6 slices stale bread, trimmed
    6 large eggs
    1 tablespoon chopped fresh parsley

Preheat the oven to 450° F.

Heat a medium-size saucepan. Add the olive oil and cook the garlic cloves until just soft. Add the tomatoes and bay leaf. Stir constantly over low heat for 3 to 4 minutes. Add the chicken stock and salt. Bring to a boil and cook over medium heat, about 20 minutes longer. Strain and set aside.

Place the bread in 6 individual heatproof dishes. Break an egg over each piece of bread, then strain the soup over. Sprinkle with fresh parsley. Bake for 5 to 7 minutes and serve piping hot.

*To defat canned broth, place can in the refrigerator. When chilled, open can and skim fat from the surface.

Black Chili

Chile Negro

Some chili purists may cringe at this version of their favorite Tex-Mex, but it's rapidly becoming a popular dish among Cubans in this country. If you prefer a vegetable version, omit the beef and pork, replacing them with rice and vegetables of your choice. The cilantro adds a distinctly Cuban flavor to this unusual version of chili. **Serves 8 to 10**

- **1 pound dried black beans**
- **1 large green bell pepper, seeded and halved**
- **1 large green bell pepper, seeded and chopped**
- **1 large red bell pepper, seeded and chopped**
- **4 tablespoons olive oil**
- **2 medium onions, peeled and chopped**
- **3 garlic cloves, peeled and chopped**
- **2 tablespoons chopped fresh parsley**
- **2 tablespoons chopped fresh cilantro**
- **1 pound lean ground beef**
- **1 pound lean ground pork**
- **2 tablespoons mild or hot chili powder**
- **1 teaspoon cumin seed, lightly toasted**
- **1 (16-ounce) can whole tomatoes, drained and crushed**
- **1 cup V-8 juice**
- **Salt and cracked pepper, to taste**
- **1 cup chopped onion, for garnish**
- **1 cup shredded queso bianco or Cheddar cheese, for garnish**

Soak beans for 8 hours or overnight in a large bowl to which a seeded and halved green pepper has been added. Pour beans with their soaking liquid into a large heavy pot or kettle.

Add enough fresh water to cover. Cover and simmer until beans are tender, about 1½ hours. Set aside.

Heat 2 tablespoons of the olive oil in a small sauté pan. Sauté onion until tender, then add the chopped green and red pepper, garlic, parsley, and cilantro.

In a separate large pot or kettle, heat the remaining 2 tablespoons olive oil and add beef and pork. Sauté for about 15 minutes. Drain fat from meat and add the onion mixture. Add chili powder and cook for about 10 minutes.

Add the cooked beans, cumin seed, canned tomatoes, and V-8 juice. Cover and simmer for about 1 hour, then uncover and cook for another 30 minutes. Skim excess fat from top. Season with salt and pepper. Serve with chopped onions and a tablespoon of shredded cheese, if desired.

Cuban Creole Stew

Ajiaco Criollo

After sampling dozens of versions of *ajiaco*, Cuba's national dish, this is my choice for the winning recipe. *Ajiaco* is a thick stew full of vegetables and meats, originally cooked in a large clay pot over an open fire.

This recipe, given to me by my friend Alicia Penabad, is lengthy and looks complicated, but it's really easy. To save time, lay out your ingredients in order. Keep tubers submerged in cold water with a few teaspoons of lemon or lime juice, so they don't discolor before they're placed in the stew. It's also a good idea to add a little lime juice to the *ajiaco* itself to prevent the tubers from turning the water brown. **Serves 8 to 10**

MEAT

¾ **pound tasajo* (salt-dried beef)**
1 **pound lean pork, cut into 1-inch squares**
1 **pound baby back ribs, cut into 2-inch pieces**
1 **pound beef flank steak, cut into 1-inch squares**
6 **to 8 quarts water**

SAUCE

½ **cup olive oil**
1 **large white onion, chopped**
8 **garlic cloves, peeled and minced**
1 **large green bell pepper, seeded and diced**
1 **cup diced red ripe tomatoes**
2 **teaspoons ground cumin**
2 **teaspoons Spanish paprika**
2 **teaspoons black pepper**

HARD VEGETABLES

1 **pound yuca, peeled and cut into 2-inch pieces**
1 **pound namé (white yam), peeled and cut into 2-inch pieces**
½ **pound white malanga, peeled and cut into 2-inch pieces**
½ **pound yellow malanga, peeled and cut into 2-inch pieces**
3 **ears young fresh corn, cut into 2-inch rounds**

SOFT VEGETABLES

1 **pound calabaza or pumpkin, peeled and seeds removed, cut into 2-inch squares**
1 **pound boniato, cut into 2-inch pieces**
2 **green (unripe) plantains, cut into 1-inch pieces**
2 **yellow-black (ripe) plantains, cut into 2-inch pieces**
2 **limes**
1 **pound white potatoes, peeled and cut into 2-inch pieces**

To remove some of the salt, soak tasajo meat overnight in a large kettle filled with 6 quarts water. Change water at least twice. Reserve the last change of water in pan so meat will not have to be salted. Pour off about 2 quarts and reserve for future use in this recipe. The amount left in the kettle will be about 4 quarts.

Remove tasajo from kettle and cut into 1-inch pieces. Remove excess fat and put back into kettle. Bring to a boil and cook on medium-high heat for about 1 hour.

Add pork, ribs, flank steak, and reserved 2 quarts salted water. Cook for about 1 hour, constantly skimming off fat, until meat becomes tender.

Meanwhile, prepare the sauce, or *sofrito*, by adding olive oil to a large heated skillet. When oil begins to smell fragrant and is hot, add onion, garlic, green pepper, tomatoes, cumin, paprika, and black pepper. Combine well and cook 2 to 3 minutes.

When meat is tender, add all the hard vegetables plus the *sofrito* and cook another 45 minutes, or until hard vegetables become soft. Add the soft vegetables, except the ripe plantains and the calabaza, and cook 20 to 25 minutes longer. Add the plantains and calabaza in the last 15 minutes and cook until soft but not mushy.

---

*Available in the refrigerated meat compartment of most Hispanic markets.

The resulting mixture will have a creamy stew-like consistency with all the pieces of meat and vegetables soft, though intact. If a more smooth consistency is desired, 2 or 3 pieces of the vegetables can be mashed and added to the broth during the last few minutes of cooking.

Serve piping hot in large pottery bowls with plenty of crusty Cuban bread.

CALABAZA

Lamb Stew

Estofado de Cordero

E l Bodegon Castilla, located on bustling Calle Ocho in Miami's Little Havana, is a celebrated gathering place of the Latin community. Cubans, Spaniards, Nicaraguans, and others from all over the world visit to sample its comforting home-style dishes. In the thirteen years I've been going to the restaurant, I've often ordered this robust lamb stew. This is a variation of that classic stew that originated in Spain, but is beloved today in Miami's Cuban community.

Serves 4 to 6

2 tablespoons olive oil
2½ pounds cubed lamb, excess fat removed
¼ cup diced white onion
2 garlic cloves, peeled and minced
¼ cup diced celery
¼ cup diced carrots
1 (8-ounce) can stewed tomatoes, drained
1 bay leaf
½ cup dry white wine
½ cup brown sauce (page 32)
Salt and coarsely ground pepper, to taste

Heat a large Dutch oven and add the olive oil. When very hot, add the lamb, onion, garlic, celery, and carrots. Mix together well and sauté for about 10 minutes, until lamb is browned. Add the tomatoes, bay leaf, white wine, and ½ cup brown sauce. Season with salt and pepper. Simmer until lamb is tender, 1½ to 2 hours. Serve in warmed heavy pottery bowls with crusty Cuban bread.

Eggs and Cheeses

Huevos y Quesos

Cuban Americans eat eggs for breakfast on occasion, but are much more likely to enjoy them with cold salads or at buffets and special occasions where they are served casserole style.

Cooking eggs Cuban style means everything from plain fried to a fanciful *revoltillo*, an omelet that can include a myriad of ingredients from zesty chorizos, to freshly caught shrimp and crab. Another favorite, lobster omelet (*tortilla de langosto*), is gratifying both for breakfast or a late night supper.

Festive Cuban Scrambled Eggs

Revoltillo Carnaval

Most of the Cuban families I know like scrambled eggs on the dry side. Although the classic recipe does not call for garlic, I often sauté a few cloves along with the fresh vegetables. Be creative and add other ingredients if you wish.

Serve with toasted Cuban bread spread with olive oil or butter. **Serves 6 to 8**

    1 tablespoon olive oil
    1 tablespoon plus 1 teaspoon butter or
        margarine
    1 medium onion, minced
    2 cups peeled, seeded, and chopped ripe
        tomatoes
    ½ cup chopped green bell pepper
    1 tablespoon chopped fresh parsley
    ½ teaspoon salt, or to taste
    1 teaspoon freshly ground pepper, or to taste
    ¼ cup baby green peas (petit pois)
    6 eggs, well beaten
    ¼ cup shredded cheese (queso blanco, Swiss,
        or Cheddar)
    Chopped fresh parsley and pimiento, for
        garnish

Heat a large skillet or sauté pan and add the oil and 1 tablespoon butter. After butter melts and oil begins to sizzle, add the onion, tomatoes, green pepper, parsley, salt, and pepper. Sauté until vegetables are soft. Drain off excess water. Stir in peas, then the eggs, plus the 1 teaspoon of butter. Stir over low heat until eggs are well scrambled. Serve in a large decorative bowl. Sprinkle with shredded cheese and top with chopped pimiento and parsley.

Ranch-Style Eggs

Huevos Rancheros

Here's a great way to start the day. The addition of black beans makes this dish decidedly Cuban. Make it mild or with hot peppers, such as jalapeño, for added zest.

Serves 4

RANCHERO SAUCE

    Olive oil, for frying
    2 tablespoons minced onion
    2 tablespoons diced green or red bell pepper
    1 bay leaf
    Tabasco sauce, to taste

    4 large corn tortillas
    Olive oil, for frying
    8 eggs
    1 cup shredded sharp Cheddar cheese

To prepare ranchero sauce, heat a large skillet and add the olive oil. When the oil begins to smell fragrant, add onion, pepper, and bay leaf. Sauté until vegetables are lightly cooked. Add Tabasco.

Brown each tortilla lightly on both sides in olive oil in a large skillet. Break 2 eggs on top of each tortilla. Pour ranchero sauce over eggs and tortilla. Top with cheese and cover pan to let cheese melt and to cook eggs to desired consistency. Serve with black beans on the side.

Fried Eggs, Cuban Style

Huevos à la Cubana

If you don't like the heaviness of olive oil with eggs, use a light variety. This doesn't mean it's lighter in calories, but lighter in flavor. **Serves 4**

½ cup olive oil
2 garlic cloves, unpeeled and crushed
8 large eggs
2 very ripe (black) plantains, peeled and
    sliced on an angle*
Cooked long-grained white rice
1 tablespoon chopped fresh parsley, for
    garnish
1 avocado, peeled and sliced, for garnish

Heat a large heavy skillet or sauté pan. Add the olive oil and garlic cloves. Remove garlic when it becomes translucent and cooked. Break the eggs into the hot oil. Spoon oil over the eggs until yolks are cooked to your liking. Remove with a slotted spoon and place on an ovenproof platter in the oven to keep warm.

Fry plantain slices in the same skillet, adding more oil if necessary. When golden, drain on brown paper bags or paper toweling.

To serve, spoon a large portion of white rice onto each plate. Place 2 of the fried eggs on top with the plantains on the side. Garnish plates with parsley sprinkled over eggs and rice and two slices of avocado.

*See page 23 for how to peel plantains.

Avocado Omelet

Tortilla de Aguacate

This omelet, filled with onion, bell pepper, tomatoes, and avocado, is perfect for a lazy summer brunch. **Serves 1**

2 tablespoons olive oil
1 tablespoon chopped onion
2 tablespoons diced green bell pepper
2 plum tomatoes, diced
1 avocado, peeled and sliced, 1 slice reserved
3 large eggs
3 tablespoons cold water
2 tablespoons unsalted butter
Salt and pepper, to taste
Fresh parsley, for garnish

Heat olive oil in a small sauté pan. When hot, add the onion, green pepper, and tomatoes. Cook until onion is translucent and slightly browned. Set aside with avocado slices.

With a fork, beat eggs to which cold water has been added.

Heat a 10-inch omelet pan and add butter. When pan becomes very hot, add egg mixture. Using a pancake turner, press sides of eggs to center so that egg runs inside and gets cooked. When egg is almost solid on top, add vegetable mixture and avocado and spread over omelette. Season with salt and pepper. Cook 1 to 2 minutes, then carefully slide omelet onto a dish so that it folds over to cover filling. Garnish with sprigs of fresh parsley and the remaining slice of avocado.

Peel eggs, slice in half lengthwise, and place on a nonstick cookie sheet with sides.

In a medium saucepan, melt butter over low heat. Add flour, a little at a time, to form a smooth thick roux. Slowly add chicken stock until thickened. When smooth, add pimiento, nutmeg, and allspice. Stir and remove from stove, cool slightly, and add egg yolks quickly to avoid curdling.

Pour sauce over eggs, covering each. Place in the refrigerator to cool overnight.

Carefully remove each egg from cookie sheet and slowly roll through cracker meal. Dip each into the beaten eggs and roll once again in cracker meal. Press fingers lightly on each to make sure cracker meal adheres.

Heat a large skillet and add about 2 inches of oil to pan. Fry coated eggs in oil until golden brown. Serve hot, garnished with fresh parsley, accompanied by chopped fresh papaya fruit.

*To defat canned broth, place can in refrigerator. When chilled, open can and skim fat from surface.
†Available at most supermarkets, or make your own by processing saltine crackers in a food processor until finely ground 36 saltines make about 1 cup crumbs.

Fried Hard-Boiled Eggs Batabano

Huevos Duros Batabano

I f you're searching for a novel yet scrumptious appetizer, this is the recipe for you. Boiled eggs are dipped into a creamy béchamel, dotted with red pimiento, then coated with a crunchy crust and fried until golden. Serve with chopped tropical fruits for a sharp contrast in taste and texture.   **Serves 4**

6 hard-boiled eggs
2 tablespoons butter or margarine
2 cups chicken stock (page 36) or defatted
  chicken broth*
½ cup all-purpose flour
1 tablespoon chopped pimiento
½ teaspoon ground nutmeg
½ teaspoon allspice
3 egg yolks, at room temperature,
  slightly beaten
Cracker meal†
2 large eggs, beaten
Chopped fresh parsley, for garnish
Light olive or vegetable oil, for frying

Garden Eggs

Huevos à la Jardinera

This classic baked dish is an ideal alternative to eggs Benedict.

The *sofrito* will have an even better flavor if prepared a day or two ahead, but keep tightly sealed in a glass jar in the refrigerator.

Serves 4 to 6

1 tablespoon olive oil
¾ pound smoked ham, diced
1 cup Sofrito Español (page 29)
½ cup baby green peas (petit pois)
6 large eggs
½ cup freshly grated Parmesan cheese
3 tablespoons cracker meal*
Pimiento strips, for garnish

Preheat the oven to 350° F.

Heat a large skillet and add the olive oil. When oil begins to smell fragrant, add ham and cook until lightly browned. Remove ham to a chopping board and dice.

Put diced ham in a bowl and mix with ¾ cup of the *sofrito*. Add peas and combine thoroughly. Pour half of the mixture into the bottom of a 2-quart Pyrex casserole.

Crack each egg and carefully drop onto the top of the *sofrito*, leaving space between each egg. Spoon the remaining ¼ cup *sofrito* over all. Sprinkle cheese over surface, followed by cracker meal. Bake for 15 to 20 minutes, or until eggs are cooked to suit. Garnish with pimiento strips. Serve with warmed Cuban bread.

*Available at most supermerkets, or make your own by processing saltine crackers in a food processor until finely ground—36 saltines make about 1 cup crumbs.

Lobster Omelet

Tortilla de Langosta

Lobster in Cuba is the spiny lobster sans claws. It is every bit as delicious as Maine lobster.

Serves 3 to 4

2 tablespoons olive oil
1 tablespoon butter or margarine
2 tablespoons finely chopped white onion
1 cup chopped raw lobster meat
1 teaspoon chopped fresh thyme
1 teaspoon finely minced scallions
1½ tablespoons chopped fresh parsley
6 eggs
¾ cup cold water
1 tablespoon white rum
Dash of Tabasco sauce
Fresh parsley sprigs, for garnish

Heat a large skillet and add the olive oil and butter. When the pan is hot and the oil begins to smell fragrant, add onion and cook just until translucent. Add lobster, thyme, scallions, and parsley. Cook just a few minutes until lobster turns white.

Meanwhile, put eggs in a small mixing bowl. Add cold water, rum, and Tabasco. Using a fork, beat mixture until frothy. Pour over lobster mixture and press into sides of omelet with a pancake turner or spatula so that egg runs back into center. Cook 1 to 2 minutes, then carefully slide omelet off pan onto a plate so that it stays in one piece. Garnish with fresh parsley sprigs.

Jalapeño Omelet

Tortilla de Huevos Jalapeños

In this updated *nuevo Cubano* version of a classic, I have used egg whites instead of whole eggs and olive oil instead of lard. The flavors are still present, but the calories are substantially reduced. This recipe also includes jalapeño, not often used in the mild-mannered Cuban cuisine.   **Serves 4**

2 to 3 tablespoons olive oil
2 garlic cloves, peeled and minced
½ cup chopped onion
½ cup chopped green bell pepper
½ cup chopped red bell pepper
2 tablespoons water
1 pickled jalapeño pepper, chopped
2 ripe plum tomatoes, seeded and diced
6 egg whites, at room temperature
2 pinches of saffron or bijol*
½ cup shredded queso blanco or any other
   white cheese
Salt and pepper, to taste
Homemade† or commercial salsa
Choppedn fresh parsley, for garnish

Heat a medium-size skillet and add the olive oil. When the oil begins to smell fragrant, add garlic, onion, green pepper, red pepper, and water. Cook until translucent. Add the jalapeño and tomatoes and cook off the liquid.

In a chilled small glass mixing bowl, beat egg whites until soft peaks form. Add the saffron or bijol and continue to beat a minute longer. Add the white cheese, then mix in the cooked vegetables and season with salt and pepper. Return mixture to the skillet and cook until omelet is set.

Cut omelet into 4 servings and top with homemade or commercial salsa. Garnish with parsley.

*See page 60
†See the recipes on pages 200 to 205.

Egg Nests

Huevos al Nido

This dish is total fun. Easy to prepare and exceedingly different, it's a colorful invitation to brunch.   **Serves 4**

8 large eggs
4 garlic cloves, peeled and mashed
½ teaspoon salt
½ teaspoon white pepper
½ cup tomato sauce
2 cups diced lean ham
⅓ cup baby green peas (petit pois)
2 cups julienned potatoes
Vegetable oil, for frying
Chopped fresh parsley, for garnish

Preheat the oven to 450° F.

Coat individual baking ramekins with olive oil. Break 2 eggs into each dish. Blend garlic, salt, and white pepper with tomato sauce.

Pour a portion of the tomato sauce around each egg yolk in each of the ramekins. Sprinkle the ham and peas over the sauce. Bake for about 10 minutes.

Fry potatoes in vegetable oil while eggs are baking. Season to taste. Drain. Place potatoes over the tomato sauce and peas so that only the yolks show through. Garnish with fresh parsley. Serve with Cuban toast.

Stuffed Eggs

Huevos Rellenos

Although many products are difficult to find in Cuba today, tourists are served eggs in a variety of styles. On a recent visit to the island, at the Hotel Plaza in Havana, I was served a version of these flavor-smothered eggs for breakfast as well as lunch.

Makes 1 dozen

12 hard-boiled eggs, shells removed
½ cup chopped cooked shrimp
1 cup light sour cream
1½ tablespoons Dijon mustard
1 teaspoon fresh lime juice
1 tablespoon chopped fresh parsley
1 tablespoon minced red onion
1 teaspoon chopped fresh cilantro
½ cup minced pimiento-stuffed manzanilla olives
¼ teaspoon salt
½ teaspoon white pepper
1 pimiento, chopped, for garnish
Spanish paprika, for garnish
⅛ cup chopped fresh parsley, for garnish

Using a very sharp knife, cut eggs in half lengthwise. Scoop out yolks and place them in a 1-quart heavy plastic bag. Reserve whites. Add remaining ingredients except garnishes to the bag. Press out air, close bag, and knead until contents are thoroughly blended. Push contents toward corner, then snip off a corner (about ½ inch) with scissors.

Gently fill the egg whites with the yolk mixture by squeezing contents upward and out of the corner of the bag. Chill the stuffed eggs to blend flavors. Dot filled eggs with pieces of pimiento and sprinkle with paprika and fresh parsley. Arrange on a bed of leafy greens.

Three-Cheese Chorizo Macaroni Bake

Macarrónes Horneados

con Tres Quesos y Chorizo

Here's a refreshing change from "ho-hum" macaroni and cheese with fewer calories and more flavor. It's a super dish to take to a buffet supper. **Serves 8 to 10**

2 cups large elbow macaroni
4 tablespoons margarine
2 tablespoons all-purpose flour
1 teaspoon cayenne pepper
3 cups low-fat milk
¾ teaspoon salt
1 tablespoon grated red onion
1 cup shredded low-fat mozzarella cheese
1 cup shredded sharp Cheddar cheese
½ cup grated Parmesan cheese
1 cup 1-inch pork chunks, fried
¼ pound chorizo sausage, sliced

Preheat the oven to 350° F.

Add macaroni to 2 quarts rapidly boiling water. Stir. When water returns to a boil, reduce heat to a slow boil and cook for 8 to 10 minutes. Drain and rinse macaroni.

In a medium saucepan, melt margarine, then whisk in flour, salt, and ½ teaspoon cayenne. Add milk and blend until smooth.

Add onion, cheeses, pork chunks, and chorizo to white sauce. Combine with macaroni and pour into a 5-quart Pyrex casserole. Sprinkle with remaining cayenne. Bake for 30 to 35 minutes, or until firm and golden brown on top.

Serve with a side of citrus chutney and a leafy green salad.

Cuba Beans and Rice

Frijoles y Arroz

Beans and rice are both blank culinary canvases. There are many ingredients you can use as flavor enhancers, and Cuban cooks are expert in this art form.

The most popular varieties of beans used in island cooking are black beans, red beans, and garbanzos, also known as chick-peas. All are extremely adaptable, easy to prepare, and rich in vitamins and fiber.

Modern packaging techniques have eliminated most of the soil, stones, and pebbles once found in boxes or sacks of dried beans, but it is still a good idea to pick through the beans before proceeding. And it is important to rinse your beans quickly to remove field dust before soaking.

When buying beans, keep these simple statistics in mind. Dried beans expand to about one and one-half their original size when soaked. A one-pound package equals two cups dried beans, five or six cups cooked. One sixteen-ounce can, drained, equals one and two-thirds cups cooked beans.

The rice dishes so enjoyed by Cubans are mostly Spanish in origin and many combine rice with a *sofrito*, a slow-cooked sauce of olive oil, tomatoes, bell peppers, onions, and other ingredients, including ham, wine, and lots of garlic.

Basic Beans

Frijoles Clásico

Here are directions for cooking beans the regular way, with the pressure cooker, or in a microwave.

1 pound (2 cups) dried beans
8 cups cold water
1 whole green pepper
1 large onion, halved

To prepare by the regular method, be sure to sort and wash beans carefully to remove foreign particles and damaged beans. Rinse quickly to remove field dust. Cover with cold water and soak with whole green pepper for 8 hours, or overnight. Do not discard liquid. After soaking, remove the green pepper and discard. Pour beans with soaking liquid into a 5-quart kettle. Add onion. Bring beans and water to a boil, cover, reduce heat, and simmer about 2 hours, or until beans are tender. Add additional water, if necessary, so that beans are covered by at least ½ inch of water at all times. Season to taste.

There are many ingredients, such as pork, ham, or bacon, that can be added during cooking to enhance the flavor. But do not add ingredients such as salt that will cause acidity, thus retarding the cooking of the beans.

QUICK-SOAKING METHOD
MÉTODO RÁPIDO

1 pound (2 cups) dried beans
8 cups cold water
1 large onion, halved

Follow directions for sorting and rinsing beans, then pour beans, water, and onion halves into a 5-quart kettle. Bring to a boil and cook for about 5 minutes, then remove from heat and allow to sit, covered, for about 1 hour. Return pot to heat, bring to a boil, and simmer until beans are done, about 2 hours. Be careful not to overcook. Add additional ingredients as above.

PRESSURE-COOKER METHOD
MÉTODO EN OLLA DE PRESIÓN

1 pound (2 cups) dried beans
5 to 6 cups cold water

Follow directions for sorting, rinsing, and soaking beans. Cover beans with water. Cook at 10 pounds of pressure for 30 to 35 minutes, or until tender.

MICROWAVE METHOD
MÉTODO EN HORNO MICROONDA

1 pound (2 cups) dried beans
8 cups hot water

You can use the microwave to soak beans by putting them in a 5-quart container with the hot water. Cover and cook at full power for 8 to 10 minutes, or until boiling. Allow to stand for 1 hour or longer, stirring occasionally, then drain.

To cook the beans, add 8 cups hot water to the beans and cover. Cook at full power for 8 to 10 minutes, or until boiling. Reduce power 50 percent and cook another 15 to 20 minutes, or until beans are tender.

Easy No-Fail Black Beans

Frijoles Negros en un Tiro Garantizados

Black beans, flavored to individual tastes, are enjoyed when served alone, in a soup, or with fluffy white rice. Here is a speedy *nuevo Cubano* recipe that your guests will savor for the spectacular taste imparted by the addition of the smoked bacon, pork, cider vinegar, and sherry.   **Serves 6 to 8**

- 2 slices smoked bacon, diced
- ½ ounce salt pork, cut into pieces
- 1 tablespoon butter or margarine
- 2 garlic cloves, peeled and pressed
- 1 onion, diced
- ½ cup diced green bell pepper
- 2 tablespoons minced celery
- 2 tablespoons cumin seed, toasted and ground
- 2 cups cooked black turtle beans (page 88)
- 1 quart chicken stock (page 36) or defatted chicken broth*
- 2 bay leaves
- ¾ cup dry sherry
- ½ cup cider vinegar
- 2 tablespoons olive oil
- Salt
- ½ cup chopped white onion

Heat a medium saucepan over medium heat and add the bacon and salt pork. When bacon is translucent, add butter. When melted, add garlic, onion, green pepper, and celery and stir constantly over medium heat until vegetables are just done. Add cumin and combine well, then add cooked black beans, chicken stock, and bay leaves. Reduce to a simmer and cook for about 15 minutes, stirring occasionally. Strain beans, reserving the liquid.

Heat another medium saucepan over high heat, then pour in sherry and vinegar. Bring to a boil and cook until reduced to half the amount of liquid. Add the reserved broth and olive oil and reduce by about a third. Add black beans and more water, if necessary, and cook for another 10 minutes. Remove 1 cup of the beans and purée or crush with a spoon. Add back to the sauce. This will thicken the beans. Season with salt, stir in olive oil, and serve with chopped onions over all.

*To defat canned broth, place can in the refrigerator. When chilled, open can and skim fat from the surface.

Erasmo's Black Beans

Frijoles Negros de Erasmo

This is my variation on a recipe served to-day at El Tocororo restaurant in Havana, a favorite of tourists. I was fortunate to spend a considerable amount of time in this beautiful residential restaurant, watching and learning from the executive chef, Tomas Erasmo, who has an international reputation for cooking the best black beans.

Erasmo claims the true secret is refrigerating the beans for 2 to 3 days. He says this period allows the flavors to develop. He calls them "still" beans. "Never," he cautioned, "serve the beans on the same day they are cooked." His recipe uses a small amount of pork and lard for flavoring, which you may prefer to include. **Serves 4**

1⅔ cups dried black beans
4½ cups cold water, or more if necessary
2 tablespoons olive oil or lard
2 white onions, minced
5 garlic cloves, peeled and minced
⅛ pound roasted pork, or small piece
   of salt pork
1 teaspoon dried oregano
1 teaspoon ground cumin
2 bay leaves
1 teaspoon granulated sugar
2 tablespoons chopped cilantro or culantro*
1 teaspoon salt, or to taste
Extra-virgin olive oil
½ cup chopped white onion

Wash beans well. Place in a large glass bowl with enough water to cover and soak overnight. The next day, transfer the beans and water to a large Dutch oven or saucepan and cook over low-medium heat for 1½ to 2 hours, or until just tender.

In a skillet, heat the olive oil and sauté minced onions and garlic until tender, but do not overcook. Add onion-garlic mixture to beans in kettle along with pork. Combine well. Add oregano, cumin, bay leaves, sugar, cilantro, and salt. Check seasoning and add more garlic and herbs as necessary. Cook for 10 to 15 minutes longer and add a little more water if mixture becomes too thick. Boil beans gently and stir carefully so that skins are not broken.

Cool beans to room temperature, then put in refrigerator. After 2 to 3 days, remove and splash with extra-virgin olive oil and garnish with chopped white onion.

*Cilantro is the Spanish name for fresh coriander, and culantro is a flat-leaf herb with a similar taste that Erasmo prefers over cilantro.

Black Bean Cakes

Tortas de Frijoles Negros

Here is still another use for leftover beans.

Serves 4 to 6

7 tablespoons olive oil
2 tablespoons all-purpose flour
⅓ cup chopped red onion
2 garlic cloves, peeled and finely minced
⅓ cup chopped red bell pepper
⅓ cup chopped green bell pepper
1 teaspoon ground cumin
2 cups cooked or canned black beans, rinsed
1 teaspoon chopped fresh cilantro
1 egg, beaten with ⅓ cup low-fat milk
½ cup fine dry bread crumbs, mixed with ½
  teaspoon confectioners' sugar
Sour cream
Chopped fresh parsley

Heat 2 tablespoons of the olive oil in a saucepan, add flour, and whisk to a light roux. Set aside.

In another pan, make a *sofrito* by sautéing the onion, garlic, and peppers in 2 tablespoons olive oil until just translucent, 3 to 4 minutes. Add the cumin and combine well, then add the cooked beans. Stir in the roux and continue to stir until the mixture becomes thickened, about 4 minutes. Remove from heat and cool. Add the chopped cilantro. Form into 6 to 8 cakes and refrigerate until firm.

Coat each cake with the egg mixture and then with bread crumbs. Sauté cakes in remaining olive oil until nicely browned. Top each cake with a dollop of sour cream and chopped parsley.

Chick-pea Sauté

Garbanzos Fritos

Garbanzo beans, often called chick-peas, have a mild flavor. When blended with the assertiveness of the chorizo sausage and fresh vegetables, they make for an especially mouth-watering side dish. It can be served as a main course, also, over fluffy white rice.

Serves 4

¼ cup olive oil
3 garlic cloves, pressed
1 white onion, chopped
1 green bell pepper, seeded and chopped
2 chorizo sausages (3 to 4 ounces each),
  sliced
¼ pound lean smoked ham, chopped
½ teaspoon Spanish paprika
1 bay leaf
2 (15-ounce) cans garbanzo beans,
  drained and rinsed

Heat a medium sauté pan and add the olive oil. When the oil starts to smell fragrant and begins to sizzle, add the garlic, onion, and green pepper and sauté until onion becomes translucent. Add chorizos, ham, paprika, bay leaf, and garbanzo beans. Cover and simmer slowly for 15 to 20 minutes. Serve hot.

Black Beans and Rice

Moros y Cristianos

Here's a classic dish that is often prepared with beans left over from the day before. A *sofrito,* or sauce, is prepared and then the beans are added. Cubans usually add their favorite flavoring agents to this dish, including salted beef and pork. Keep in mind that the quality of this dish has everything to do with the combination of flavors, which often range from very mild to somewhat spicy.   **Serves 6 to 8**

½ cup olive oil
½ cup chopped green onion
½ cup chopped white onion
¼ cup chopped green bell pepper
1 (4-ounce) jar red pimientos, drained and chopped
8 garlic cloves, peeled and crushed
2 cups cooked black beans (page 88) or use rinsed canned beans
4 cups chicken stock (page 36) or defatted chicken broth'
3 cups long-grain rice
1 teaspoon ground oregano
1 teaspoon ground cumin
1 tablespoon chopped fresh cilantro or culantro
2 tablespoons olive oil
Salt, to taste

Heat a large pot and add olive oil. Prepare a *sofrito* by adding the green and white onion, green pepper, pimientos, and garlic. Sauté about 5 minutes. Add black beans and mix well. Add chicken stock and bring to a boil, then add rice, salt oregano, and cumin. Cover pan with a sheet of wax paper, then with a sheet of paper towels, and finally the lid. Cook over low heat for about 30 minutes, or until rice is tender but still moist. Five minutes before serving, add cilantro or culantro and olive oil. Add salt to taste and serve steaming hot.

*To defat canned broth, place can in refrigerator. When chilled, open can and skim fat from the surface.

Garbanzo Mélange

Garbanzos Salteados

This is a satisfying comfort dish that is almost a bean and vegetable stew. The use of potatoes thickens the sauce naturally, while the bacon imparts a delicate smoked flavor.   **Serves 4 to 6**

2 cups dried garbanzo beans
Few strands of saffron or bijol*
2 slices slab bacon, diced
6 new potatoes, diced with skins on
2 tablespoons olive oil
1 white onion, minced
2 garlic cloves, peeled and crushed
2 (16-ounce) cans plum tomatoes, drained and crushed
1 tablespoon chopped fresh parsley
½ teaspoon Spanish paprika

Soak and cook garbanzo beans according to directions on page 88. Drain the liquid, reserving about 1 cup. Put beans, reserved liquid, and saffron or *bijol* in a saucepan. Cook about 10 minutes.

Cook the bacon in a large skillet until very crisp. Remove bacon to drain. Add the potatoes, olive oil, onion, garlic, tomatoes, and parsley. Cook until potatoes are tender, about 15 minutes. Add cooked beans with saffron to skillet, and cook a few minutes. Crumble bacon and add, then sprinkle with paprika and serve piping hot.

*See page 6.

Fried White Bean Cake

Judías en Munyetas

Visitors to Spain's Catalonia region will surely recognize this dish. Catalonian immigrants brought this cooking method with them to Cuba many generations ago, and it has become a standard on the island, although many of these products are difficult to find today in Cuba. The presentation of this beautifully browned and wonderfully aromatic bean cake will surprise your guests.

Serve alone with a small salad, or as an accompaniment to a main course.   **Serves 4**

> 1 pound dried white beans, preferably
>   Great Northern
> ¼ cup plus 2 tablespoons olive oil
> 2 tablespoons butter or margarine
> 1 (4 × 4-inch) piece salt pork, diced
> ¼ pound lean smoked ham, or cooking ham,
>   chopped
> ½ pound chorizo, or other smoked sausage,
>   cooked and drained
> 3 garlic cloves, peeled and chopped
> ½ cup chopped onion
> 1 tablespoon chopped flat-leaf fresh parsley

Cook beans until tender according to package directions. When well done and soft, drain off water in a colander.

Heat a large sauté pan and add ¼ cup olive oil, 1 tablespoon butter, and salt pork. Fry salt pork until it begins to brown. Add ham, sausage, garlic, onion, and parsley and combine well. Add beans and mix all together thoroughly.

Remove mixture to a large bowl, allow to cool a few minutes, and then form into one large patty. Meanwhile, add 2 tablespoons of olive oil mixed with 1 tablespoon remaining butter to the same sauté pan. When the oil begins to smell fragrant and sizzle, carefully add the large bean cake. Cook about 15 minutes on each side. Slice into wedges to serve. If you prefer individual servings, make small patties and serve 1 per guest.

Bodeguita del Medio's Black Beans and Rice

Moros y Cristianos de Bodeguita del Medio

Ernest Hemingway's favorite stop-off for conversation and cocktails was Bodeguita del Medio, a cozy bar-restaurant in Havana that is as packed today as it was in the 1950s. Three of the cooks at Bodeguita have been there for 42 years, preparing the same recipes day after day for thousands of hungry patrons. One of these dishes is this version of black beans and rice, created by Angel Martinez, the restaurant's founder.   **Serves 4**

> 4 to 5 tablespoons pork fat*
> 6 garlic cloves, peeled
> 1 large onion, chopped
> 1 green bell pepper, seeded and chopped
> 1 cup cooked black beans
> 2½ cups long-grain white rice
> ½ to 1 cup pork cracklings*
> 4½ cups heated water
> 1 teaspoon salt, or to taste

Preheat the oven to 325°F. Heat a large skillet and add pork fat. When oil begins to smell fragrant, add garlic, onion, and green pepper and sauté until tender. Add the cooked beans, rice, pork cracklings, salt, and water and stir once. Cover and cook on medium-low heat for about 20 minutes or longer. When rice is soft and cooked, place in a casserole and bake for about 10 minutes. Season with salt.

*The restaurant uses fresh pork fat to make its cracklings, but you may substitute packaged cracklings, bacon or, for health reasons, olive oil.

Potato and Black Bean Pancakes

Panqué de Papas y Frijoles Negros

In this modern-day recipe, bacon spices up the otherwise bland beans while the onion, garlic, and green peppers join in to create a luscious potato-bean cake.

You can prepare these several hours ahead, then fry or bake and serve in just a few minutes. Served with a pork roast or baked chicken, they're a real show stopper. **Makes 2 dozen cakes**

4 Idaho potatoes, finely grated (about 3 cups)
2 eggs, slightly beaten
⅓ cup chopped scallions
1 teaspoon chopped fresh parsley
2 tablespoons minced red onion
2 tablespoons minced green bell pepper
2 garlic cloves, minced
2 cups cooked black beans, or 2
** (15-ounce) cans, rinsed**
2 tablespoons red wine vinegar
1 cup all-purpose flour
1 teaspoon salt
½ teaspoon freshly ground pepper
All-purpose flour, for dredging
Cracker meal,* for dredging
Olive oil, for frying
4 slices bacon
1 cup light sour cream
Chopped fresh parsley, for garnish

Squeeze liquid from grated potatoes and put in a large glass bowl. Add the eggs, scallions, parsley, onion, green pepper, garlic, black beans, vinegar, flour, salt, and pepper. Stir well to blend all ingredients. Chill for 1 to 2 hours so mixture will become firm.

Using an ice cream scoop or a large spoon, form into balls. Roll balls in flour, then flatten into thin patties with a pancake turner. Coat each patty on both sides with cracker meal.

Heat a large sauté pan. Preheat the oven to 350°F.

Add olive oil and bacon to heated pan and cook until bacon is crisp. Remove bacon and, when cooled, crush for garnish. Fry cakes for about 3 minutes on each side, until crisp, then season with salt and pepper. Drain on brown paper bags or paper towels, then place on a sheet pan. Bake for about 5 minutes. Serve with a dollop of sour cream, the crushed bacon bits, and chopped fresh parsley. Serve with a side dish of homemade chutney.

*Available at most supermarkets, or make your own by processing saltine crackers in a food processor until finely ground—36 saltines make about 1 cup crumbs.

Cuban Rice

Arroz à la Cubana

Here's your basic rice without a lot of outside enhancement. The fresh garlic, tomato sauce, and stock are enough to make it a very satisfying side dish or main vegetarian choice.   **Serves 4**

1 tablespoon olive oil
½ medium onion, chopped
2 garlic cloves, minced
2 cups long-grain white rice
1 cup tomato sauce
1 bay leaf, crushed
1 teaspoon dried oregano
1 cup chicken stock (page 36) or defatted
  broth*
Salt, to taste

Preheat the oven to 325°F. Heat a large skillet or sauté pan and add olive oil. When oil is heated, add onion and garlic and cook until not quite brown. Add rice, tomato sauce, bay leaf, oregano, and stock. Reduce heat to a simmer, cover, and place in oven for about 20 minutes. Season with salt to taste.

Remove from oven. Remove bay leaf and serve piping hot.

*To defat canned broth, place can in refrigerator. When chilled, open can and skim fat from the surface.

Yellow Rice

Arroz Amarillo

Ounce for ounce, saffron is the most expensive spice in the world. Its cost is reason enough to use it sparingly. If your budget doesn't permit this luxury, then use *bijol,* a satisfactory substitute. It's readily available at most Hispanic markets and is far superior to yellow food dye, which is often used to color the grains.

For best results, use a good Spanish sherry and a homemade or quality tomato sauce.

Serves 4

½ cup olive or vegetable oil
4 garlic cloves, peeled and mashed
1 cup minced white onion
¼ cup diced green bell pepper
¼ cup diced red bell pepper
½ cup dry sherry
8 ounces tomato sauce
8 to 10 saffron threads, or ½ teaspoon bijol *
4 cups chicken stock (page 36) or defatted
  chicken broth†
1½ cups long-grain rice
1 (4-ounce) jar pimientos soaked in olive oil
2 tablespoons chopped fresh parsley

Heat a large skillet and add the olive oil. When oil is fragrant and hot, make a *sofrito,* or thick sauce, by adding garlic, onion, and peppers and stirring constantly until vegetables are soft and translucent, about 10 minutes. Add the sherry, tomato sauce, saffron, and chicken stock. Combine well and raise the heat to high, bringing mixture to a boil. Add rice. Bring to another boil then cover, lower heat to a simmer, and cook for about 20 minutes, or until liquid is absorbed and rice is slightly moist and fluffy. Do not overcook. Garnish with sliced pimientos that have been soaked in olive oil and sprinkle with parsley.

*See page 6.
†To defat canned broth, place can in refrigerator. When chilled, open can and skim fat from the surface.

Miami Rice

Arroz Miami

Before moving to my home in Tampa Bay, I lived in Miami for five years, seizing every opportunity to sample the cuisine in a melting-pot community made famous by the popular television episodes of *Miami Vice* starring Don Johnson. This recipe is one that became popular during those times when the actor propelled the city's reputation to international heights, both political and culinary.

Serves 6

4 slices bacon, each slice cut into fourths
¼ cup olive oil
4 tablespoons butter or margarine
1 cup minced white onion
1 cup thinly sliced mushrooms
3 cups warm cooked white rice
Salt and coarsely ground pepper, to taste
Fresh Italian parsley sprigs or cilantro,
**   for garnish**

Fry bacon until crisp. Drain. Heat a large skillet and add the olive oil. When oil becomes fragrant and hot, add the butter and blend together. Add the onion and mushrooms and cook on medium high, stirring until the mushroom liquid is reduced by half. Add the bacon, rice, and salt and pepper. Decorate with fresh parsley or cilantro sprigs.

Salads

Ensaladas

With the tropical climate of the beautiful island so favorable to growing fruits and vegetables, it is little wonder that salads are becoming popular with Cubans. But it was not always so. Until the American influence on the island in the 1950s integrated more healthful salads into the cuisine, salad to many Cubans meant canned vegetables, ham, or fish mixed with mayonnaise, molded, and decorated with bright garnishes such as pimientos, canned asparagus, and bright green garden baby peas. Green salads as we know them were rarely served, the exception being a Basque-style salad that was tossed with olives, cheese, and radishes. Fruit salad was often canned fruit cocktail combined with a few fresh mangoes and cream cheese, molded and coated heavily with mayonnaise.

Today all that has changed and there are many types of salads available at the Cuban table, from the simple and classic sliced avocado topped with a basic vinaigrette dressing, to the more complex lobster salad prepared with a mild dressing of herbs and spices.

Avocado Salad

Ensalada de Aguacate

The creamy dressing in this unusual salad should be fixed 1 to 2 hours ahead, so that the lime, mustard, and honey have time to meld. But do not toss with salad greens until ready to serve so that the avocado remains firm. Since avocados are harvested unripe, it may be necessary to quicken the process by wrapping them in aluminum foil or newspaper for a day or so. In totally ripe fruit, the stone is loose and the fruit will rattle when shaken.   **Serves 6 to 8**

DRESSING

¼ cup mayonnaise or aïoli (page 32)
1½ tablespoons fresh lime juice
2 tablespoons Dijon or Pommery mustard
2 tablespoons honey
3 tablespoons sour cream
Salt, to taste

SALAD

2 ripe avocados, peeled and diced
2 cups thinly sliced red cabbage
2 cups thinly sliced green cabbage
1 carrot, peeled and grated
Watercress, for lining plates

In a medium bowl or the container of a food processor, combine all dressing ingredients. In a glass salad bowl, combine all salad ingredients. Pour dressing over all and toss well. Serve on a bed of watercress as soon as possible so that the avocado remains firm.

Avocado, Tomato, and Onion Salad

Ensalada de Aguacate, Tomate, y Cebolla

This is one of my favorite ways to serve avocado. Its delicate sweetness plays against the citrus flavors and the acidity in tomatoes and oranges, while onion and radicchio add a crunchy texture.   **Serves 4**

2 avocados, peeled and sliced into
  ½-inch wedges
2 large navel oranges, peeled and sectioned
1 large red onion, peeled and thinly sliced
  into rings
Radicchio, watercress, or lettuce for lining
  plates
2 tablespoons red wine vinegar
¼ cup extra-virgin olive oil
Freshly ground black pepper, to taste
Chopped fresh parsley, for garnish

Chill four glass salad plates. Carefully arrange avocado slices, then the orange and onion slices, in spiral fashion on the plates lined with radicchio pieces. Mix together the vinegar, olive oil, and black pepper and sprinkle over all. Garnish with chopped fresh parsley.

1905 Tossed Salad

Ensalada Mixta 1905

When the famous Columbia in Ybor City, in Tampa, the world's largest Spanish-Cuban restaurant, celebrated its 88th anniversary, the owners, the Gonzmart family, created this special salad. The combination of shrimp, cheese, and tomatoes together with the piquant garlicky dressing will make you repeat this again and again.   **Serves 4 to 6**

SALAD

½ chilled head lettuce, torn into
   small pieces
½ cup manzanilla olives*
2 plum tomatoes, cut into fourths
3 ounces light Swiss cheese, julienned
12 large shrimp, shelled, deveined, cooked,
   and cut in half lengthwise
1 tablespoon freshly grated Romano or
   Parmesan cheese

DRESSING

5 garlic cloves, peeled and minced
2 teaspoons chopped fresh oregano, or
   1 teaspoon dried
1 tablespoon Worcestershire sauce
½ cup olive oil
2 tablespoons red wine vinegar
Juice of 1 lemon or lime
Salt and cracked pepper, to taste

Wash and dry lettuce well. In a large bowl, toss all salad ingredients together except the cheese.

To prepare the dressing, using a mortar and pestle, mash and then mix together garlic, oregano, and Worcestershire. Using a fork or whisk, beat briskly until smooth. Add in olive oil slowly, whisking well. Add vinegar and lemon juice. Season with salt and pepper.

Pour dressing to salad mixture in bowl. Toss several times so greens are well coated with dressing. Add cheese and toss once more. Serve while greens are still very cold.

*You may use any type of Spanish olives, but I prefer the intense flavor of the small manzanilla type in salads and the "queens," or larger variety, to eat whole.

Basque Tossed Salad

Ensalada Vasca

Use a large assortment of mixed greens, including leafy red lettuce, spinach leaves, romaine, and escarole, as a bed for this Basque salad brought to the island of Cuba by Spanish-Basque ancestors. Egg, capers, ripe tomatoes, and manzanilla olives make this a superb luncheon dish.   **Serves 4**

DRESSING

½ teaspoon kosher salt
½ teaspoon dried oregano
3 garlic cloves, peeled
1 tablespoon minced red onion
½ teaspoon granulated sugar
1 teaspoon fresh lime juice
1 teaspoon Worcestershire sauce
2 tablespoons red wine vinegar
¾ cup extra-virgin olive oil

SALAD

2 large tomatoes, chopped
½ cup chopped green bell pepper
1 large cucumber, peeled, seeded, and
   chopped
1 teaspoon small capers, finely chopped
2 tablespoons finely chopped pimiento-stuffed
   manzanilla olives
4 cups finely shredded salad greens, chilled
2 boiled eggs, peeled and finely chopped,
   for garnish
Chopped fresh parsley, for garnish
1 large ripe tomato, chopped, for garnish

Using a mortar and pestle, mash the salt and oregano with the garlic. Add onion, sugar, lime juice, Worcestershire, vinegar, and olive oil and whisk well with a wire whisk for 2 to 3 minutes. Pour dressing into a bowl. Add tomatoes, bell pepper, cucumber, capers, and olives and combine well. Serve on a decorative platter over chilled shredded salad greens. Garnish with chopped eggs, parsley, and chopped tomato.

Mango Salad

Ensalada de Mango

This is a noble yet healthy innovation that uses mango as both a base ingredient in the salad as well as the key component in the tangy dressing.   **Serves 4 to 6**

DRESSING

> ½ medium mango, peeled and cut into chunks*
> ¼ cup vegetable oil
> 2 tablespoons orange juice
> 2 tablespoons lemon juice
> 2 teaspoons grated fresh ginger

SALAD

> 3 mangoes, peeled, seeded, and sliced*
> 2 bananas, peeled and sliced diagonally
> 1 tablespoon fresh lime juice in 1 cup cold water
> 2 rounds fresh pineapple, peeled and cut into wedges
> Salad greens

Combine all dressing ingredients in the container of a blender or food processor and purée until smooth. Chill.

To prepare salad, dip mango and banana slices into fresh lime juice mixture. Arrange fruit on chilled glass plates lined with greens. Pour dressing over all.

*See page 23 for how to cut a mango.

Tropical Fruit Salad with Avocado Dressing

Ensalada de Frutas con Aderezo de Aguacate

As an ingredient in this dressing, avocado gives body to the sour cream and honey. With the addition of lime juice and Tabasco, there is a sweet and sour flavor added to the medley of tropical fruits.   **Serves 4**

DRESSING

> 1 ripe avocado, peeled and cubed
> ⅔ cup sour cream
> 3 tablespoons fresh lime juice
> 1 tablespoon honey
> Dash of Tabasco sauce
> Pinch of salt

SALAD

> 1 head red leaf lettuce
> 1 avocado, thinly sliced
> 2 bananas, thinly sliced
> 2 cups fresh or canned pineapple chunks
> 1 cup 1-inch mango chunks*
> 1 cup 1-inch papaya chunks
> 1 cup seedless white grapes
> ½ cup chopped pecans or toasted almonds

Chill all dressing ingredients.

Line a large serving platter with leafy red lettuce. Arrange fruit in a circular fashion beginning with the avocado on the outside. Follow with the bananas, pineapple, and mango chunks. Arrange papaya chunks last with seedless grapes in the center. Sprinkle with chopped nuts.

Place chilled dressing ingredients in the container of a blender. Blend until smooth. Pass fruit and bowl of dressing separately, or pour over all.

*See page 23 for how to cut a mango.

Papaya Salad

Ensalada de Papaya

I've made many converts to papaya, a favorite of Cubans, by serving this fantastic fruit salad. You can use fresh ripe pineapple, but canned pineapple is usually top quality and sweeter than fresh. No need to peel the kiwi.

Serves 4

2½ cups peeled and diced firm ripe papaya
2 bananas, peeled and sliced
1 cup fresh orange segments, pith and seeds removed
½ cup halved red seedless grapes
1½ cups pineapple chunks
1 kiwi, sliced
1 tablespoon honey
Fresh lime juice, to taste
½ cup freshly grated coconut or unsweetened canned coconut

In a large attractive glass serving bowl, combine all fruits and blend well. Add honey and lime juice and gently toss again to coat all pieces with honey and lime. Chill for a few hours. Add grated coconut just before serving.

Mixed Vegetable Salad

Ensaladilla Rusa

This recipe, borrowed from Spanish ancestors, has many variations, but is always made with cooked vegetables. You can use just about any firm vegetables you have in the house. Place this domed-style salad on a very large plate so there's room to decorate the border with pieces of parsley, olives, asparagus, and egg wedges.

Serves 8 to 10

1 pound white potatoes, cooked, peeled, and diced
1 pound red beets, cooked and diced
4 carrots, cooked and diced
1 turnip, cooked and diced
½ cup diced lean ham
½ cup mayonnaise
2 tablespoons dry sherry
Salt, to taste
½ cup thinly sliced pimiento-stuffed manzanilla olives
Mayonnaise
Canned thin green asparagus, for garnish
5 hard-boiled eggs, sliced, for garnish
Sliced dill pickle, for garnish
2 tablespoons chopped pimientos, for garnish
1 tablespoon chopped fresh parsley, for garnish
Small cooked green peas, for garnish

Cook all the vegetables separately until slightly al dente, then dice.

Add the cubed vegetables and ham to a large glass bowl. Add just enough mayonnaise so that mixture binds together. Toss well. Add sherry, salt, and olives.

Using your hands, mound the mixture to resemble a dome. Using a rubber spatula, cover the dome with a thin coat of mayonnaise so that it looks somewhat like an igloo. Decorate artistically using the asparagus spears to form triangles. Pat the egg slices into the triangles. Place olives on eggs to decorate. Place thin pickle slices in a circular fashion around the edge of the plate. Dot with small pieces of pimiento in the center of each pickle. Sprinkle with small peas and fresh parsley.

Mixed Greens with Yogurt Dressing

Verduras Mixtas con Aderezo de Cilantro y Yogurt

This is a simple Cuban salad that I've augmented with a variety of lettuces and a contemporary fresh cilantro dressing.

Serves 6 generously

DRESSING

2 cups plain nonfat yogurt
½ cup chopped fresh cilantro
½ teaspoon pepper, or to taste
2 garlic cloves, peeled and mashed
½ teaspoon Worcestershire sauce
Dash of Louisiana Hot Sauce

SALAD

1 head bibb lettuce
1 head romaine lettuce
1 head red lettuce
½ cup grated carrots
2 tablespoons grated red onion
1 cucumber, peeled and thinly sliced
4 plum tomatoes, diced
½ cup thinly sliced mushrooms

Combine all dressing ingredients in a glass bowl and blend well using a wire whisk. Refrigerate.

To prepare the salad, wash lettuces well and drain. Add remaining ingredients and toss well. Serve chilled with the cilantro dressing.

Garbanzo Bean Salad

Ensalada de Garbanzos

This typical Cuban salad uses ingredients and seasonings native to the island, with the possible exception of the manzanilla olives and English mustard.

The vinaigrette dressing, one of my favorites, contains cilantro and extra-virgin olive oil, which greatly enhance the nutlike flavor of the firm-textured beans.

Serves 8

1½ cups dried garbanzo beans, or use canned beans
1½ cups chopped ripe tomato
½ cup sliced black olives
½ cup sliced pimiento-stuffed manzanilla olives
3 scallions, chopped
2 tablespoons chopped pimientos, for garnish

CILANTRO VINAIGRETTE

2 garlic cloves, peeled and crushed
½ teaspoon kosher salt
1 teaspoon Dijon mustard
½ cup extra-virgin olive oil
2 tablespoons red wine vinegar
1½ tablespoons chopped fresh cilantro or culantro

Soak and cook beans according to directions on page 88. Drain in a colander.

To prepare vinaigrette, place garlic and salt in a small mortar. With a pestle, grind the salt into the garlic. Add the mustard and combine well. Whisk in olive oil and red wine vinegar. Mix in cilantro.

In a medium bowl, combine cooked beans and tomato, olives, and scallions. Mix well. Add vinaigrette and combine thoroughly. Cover and refrigerate for 2 to 3 hours, stirring occasionally.

Serve in attractive salad ramekins. Garnish with pimientos.

Marinated Garbanzos

Garbanzos en Escabeche

The subtle nutlike flavor of garbanzo beans in this gratifying side dish is enhanced by the ingredients in the marinade. The two vinegars bring it all together.   **Serves 4 to 6**

¾ cup chopped white onion
2 garlic cloves, peeled and minced
2 tablespoons olive oil
¼ cup cider vinegar
¼ cup red wine vinegar
½ cup water
1 teaspoon chopped fresh thyme, or
    ½ teaspoon dried
½ teaspoon coarsely ground black pepper
1 teaspoon chopped fresh parsley
2 cups cooked garbanzo beans, or 1 (15-
    ounce) can, drained
Lettuce leaves

Prepare the marinade by sautéing the onion and garlic in the olive oil for 4 to 5 minutes. Add the cider and red wine vinegars, water, thyme, black pepper, and parsley and cook another 10 minutes. Pour mixture into a large glass bowl with the beans and marinate overnight. Serve as an appetizer or a salad over leafy lettuce.

Chicken in Tomato Cups

Pollo en Copitas de Tomate

Here's a colorful presentation for a light salad luncheon.   **Serves 4**

4 skinless boneless chicken breast halves
1 (2-inch) piece of gingerroot, peeled
2 pounds potatoes, diced and boiled
1 hard-boiled egg, chopped
¼ cup chopped black olives
¼ cup sliced pimiento-stuffed manzanilla
    olives
½ cup chopped canned artichokes
1 cup baby green peas (petit pois)
1 Granny Smith apple, peeled and chopped
1 cup mayonnaise
1 (6-ounce) can asparagus tips, drained
4 large ripe tomatoes, halved, with pulp
    removed
Chopped green manzanilla olives for garnish
Chopped fresh parsley, for garnish

Cook chicken breasts in a pot of boiling water with the ginger. This will add flavor to the chicken. Do not overcook. Cool. Cut into bite-size pieces.

Combine all ingredients except the tomatoes and garnish. Mix well, then spoon into the tomato cups. Serve each on a bed of leafy greens. Garnish with chopped green olives and freshly chopped parsley.

Potato and Tuna Salad

Ensalada de Papas y Atún

This is an easy-to-prepare tuna and potato salad, with a smooth texture and a tangy flavor, that can be turned into a fancy luncheon or buffet item by some simple decorative tricks. Coat the top of the molded salad lightly with mayonnaise and then form the pimiento slices into a grid of squares and place a thinly sliced olive in each center. Or do your own thing.

Serves 4

1 (6-ounce) can white tuna packed in water, drained and mashed

1½ cups mayonnaise or aïoli (page 32)

3 large white potatoes, peeled, boiled, diced, and cooled

3 large carrots, peeled, boiled, diced, and cooled

1½ cups cooked fresh or canned green peas, cooled

1 (3-ounce) jar sliced pimientos, drained

4 hard-boiled eggs, cooled and chopped

1 tablespoon cider vinegar

Leafy lettuce, for lining the plate

Eggs, asparagus, olives, and pimientos, for garnish

Mix the mashed tuna with mayonnaise. Add potatoes, carrots, peas, half of the pimientos, chopped egg, and vinegar and blend well.

Place in a mold, or mound into a dome shape using your hands. Chill for a few hours. Unmold and place dome on a bed of leafy lettuce and decorate creatively with eggs, asparagus, olives, and remaining pimientos.

Corn Salad

Ensalada de Maíz

Corn may be the prime ingredient in this simple to prepare salsa-style salad, but the key is the cilantro. The tangy herb intensifies the flavor of the corn.

For added dimension, grill whole cobs (8 ears) fresh corn, slice it from the cob, and use in place of canned kernels.

Serves 4

2 tablespoons extra-virgin olive oil

2 tablespoons red wine vinegar

1 tablespoon chopped fresh cilantro

½ teaspoon granulated sugar

Salt, to taste

2 (17-ounce) cans (4 cups) whole kernel yellow corn with red and green peppers, drained and rinsed to remove excess salt

Fresh cilantro sprigs, for garnish

Whisk together the olive oil, vinegar, cilantro, sugar, and salt.

Add corn, mix well, and chill. Garnish with cilantro sprigs. Serve as a salad or as a salsa with fresh fish or meats.

Black Bean and Rice Salad with Cilantro Vinaigrette

Ensalada de Moros y Cristianos Cilantro

Vinaigretta

This tart salad constitutes a modern-day use of rice and black beans, so loved by Cuban Americans. You can prepare the dish ahead, then toss the fresh dressing in at the last minute. **Serves 4**

2 cups cooked long-grain rice, cooled
1 cup cooked black beans, drained
1¼ cups chopped ripe plum tomatoes
½ cup shredded queso banco or other mild white cheese
1 tablespoon chopped fresh parsley
¼ cup cilantro vinaigrette (page 102)
1 tablespoon fresh lime juice
Salt and cracked black pepper, to taste
Watercress or mixed lettuce leaves

Combine cooked rice, black beans, chopped tomatoes, cheese, and parsley in a large glass bowl. Pour dressing and lime juice over rice mixture. Season with salt and pepper. Toss and serve on watercress or mixed lettuce leaves.

Saffron Rice Salad

Ensalada de Azafrán Santa Cruz

Turmeric, *bijol* made from *achiote* seed, or yellow food coloring are often suggested as reasonable substitutes for priccy saffron. They will put forth a similar color, but never the pungent aroma and flavor of this extraordinary flower spice. **Serves 4**

2 tablespoons cider vinegar
1 teaspoon red wine vinegar
2 tablespoons extra-virgin olive oil
3 drops of Tabasco sauce
1 cup rice, cooked in chicken stock with ½ teaspoon saffron threads, then cooled to room temperature
1 cup diced green bell pepper
½ cup diced red bell pepper
¼ cup sliced pitted ripe olives
¼ cup sliced pimiento-stuffed manzanilla olives
2 scallions, chopped
4 to 5 sprigs fresh flat-leaf parsley
1 tomato, chopped
Spinach, lettuce or kale leaves

In a large decorative bowl, thoroughly mix together the vinegars, olive oil, and Tabasco. Add the rice, green and red bell peppers, olives, and scallions. Toss well.

Serve on chilled leaves and garnish with parsley and chopped tomatoes.

Paella Salad

Ensalada de Paella

You can add more fresh seafood to this salad, just as you would a regular paella, the renowned saffron rice dish borrowed from the Spanish that is served in so many Cuban restaurants. When you make this for a special occasion, serve it in a regular paella pan, a special two-handled wide shallow pan after which the dish is named.   **Serves 4 to 6**

> 1 cup cooked long-grain rice
> ½ pound chicken, cooked and cut into
>   medium-size chunks
> 1 cup sliced scallions
> ¼ pound medium shrimp, peeled and cooked
> 2 tablespoons olive oil
> 2 garlic cloves, peeled and minced
> 1 cup chopped green bell pepper
> 1 (14 ½-ounce) can stewed tomatoes
> ½ teaspoon Tabasco sauce
> 1 teaspoon Spanish paprika
> 1 teaspoon ground cumin
> Salt and coarsely ground pepper, to taste
> ½ teaspoon saffron threads, or small envelope
>   bijol*
> ½ pound chorizo sausage, sliced, each slice
>   cut into quarters
> Fresh spinach leaves
> 1 red bell pepper, seeded and cut into rings
> 1 fresh lime, cut into 8 thin wedges

In a medium bowl, combine the rice with the chicken, scallions, and shrimp. Heat a large sauté pan and add the olive oil. When oil becomes fragrant and starts to sizzle, add garlic and green pepper and sauté for about 1 minute, then add the tomatoes, Tabasco, paprika, cumin, salt and pepper, and saffron threads. Bring to a boil and cook over high heat for about 4 minutes, or until mixture thickens. Remove from heat and cool about 5 minutes. Add to rice mixture and combine well. Add chorizo and mix again.

Chill thoroughly. Serve over a bed of fresh spinach leaves and garnish with circles of red pepper and lime wedges.

*See page 6.

Black and White Bean Medley

Combinación de Frijoles Negros y Blancos

Colorful sweet peppers against a backdrop of checkered beans make this creation an ideal centerpiece for a buffet luncheon.   **Serves 6 to 8**

> 1 (7-ounce) package dried white beans
> 1 (7-ounce) package dried black turtle beans
> ½ cup chopped green bell pepper
> ½ cup chopped red bell pepper
> ½ cup chopped yellow bell pepper
> ½ cup chopped red onion
> 4 plum tomatoes, seeded and diced
> ¼ cup chopped fresh cilantro
> 1 teaspoon chopped fresh basil
> 4 garlic cloves, peeled and chopped
> ¼ cup red wine vinegar
> 1 teaspoon Dijon mustard
> 2 tablespoons extra-virgin olive oil
> ½ teaspoon salt
> Kale or lettuce leaves
> Red and green pepper rings, for garnish

Wash beans and put each color in a separate large saucepan with water to cover. Bring each to a boil and cook for 5 to 10 minutes. Remove from heat and allow to soak in the water for about 1 hour. Return the beans to the heat and add more cold water so that beans are well covered.

Bring to a boil, then turn heat down to medium-low and cook for another 1½ to 2 hours, or until beans are tender. Drain and allow to cool, so that skins remain intact. Combine beans in a large mixing bowl.

In a separate bowl, combine the peppers, onion, tomatoes, cilantro, and basil. Mix together well and stir into the bowl of beans.

In the container of a food processor or a blender, combine the garlic, vinegar, mustard, olive oil, and salt. Blend for about 10 seconds and then pour over beans. Marinate mixture for at least 1 hour, or more. Serve on a bed of kale or lettuce garnished with red and green pepper rings.

Lobster Salad Calle Ocho

Ensalada de Langosta Calle Ocho

My love for lobster knows no bounds. I eat it several times a week, even at breakfast in omelets. In researching the recipes for this book I encountered several that called for lobster and pineapple and discovered that it was an ideal combination.

This recipe is named after Eighth Street, or Calle Ocho, in Miami's celebrated Little Havana district. **Serves 4**

2 cups cubed cooked lobster
2 ripe pineapples, halved lengthwise, fruit cut into small chunks, shells reserved
½ cup peeled and diced celery
½ cup toasted blanched slivered almonds
¼ cup shredded coconut
⅓ cup or more light mayonnaise
¼ cup peeled and diced kiwi fruit
Leafy red lettuce
1 kiwi fruit, thinly sliced, for garnish

In a large glass mixing bowl, combine lobster, pineapple chunks, celery, almonds, coconut, mayonnaise, and kiwi fruit. Mix well.

Fill the pineapple halves with mixture. Place halves on a bed of leafy red lettuce and garnish with sliced kiwi.

Lobster Salad Seviche

Ensalada de Langosta Seviche

There is nothing better than a succulent seasoned lobster salad, and the combination of flavors in this recipe is a perfect example. It's an ideal entrée for a hot summer night. **Serves 4**

2 pounds cooked lobster meat, cubed
3 tablespoons fresh lime juice
½ cup olive oil
¼ teaspoon Tabasco sauce
1 cup diced peeled celery
1 tablespoon minced green bell pepper
½ cup minced red onion
1 teaspoon chopped fresh cilantro
2 scallions, trimmed and very thinly sliced
⅓ cup mayonnaise
½ cup light sour cream
½ cup pimiento-stuffed manzanilla olives
Curly endive or escarole
1 tablespoon chopped fresh parsley, for garnish
1 lime, very thinly sliced, for garnish

Combine the lime juice, olive oil, and Tabasco in a nonmetallic bowl. Marinate the lobster in the mixture in the refrigerator for 1 to 2 hours. Drain the marinade and discard.

Add the celery, green pepper, red onion, cilantro, scallions, mayonnaise, sour cream, and olives. Toss well. Line a large bowl with a bed of curly endive or escarole. Garnish with chopped parsley and wafer-thin lime slices.

Codfish Salad

Bacalao de Almeria

Cubans use *bacalao*, or dried salt cod, in many forms, a tradition that began when refrigeration did not exist on the island.

I know you'll enjoy the bold cod taste melded with the piquant flavor of Spanish olives. Present this well chilled on a bed of fresh lettuce for a light meal on a warm day.   **Serves 4**

½ pound salted cod, soaked and cooked*
12 pimiento-stuffed manzanilla olives
1 cucumber, peeled and diced
1 large red tomato, peeled and diced
1 medium red onion, diced
2 garlic cloves, peeled and finely minced
1 red bell pepper, seeded and diced
1 green bell pepper, seeded and diced
1 tablespoon water
2 tablespoons extra-virgin olive oil
1 tablespoon red wine vinegar
Leafy red lettuce or other leafy lettuce
1 hard-boiled egg, chopped
2 tablespoons finely chopped fresh parsley
Pimiento strips, for garnish

Flake the cooked codfish and mix together with the olives, cucumber, tomato, onion, garlic, peppers, and water. Mix the olive oil and vinegar together and add to cod. Mix well and chill for at least 1 hour. Line four glass plates with lettuce. Mound the salad on the bed and then sprinkle egg and parsley over the fish and garnish with strips of pimiento.

*See page 25 for how to prepare salted cod.

Curried Chicken Salad

Ensalada de Pollo al Curry

This salad is a cinch to prepare and the flavors, both tart and sweet, blend beautifully.   **Serves 4**

1 (12½-ounce) can chunk white chicken, drained, or ¾ pound thoroughly cooked chicken chunks
1 cup canned pineapple slices with juice, cut into ½-inch pieces
3 tablespoons mango chutney*
¼ cup light mayonnaise
Juice of ½ lime
1 tablespoon mild curry powder cooked with 2 tablespoons olive oil
4 scallions, finely chopped
½ cup chopped green bell pepper
Salt, to taste
Red leaf lettuce or fresh pineapple shells
½ red bell pepper, seeded and thinly sliced into rings, for garnish

In a glass bowl, mix together the chicken, pineapple, and juice. Add mango chutney and mayonnaise and then blend gently, but thoroughly. Add remaining ingredients. Toss well. Serve on a bed of red leaf lettuce or in fresh pineapple shells, garnished with thin red bell pepper rounds.

*Use the recipe on page 207, or a good thick commercial brand.

Sherry Vinegar Dressing

Aderezo de Jerez Vinagre

Use a moderately dry, medium-body sherry, such as Amontillado, in this dressing. Produced in the Jerez de la Frontera region of Spain, this historic wine has a unique flavor that is rarely duplicated. Mix this light and lovely dressing a few hours ahead so that the flavors meld.

Makes 1¼ cups

2 tablespoons dry sherry
1 tablespoon white vinegar
1 cup extra-virgin olive oil
1 tablespoon heavy whipping cream
½ teaspoon finely chopped fresh cilantro
1 teaspoon finely chopped fresh parsley
2 tablespoons finely minced red onion
Salt and pepper, to taste

Pour sherry and vinegar into a small bowl, then whisk in the olive oil. Slowly add the cream, cilantro, parsley, onion, and salt and pepper. Serve over fresh greens.

Simple Vinaigrette

Vinagreta Sencilla

Some recipes in Cuban cuisine are adaptations of familiar foods and sauces introduced by visitors and immigrants over the years. This vinaigrette, basically French in origin, gets a Cuban touch with the addition of lime and cilantro as flavoring agents. It is best prepared a day ahead. You really should use a mortar and pestle to extract the flavors most fully, but a food processor will provide an adequate alternative.

Makes about 1 cup

3 garlic cloves, peeled
½ teaspoon dried oregano
1 teaspoon kosher salt
1 teaspoon Pommery or Dijon mustard
2 tablespoons red wine vinegar
Juice of 1 lime
1 cup extra-virgin olive oil
1 teaspoon finely chopped fresh parsley
½ teaspoon finely chopped fresh cilantro
Salt and cracked pepper, to taste

Using a mortar and pestle or a food processor, mash garlic and oregano with kosher salt. Add mustard, vinegar, and lime juice and combine well. Slowly add the oil. Add parsley and cilantro and blend well. Add salt and pepper to taste. Allow to marinate in refrigerator overnight. Keep tightly closed in a glass jar. Adjust seasoning, if necessary, before using.

Papaya Salad Dressing

Vinagreta de Papaya

In this New World recipe, papaya seeds bestow an especially lively flavor on the dressing. Served over raw papaya fruit or fresh greens, its sweet and sour taste whets one's appetite for the meal to follow.

Makes about 2½ cups

1 cup cider vinegar
1 teaspoon dry mustard
¼ cup granulated sugar
½ teaspoon salt
2 cups canola oil
1 white onion, minced
2 tablespoons fresh papaya seeds

Pour vinegar, mustard, sugar, and salt into the container of a blender or food processor. Process for 20 to 25 seconds. Slowly add oil and onion and blend until smooth. Add papaya seeds and blend until they are about the size of coarsely ground pepper, about 15 seconds. Will keep for 4 to 5 days refrigerated.

Vinaigrette Sauce

Salsa Vinagreta

This hearty yet light dressing blends boiled egg, capers, and red wine vinegar in a lovely olive oil sauce. It is spectacular served over salad greens, and is equally good over fried or broiled fish.   **Makes about 1 cup**

½ cup olive oil
¼ cup red wine vinegar
1½ tablespoons chopped fresh parsley
3 garlic cloves, peeled and finely chopped
2 tablespoons capers, drained
1 tablespoon finely chopped pimientos*
2 tablespoons minced red onion
Salt, to taste
½ teaspoon freshly ground black pepper
1 hard-boiled egg, finely chopped

Put all ingredients, except the egg, in the container of a food processor. Blend for 3 to 4 seconds, or until all ingredients are well combined. Store in a tightly closed glass jar. Just before serving, add the chopped egg. Serve over chilled greens.

*To store after opening the typical 4-ounce jar, cover remaining pimientos with water, add ½ teaspoon vinegar, and reseal tightly.

Fish and Shellfish

Pescados y Mariscos

Who should know better about preparing great seafood than those who live by the sea? With nine hundred species of fish, the waters surrounding Cuba make it a popular destination for fishermen from all over the world. The Hemingway Marina, just outside Havana, is renowned as one of the best deep-sea fishing marinas in the Americas. Sea bass and snapper are two of the most popular fish, but there is also grouper, swordfish, yellowtail, and kingfish.

Crab is a very popular shellfish, as are shrimp. My favorite is the spiny lobster, or *langosta*, found in warm waters, equaling and surpassing Maine lobster in flavor.

Despite the wealth of fresh fish nearby many Hispanic cities, Cubans still cherish their *bacalao*, the dried salted cod that was used for centuries before refrigeration came to the island.

The following "treasures of the sea" include a number of classic fish and shellfish dishes, as well as a selection of those with a more modern style. As with much Cuban cookery, tropical fruits and island vegetables play an important role. When prepared Cuban style, seafood presents an array of flavors and textures with intriguing subtleties and immense variety.

becomes fragrant, gently slide 2 fillets into each skillet with a spatula, crust side up, taking care to keep crust intact. Fry for about 2 minutes, then flip the fillets quickly and carefully and fry crust-side down until golden brown, 2 to 3 minutes, or longer, depending on thickness.

Remove fillets to each plate or one attractive large serving plate. Sprinkle with chives and serve hot.

*See Page 11.
†Also excellent with finely ground macadamia nuts.

Red Snapper with Malanga Crust

Pargo Envuelta Malanga

One of the interesting and flavorful techniques in the *nuevo Cubano* cuisine is coating fresh fish with the wonderful tubers of the Caribbean, such as malanga, boniato, and yuca. This recipe, a variation on one shared with me by Carole Kotkin, has the nutty taste of the malanga coating, somewhat like a black walnut flavor, which brings the snapper to a higher level of flavor and provides a lovely crunchy texture.

It may take a while to get the knack of coating the fillets, but when you master it, the results are well worth the effort.   **Serves 4**

   4 (6- to 8-ounce) red snapper fillets
   Salt and coarsely ground pepper, to taste
   1 tablespoon Pommery or any other grainy
      mustard
   3 pounds malanga, peeled and grated*
   ¼ cup finely ground pecans†
   ½ cup olive oil
   ¼ cup snipped fresh chives

Season fillets with salt and pepper. Spread 1 teaspoon of Dijon mustard on each fillet, back and front. Using clean hands, firmly pat a ¼-inch coating of malanga on top of each fillet.

Heat two nonstick large skillets and add ¼ cup of olive oil to each. When oil is heated and

Red Snapper with Cilantro-Lime Sauce

Pargo con Salsa de Cilantro y Limón
Verde

Red snapper, know as *pargo*, is delicious by itself, but this cilantro-lime sauce bestows a richly pungent flavor that greatly enhances the fresh qualities of the fish. It is equally exquisite over broiled or fried fish.   **Serves 4**

   2 to 3 tablespoons butter or margarine
   2 garlic cloves, peeled and chopped
   2 pounds red snapper or other firm
      white fish fillets
   1 cup cilantro-lime sauce (page 34)
   1 sweet white Bermuda onion, thinly sliced,
      for garnish
   Fresh cilantro sprigs, for garnish
   1 lemon and 1 lime, sliced lengthwise, for
      garnish

Melt the butter in a skillet and add garlic and fish. Sauté until fish flakes when tested with a fork. Do not overcook. Place fish on a warmed serving platter. Pour sauce over fish, or serve on the side. Garnish dish with Bermuda onion slices, cilantro sprigs, and lemon and lime slices.

Baked Red Snapper with Garlic and Cumin

Pargo al Horno con Ajo y Comino

At least twice a year I journey to the Florida Keys to purchase fresh whole snapper from the local fishermen. Agreeably forgetting any cholesterol concern whatsoever, we bake it whole with a large batch of butter-garlic-parsley sauce for dousing. By baking the fish, the moisture is retained inside the skin and makes for an outrageous meal.   **Serves 6**

½ tablespoon Spanish paprika
12 to 14 garlic cloves, peeled and crushed
½ teaspoon dried oregano
1 teaspoon dried thyme
½ teaspoon toasted and ground cumin seeds*
2 teaspoons dried rosemary, crushed
½ teaspoon sea salt
½ teaspoon coarsely ground black pepper
3 to 4 tablespoons sour orange juice†
½ cup dry white wine
1 cup plus 4 tablespoons olive oil
1 (6- to 8-pound) red snapper, cleaned and scaled
10 to 12 tiny new red potatoes, thinly sliced
1 large red bell pepper, seeded and julienned
2 large green bell peppers, seeded and julienned
2 large white onions, thinly sliced
Kale or endive
8 ripe cherry tomatoes, quartered, for garnish
Fresh cilantro or parsley sprigs, for garnish
2 quartered limes, for garnish

In a mortar or small glass bowl, combine the paprika, garlic, oregano, thyme, cumin seeds, 1 teaspoon rosemary, salt, and pepper. Crush together well with the pestle or the back of a spoon. Add sour orange juice and white wine and mix well. Slowly pour 1 cup of the olive oil into the marinade and whisk well to combine.

Clean the fish well in a solution of lime juice and water. Drain and place fish on a large platter and, using your hands, rub the marinade inside the fish to coat cavity and then the surface. Cover and refrigerate for 1 to 2 hours.

Preheat the oven to 350° F.

In a medium glass bowl, toss the potatoes and remaining rosemary in 2 tablespoons of olive oil and coat well. Place the potatoes on the bottom of a large baking pan or dish. Toss the peppers with 2 tablespoons of olive oil. Place a layer of the peppers and then the onions over the potatoes, then set the whole fish on top of the vegetables. Cover with aluminum foil. Bake for about 1 hour, or until flesh turns opaque and flakes easily.

To serve, place the whole fish on a bed of kale and garnish with quartered cherry tomatoes, cilantro or parsley, and limes.

*Toast and then grind in a mortar.
†Mix 2 tablespoons orange juice with 1 tablespoon lime juice if sour orange juice is not available.

Red Snapper, Alicante Style

Pargo Alicante

One of my favorite dishes is this red snapper, which is served daily at the world-famous Columbia Restaurant in Ybor City. This fabulously ornate institution of fine dining is the oldest and largest Hispanic restaurant in the United States, but is best known for its fine Cuban-Spanish cuisine. Alicante is the name of a town in Cuba as well as the name of this recipe.

There are many variations on this mouth-watering dish in which the snapper is roasted for a short time, seasoned with a brown sauce, olive oil, Sauterne, and fresh mild peppers. The garnish of fresh shrimp, eggplant, and golden toasted almonds becomes an integral part of the dish.

Serves 4

SHRIMP SUPREME

16 large shrimp, peeled and deveined
Juice of 1 lemon
2 garlic cloves, peeled and minced
1 teaspoon salt, or to taste
1 teaspoon cracked pepper
8 lean bacon strips
1 egg
½ cup milk
All-purpose flour, for dredging

ALICANTE

2 pounds red snapper
2 red onions, thinly sliced
2 garlic cloves, peeled and minced
½ cup olive oil
1 cup Sauterne wine
¾ cup brown sauce (page 32)
Salt and freshly cracked pepper, to taste
4 green bell peppers, seeded and thinly sliced

GARNISH

8 thin slices eggplant, breaded and fried
¼ cup toasted sliced almonds
Chopped fresh parsley

Pat the shrimp dry and marinate in the lemon juice, garlic, salt, and pepper for about 15 minutes. Cut the bacon strips in half, then wrap each half around the shrimp and secure with a toothpick.

Beat together the egg and milk. Dip the shrimp in the egg mixture, then into the flour. Deep-fry at 300° F until golden brown, 5 to 8 minutes. Drain and keep warm.

Heat oven to 350° F.

To assemble the *alicante,* place the red snapper on top of the onions and garlic in a large casserole. Pour on the olive oil, wine, and brown sauce to cover, and season with salt and a pinch of pepper. Top with green pepper slices. Bake in the oven for about 20 minutes. Garnish each with eggplant, 4 shrimp, almonds, and parsley.

In a small mixing bowl, combine the olive oil, paprika, garlic, thyme, wine, orange juice, and lime juice. Pour over fish and, using clean hands, spread inside and on the outside of fish. Insert thyme sprigs into fish cavity. Marinate, refrigerated and covered, for 1 to 2 hours, turning occasionally.

Preheat the oven to 350° F.

Mix the bell peppers with the onions and olive oil and set in a large rectangular ovenproof baking pan. Place fish on top of the peppers and onions and pour over marinade. Bake, covered with aluminum foil, until fish is opaque and flakes easily with a fork.

Garnish with fresh cilantro sprigs and lime wedges.

*Dried whole thyme is available at most Hispanic or Caribbean specialty stores. If not available, dried thyme leaves will suffice.

Baked Red Snapper with Paprika and Garlic Sauce

Pargo al Horno con Pimentón y

Salsa de Ajo

When fish is marinated, herbs and spices have the opportunity to enhance the natural qualities of the fish. And keeping the skin on this mild-tasting whole fish helps lock flavors in and protects the moistness of the fish. The foil helps to further seal in flavor.

Lake trout, whitefish, and rockfish also work well as an alternate in this very typical Cuban dish borrowed from the Spanish.　　　**Serves 4 to 6**

¾ cup olive oil

1 teaspoon Spanish paprika

6 garlic cloves, peeled and crushed

1 teaspoon crushed dried thyme

¼ cup dry white wine

1 tablespoon orange juice

1 tablespoon lime juice

1 (4- to 6-pound) whole red snapper, cleaned
  and scaled, head intact

2 to 3 sprigs of dried thyme*

1 red bell pepper, seeded and thinly sliced

1 green bell pepper, seeded and thinly sliced

1 yellow bell pepper, seeded and thinly sliced

2 red onions, thinly sliced

2 tablespoons olive oil

Fresh cilantro sprigs, for garnish

1 lime, thinly sliced into 8 wedges, for garnish

Fish Sautéed in Almond Sauce

Pescado en Salsa de Almendras
de Obatalá e Inle

This dish is especially meaningful to those Cubans practicing the Santeria religion and is named after two of their African gods. The popular Cuban folktale relates how Obatalá was sent to get just one fish to help cure his father's blindness. The fish was found and this dish was created. Because of it the blindness was cured, and ever since, so goes the fable, all peoples have worked together for humankind's welfare.

Serve this with boiled yuca with a hot garlicky *mojo criollo* (page 30) and black beans.

Serves 4

Juice of 2 limes (about ¼ cup), plus whole
   limes, for garnish
3 pounds fillet of red snapper, or other firm
   white fish
3 garlic cloves, peeled and crushed
½ teaspoon salt
½ cup cracker meal*
¾ cup yellow whole ground cornmeal
   (harina de maiz)
3 eggs, slightly beaten
¼ cup olive oil

SIMPLE ALMOND SAUCE

¼ pound plus 4 tablespoons unsalted butter
   or margarine
¾ cup blanched slivered almonds
1 teaspoon chopped fresh parsley
Salt, to taste
Fresh parsley sprigs, for garnish
Lime wedges, for garnish

In a large nonmetallic bowl, squeeze the lime juice over fillets and season well by rubbing in garlic and salt. Refrigerate and allow to marinate for 1 hour, turning several times so that juice penetrates all parts of fillets.

In a separate bowl, combine cracker meal with cornmeal. Dredge marinated fish with mixture, then dip in beaten eggs, then back into mixture again. Chill fillets for 15 to 20 minutes.

Heat a large skillet and add the olive oil. When oil is heated and begins to smell fragrant, add the fillets and sauté until golden brown, taking care not to overcook. You will need to do this in two batches and keep first batch warm while cooking the second. Add extra olive oil to the second batch, if necessary.

To prepare the almond sauce, melt butter in a medium skillet. Cook over medium-low heat until butter just begins to turn brown, then add almonds and sauté for 2 minutes. Stir in parsley and season with salt.

Pour sauce liberally over fish on a decorative platter garnished with sprigs of parsley and wedges of lime.

*Available at most supermarkets, or you can make your own by processing saltine crackers in the container of a food processor until finely ground—36 saltines make about 1 cup crumbs.

Grilled Snapper with Mango–Black Bean Relish

Pargo a la Parrilla con Mango y Frijoles Negros

In rural Cuba, residents often prepare fish over a pit fire made with red mangrove-growth charcoal. The mangrove wood, processed by very slow smoking over a period of time, imparts a wonderful flavor to the fish. Although this wood is not readily available, there are many woods and charcoals on the market, like mesquite, for example, that help impart such a flavor to the foods being grilled.

In the United States, there's a hotbed of young and talented chefs who borrow these traditional Cuban techniques and combine them with the new. Hubert Des Marais's *nuevo Cubano* recipes have been popular with Palm Beach aficionados, as well as those who simply enjoy splendidly seasoned foods.

This recipe is my adaptation of one of Hubert's favorites.   **Serves 4**

4 (6-ounce) red snapper fillets, or other firm white fish
¾ cup olive oil
1 pound medium shrimp, peeled and deveined
3 garlic cloves, peeled and chopped
1 Scotch bonnet pepper, seeded and minced*
4 cups mango–black bean relish (page 206)
1⅓ cups puréed roasted yellow bell pepper †
4 fresh thyme or parsley sprigs

Brush each snapper fillet with 1 tablespoon olive oil. Grill over medium-high heat for about 2 minutes on each side, or until fish turns white and is tender. Do not overcook. Keep warm while preparing shrimp.

Heat a large skillet or sauté pan and add 3 tablespoons olive oil. When hot, add shrimp, garlic, and scotch bonnet pepper and sauté for a few minutes, until shrimp turn pink and are just cooked.

To serve, place 2 heaping tablespoons of mango–black bean relish in the center of a large plain-colored serving platter. Arrange the fillets on top. Ladle yellow pepper purée around the fish and relish. Top with the shrimp and fresh thyme.

---

*Wear rubber gloves and protect eyes when seeding and chopping Scotch bonnet peppers, the highest on the capsicum scale. If a milder pepper is desired, substitute a medium cubanella pepper, or ½ red bell pepper.
† See page 24 for how to peel and roast peppers.

Preheat the oven to 400° F.

In a large skillet, sauté garlic, onion, and parsley in olive oil over moderate heat for 4 to 5 minutes, until onion turns translucent. Whisk in cornstarch. Add the fish stock, wine, and bay leaf. Bring to a boil and stir until smooth. Add more wine if necessary.

Put the sea bass, shrimp, clams, potatoes, and asparagus in a large casserole dish and add the sauce, mixing gently to cover. Salt and pepper to taste. Bake for 20 to 25 minutes, or until fish is translucent. When that stage is reached, immediately stop cooking.

Remove bay leaf before serving and arrange on an attractive flowered platter. Garnish with capers, olives, and egg. Serve hot.

*To defat canned broth, place can in refrigerator. When chilled, open can and skim off fat from the surface.

Sea Bass in Green Sauce

Lubina en Salsa Verde

This classic fish dish was brought to Cuba via Spain. Fresh fillets are baked together with a smattering of garden-fresh vegetables and herbs. Fresh parsley takes the flavor lead, but garlic, red onion, and dry white wine join in to help fashion this hearty stewlike dish.

Serves 4

2 garlic cloves, peeled and minced
1 tablespoon chopped white onion
1 bunch of fresh parsley, stems removed, minced
1 tablespoon olive oil
1 teaspoon cornstarch
2 cups fish stock (page 37) or defatted chicken broth*
¼ cup Spanish dry white wine
1 bay leaf, cracked
2 pounds sea bass, red snapper, or any firm white fish fillets
8 large shrimp, shelled and deveined
8 littleneck or other clams in the shell, thoroughly scrubbed
12 small red potatoes, peeled around the middle with a vegetable peeler and boiled
8 fresh green asparagus spears, cooked al dente
Salt and coarsely ground pepper, to taste
1 tablespoon brine-packed Spanish capers, drained, for garnish
¼ cup halved, drained pimiento-stuffed manzanilla olives, for garnish
1 hard-boiled egg, chopped, for garnish

Grilled Swordfish with Mango and Blueberries

Pez Espada a la Parrilla

con Mango y Arándanos

The ability to create dishes that combine the most tantalizing flavors of a variety of cuisines is no more evident than in Miami. In this melting pot by the sea, innovative chefs are choosing foods indigenous to the area and blending them with techniques and preparations from other cuisines. Case in point: this lovely swordfish creation.

Mangoes are puréed with dry sherry and then slowly simmered with other flavorings to produce a lovely sauce. Flavors vary tremendously from one fruit to another, so carefully select the mangoes you will be using. You can tell ripeness by feeling top and bottom; if soft and fragrant, it should be ripe.

This swordfish, with its firm white flesh, wins accolades, but the dish is also excellent when prepared with mahi mahi (dolphin) or any firm fish steak. Because I live in Florida, I often prepare it with the readily available grouper or red snapper.

Serves 4

4 (8-ounce) swordfish steaks, cut about
  1 inch thick
1 cup mojo criollo (page 30)
3 tablespoons unsalted butter or margarine
4 garlic cloves, peeled and minced
2 tablespoons minced white onion
1 cup chicken stock (page 36) or defatted
  chicken broth*
½ teaspoon dried tarragon
1 teaspoon chopped fresh thyme, or
  ½ teaspoon dried
¼ teaspoon crushed oregano
1 teaspoon chopped fresh rosemary, or
  ½ teaspoon dried

1½ cups peeled and diced fresh mangoes†
½ cup very dry sherry
2 tablespoons fresh lime juice
¼ cup raw honey
Salt and freshly ground pepper, to taste

GARNISH

1 cup fresh peeled and diced mango†
¼ cup fresh blueberries
12 fresh chive stems
1 lime, cut into 4 wedges

Put swordfish steaks in a shallow nonmetallic dish and pour over *mojo criollo*. Refrigerate for 1 to 2 hours.

Melt butter in a heavy saucepan over medium heat. Add garlic and onion and sauté until soft. Add stock, tarragon, thyme, oregano, and rosemary. Bring to a boil. Reduce mixture to about half. Remove from heat and set aside.

In the container of a food processor, purée diced mangoes with the sherry until medium thick. Add lime juice and honey. Process for 5 seconds and stir into the sauce. Place pan back onto the stove and simmer. Season with salt and pepper.

Grill the swordfish at moderate heat over fire to which fragrant charcoal has been added. Press steaks onto grill to achieve grilling marks. A 1-inch-thick fish should take 10 to 12 minutes to be fully cooked. Turn fish several times, constantly basting with the marinade or with butter sauce.

To serve, spoon a quarter of the sauce into the center of 4 oversized plates and place a swordfish steak on top of each. Garnish with a spoonful of diced mango, a few blueberries, and fresh chives. Serve with a wedge of lime on each plate.

*To defat canned broth, place can in refrigerator. When chilled, open can and skim fat from the surface. If using your own stock, be sure it is fat free.
†See page 23 for how to cut a mango.

Fish, Russian Style

Trucha à la Rusa

This fish was a favorite in Spain and was brought to Cuba, where it continued to be a favorite. The use of melted butter, chopped eggs, parsley, and bread crumbs was borrowed from the Russian culture. Today this dish is served in many Cuban and Spanish restaurants throughout the United States, often accompanied by rice and beans.

If you're squeamish about serving whole fish, cover the eyes with olives, or substitute 3 small fillets for each whole fish.   **Serves 4**

4 (1-pound) whole brook, brown, or rainbow trout, scaled and dressed
2 tablespoons minced fresh flat-leaf parsley
2 tablespoons chopped fresh thyme, or 1 tablespoon dried
2 garlic cloves, peeled and crushed
Olive oil
Salt and cracked pepper, to taste
¼ pound unsalted butter or margarine, melted and slightly browned
Fresh fine bread crumbs
2 hard-boiled eggs, chopped
1 (4-ounce) jar pimientos
4 fresh flat-leaf parsley sprigs
Lemon, orange, and lime slices, for garnish

Wash and then score trout by slashing diagonally 3 to 4 times. Combine parsley, thyme, and garlic and stuff in the slashes of the trout. Season with salt and pepper. Rub trout with olive oil so that all pieces are well saturated. Cover and marinate in refrigerator for about 2 hours. Drain off oil.

Preheat the oven to 400° F.

Place fish side by side in a large Pyrex baking dish. Pour butter over all, being careful to coat all pieces. Bake, turning fish several times, until fish turns translucent, 8 to 10 minutes, depending on thickness of trout. Lightly sprinkle fish with bread crumbs.

Garnish with hard-boiled egg, pimiento, parsley, and lemon, orange, and lime slices. Serve piping hot.

Fish with Almonds, Villaclarense Style

Pescado Villaclarense

In this classic recipe, the coating seals moisture into the fish, while the herbs and spices in the coating subtly flavor it. If grouper, a relatively lean fish, is not available, use any firm white fish. Macadamia nuts can be substituted for the almonds for an alternative taste. Use a good port wine; it will make a difference.

Serves 4

¾ cup chopped white onion
3 garlic cloves, peeled and minced
½ teaspoon white pepper
1 teaspoon ground cumin
1 tablespoon chopped fresh parsley
1 teaspoon fresh lime juice
⅔ cup chopped almonds, toasted
1 tablespoon dry port wine
4 (8-ounce) fresh grouper or other firm white fillets (2 pounds)
1 teaspoon Spanish paprika
1 tablespoon olive oil
2 tablespoons butter or margarine
Salt and coarsely ground pepper, to taste
1 lemon, sliced lengthwise
1 lime, sliced lengthwise
Watercress, for garnish

In the container of a food processor or blender, process the onion, garlic, white pepper, cumin powder, parsley, lime juice, and almonds into a paste. Slowly add wine. Using your hands, coat both sides of fish with paste. Cover completely and refrigerate for 10 to 15 minutes. Sprinkle liberally with paprika and season with salt and pepper.

Heat a large skillet and add the olive oil and butter. When the pan is heated and the oil begins to smell fragrant, use a wooden spoon to combine the butter with the oil. Sauté the fish, turning it very carefully at least once to brown, and then add more olive oil if necessary. Fish is cooked if it flakes easily when pricked with a fork. Cooking time will depend on thickness of fillet.

Garnish with lemon and lime slices and fresh watercress.

Fish with Avocado and Black Bean, Jícama, and Corn Salsa

Pescado con Aguacate y Salsa de Frijoles Negros, Jícama, Salsa de Maíz

The *nuevo Cubano* style of cooking is rapidly evolving in the United States. It stresses the use of spicy salsas and relishes, along with a number of glazes and butter sauces. Using traditional Cuban ingredients and an abundance of those indigenous to the region makes for some wildly wonderful creations. Case in point: this delicate fish assembly with its potpourri of flavors. **Serves 4**

1 ripe avocado, peeled and cut into chunks
1 teaspoon chopped fresh parsley
2 tablespoons fresh lime juice
1 garlic clove, peeled and minced
1 jalapeño pepper, seeded and diced
Ají cachucha pepper* or ½ Scotch bonnet,† seeded and diced
4 (8-ounce) firm white fish fillets
2 tablespoons olive oil
Ground cumin
Salt and cracked black pepper, to taste
4 cups black bean, jícama, and corn salsa (page 200)
Avocado slices, mango slices, and fresh cilantro sprigs, for garnish

To prepare the fish, purée the avocado in the container of a food processor together with the parsley and lime juice. Add garlic, jalapeño, and *ají cachucha* pepper. Chill.

Rub each fillet with olive oil on both sides and coat lightly with cumin, cracked pepper, and salt. Place fish on a hot grill or broil about 6 inches from broiling element. Carefully turn several times until fish turns from translucent to white.

To assemble the dish, place a portion of the jícama salsa on each serving plate. Place 1 fillet on top of each. Top with the avocado purée and garnish with avocado slices, mango slices, and sprigs of cilantro.

*Can be found at most Hispanic markets, or substitute any hot pepper.
†Wear rubber gloves when seeding this pepper because it is very hot.

Minute Fish

Pescado al Minuto

Minute fish refers both to their size and the amount of time it takes to cook them. The small fish, which were once very popular in Havana, were split open, removing the head and bones. Served in sandwich form, they were a favorite of many workers who would buy three or four for themselves and friends. For the evening meal, a huge plate of the fried finfish would be served, accompanied by rice, beans, and a bounty of fruits and vegetables.

This recipe is excellent for using small whole fish, preferably those with superior flavor, that you've caught or purchased. They're a crowd-pleaser, too, when made with fish fillets. You can prepare the fish a few hours ahead, then fry just before you're ready to serve, but be sure to keep them covered and refrigerated. **Serves 4**

    8 to 10 small fish, boned, cleaned,
       heads removed
    Juice of 2 limes
    ¼ cup olive oil
    ¾ cup all-purpose flour, for dredging
    Salt and pepper, to taste
    3 eggs, slightly beaten
    ¾ cup fine bread crumbs mixed with 1
       tablespoon chopped fresh parsley
    Vegetable oil, for frying
    1 lime, sliced lengthwise
    2 tablespoons chopped fresh parsley
    1 (4-ounce) jar pimientos, drained and
       chopped

Wash and clean fish thoroughly. Marinate whole fish in lime juice mixed with olive oil for about 10 minutes. Drain and discard marinade. In a separate glass bowl or large glass dish, mix the flour with salt and pepper. Thoroughly dredge fish in a coating of flour, then in beaten egg, then in the bread crumbs.

Heat a large frying pan and add vegetable oil for frying. Fry fillets until golden brown, or you may deep-fry. Serve with lime slices and sprinkle with fresh parsley and chopped pimientos.

Baked Cod Cakes with Cilantro-Lime Sauce

Tortas de Bacalao
con Salsa de Cilantro y Limón Verde

Cod is a popular saltwater fish that is mild-flavored and firm. These cod cakes are served with a delightful sauce made from the fragrant leaves of the coriander plant.

Serves 6 (24 patties)

    2 cups cooked and flaked fresh cod
    2 cups mashed white potatoes
    1 cup minced white onion
    2 eggs, well beaten
    3 cups corn flake crumbs
    Salt, to taste
    1 cup cilantro-lime sauce (page 34)

Preheat the oven to 400° F. Line 2 cookie sheets with foil. Brush lightly with oil and set aside.

In a medium glass bowl, mix the fish with potatoes and onion. Add salt to taste. Form into 2-inch patties by rolling first into balls, then flattening. Dip patties first in the egg, then the corn flakes. Gently place on cookie sheets, 1 inch apart. Bake for about 10 minutes, or just until done. Do not overcook. Serve with hot cilantro-lime sauce poured over each piece.

Plantain-Coated Fresh Fish

Pescado Revestido en Plátanos

Purchase plantains when the peel is green to yellow for this recipe. The fruit, which will have a slightly nutty flavor at this stage, serves two purposes. First, it acts as a coating for the fish, and second, it seals in its natural moistness.

Any firm white fish will do for this recipe, but grouper, red snapper, cobia, wahoo, or shark meat marry particularly well with the plantain.

Serves 4

4 green to slightly yellow plantains, peeled and thinly sliced*
Vegetable oil, for deep-frying
1 cup all-purpose flour
½ teaspoon cayenne pepper
1 teaspoon ground cumin
½ teaspoon salt
½ teaspoon pepper
6 (8-ounce) portions any firm white fish
4 eggs, slightly beaten
Thinly sliced lemon and limes, for garnish

Deep-fry plantains in vegetable oil until lightly browned, 2 to 3 minutes. Cool until room temperature or cooler. Process in the container of a food processor until plantains are ground into very small pieces, almost a flour, although it will be somewhat moist.

In a medium bowl, mix the flour together with cayenne, cumin, salt, and pepper and pour into a large plate or pan. Dredge fish pieces in flour mixture, then eggs, then the plantain flour, being careful to coat the surface almost completely. You may have to use your fingers to press the mixture on the skin of the fish. Deep-fry in batches until golden brown.

Serve with a chutney or tartar sauce on the side. To add color, garnish with fresh slices of lemon and lime.

*See page 23 for how to cut a plantain.

Cod with Annatto Oil

Bacalao en Aceite de Achiole

This recipe combines *bacalao* with annatto oil, a seasoning that is incorporated into many *nuevo Cubano* recipes. **Serves 4**

Juice of ½ lime
4 (6-ounce) salted cod fillets, soaked and boned*
½ cup annatto oil (page 28)
4 whole cloves
½ cup toasted blanched slivered almonds
1 tablespoon chopped fresh parsley

Squeeze lime juice over cod fillets just before cooking.

Heat a large sauté pan. Add annatto oil. When oil becomes fragrant, add cod fillets and cloves. Cook until just done, turning at least once. Remove to plates. Garnish with toasted almonds and parsley. Serve with white rice.

*See page 25 for on how to prepare salted cod.

Rice with Salted Cod

Arroz con Bacalao

Salted cod, *bacalao,* was often used in Cuba since refrigeration was a rarity, and it has become a tropical staple in most Cuban households.

This recipe, which has many variations, is especially good on a cold day. Fresh peppers and tomatoes and long-grain rice combine to produce a richly flavored one-dish supper.

It is important to soak the cod so that much of the salt is removed.   **Serves 6 to 8**

2 pounds salted cod, soaked and boned*
All-purpose flour, for dredging
¼ cup olive oil
1 cup finely chopped onion
½ green bell pepper, seeded and diced
½ red bell pepper, seeded and diced
1 bay leaf, crushed
1 teaspoon cumin seeds, toasted and mashed
¾ teaspoon Spanish paprika
3 garlic cloves, peeled and mashed
A few threads of saffron or bijol†
1½ cups peeled and chopped ripe tomatoes
½ cup red Burgundy wine
2½ cups water
½ teaspoon granulated sugar
2¼ cups long-grain rice
Salt and pepper, to taste (only if needed)

Cut boned codfish into 2-inch squares. Dredge in flour. Heat a large skillet and add olive oil. When heated and oil begins to smell fragrant, fry squares, turning gently several times. Remove from pan with a slotted spoon and drain on brown paper bags or paper towels. Keep warm in oven.

Add onion, peppers, bay leaf, cumin, paprika, garlic and saffron threads to the oil in which the cod was browned, stirring to combine. Cook 5 to 10 minutes, until vegetables are tender. Add tomatoes and incorporate well. Cover and cook for about 15 minutes. Add wine, water, sugar, and rice. Bring to a boil, then lower heat, cover, and cook for about 45 minutes, stirring at intervals. When rice is soft and water has evaporated, dish is ready. Return cod squares to the rice mixture and combine gently. Serve on a large decorative platter. Serve with green vegetables and fruit salad.

*See page 25 for how to prepare salted cod.
†See page 6.

Salted Cod, Pedro López

Bacalao Pedro López

Bacalao has a unique flavor that is enhanced by the intensity of the anchovies in this robust dish.   **Serves 4**

2 pounds salted cod, soaked and boned*
1½ tablespoons olive oil
1 large onion, sliced into rings
4 garlic cloves, peeled and chopped
1 (4-ounce) can pimientos
1 (28-ounce) can tomato purée
1 tablespoon red wine vinegar
½ teaspoon ground cumin
½ teaspoon cayenne pepper
Salt and black pepper, to taste
1 pound white potatoes, peeled, boiled,
   and sliced
1 tablespoon extra-virgin olive oil
1 tablespoon red wine vinegar
1 can anchovies, drained and chopped,
   for garnish
Fresh parsley sprig, for garnish

Cut the boned cod into 8 pieces. Heat a large skillet and add the olive oil. When oil smells fragrant, add the onion, garlic, and all the pimientos except several slices for garnish. Sauté until the onion is wilted. Add the purée, red wine vinegar, and spices. Cook over low heat for 20 to 25 minutes. Adjust seasoning.

Sprinkle potatoes with olive oil and vinegar. Place potatoes on four separate plates. Place cod on each and garnish with anchovies and a sprig of parsley.

*See page 25 for how to prepare salted cod.

Rice with White Tuna

Arroz con Atún Blanco

This innovative cold buffet dish is a favorite of many Cuban home cooks I know who live in Miami. Not only is it easy and inexpensive to prepare, but it contains many of the fresh flavors so familiar to the Cuban lifestyle. Any kind of canned tuna will do, but it works best with a good solid white variety packed in water.

The garnish is one typically used in many of the very colorful party dishes—a coat of garlic mayonnaise or *aïoli*, small peas, and chopped pimientos.   **Serves 4 to 6**

¼ cup olive oil
1 cup chopped white onion
1 red bell pepper, seeded and halved
1 scallion, chopped
¼ cup chopped small capers
2 (7-ounce) cans white tuna, packed in water
2 cups long-grain white rice
4 cups water
1 teaspoon sea salt
Light olive oil
1 cup garlic mayonnaise (page 32)
1 cup baby green peas (petit pois), drained
1 (4-ounce) jar diced pimientos

Heat a large sauté pan or skillet and add olive oil. When oil becomes fragrant, add onion, red pepper, scallion, and capers. Cook over medium heat until onion is translucent. Add the tuna. Mix together well. Add the rice, water, and sea salt. Reduce heat to a simmer and cook for about 40 minutes, or until water is absorbed and rice is tender.

Place rice mixture in a mold greased with light-flavored olive oil and press. Chill for 1 to 2 hours. Carefully unmold onto a large plate. Cover with a thin coat of garlic mayonnaise. Garnish with petit pois and red pimientos.

Fish Flan

Pudín de Pescado

Although this puddinglike dish is most typically served cold, coated with mayonnaise and beautifully garnished, it is also moist and lovely served warm just out of the oven. The addition of tomato, parsley, and egg yolk not only adds luscious flavor, but also makes for a very attractive dish.

Atlantic black sea bass, the sole member of the Pacific rockfish family found in Atlantic waters, is perfect for this dish, but any firm white fish, such as cod or grouper, will work well here.

Serves 10 to 12

2 pounds sea bass or any firm white fish
  fillets
Juice of 1 lime
1 teaspoon fresh thyme, or ½ teaspoon dried
2 bay leaves
1 teaspoon chopped fresh tarragon, or
  ½ teaspoon dried
¼ cup olive oil
1 cup finely chopped white onion
1 (16-ounce) can tomatoes, drained and
  chopped
1 teaspoon sea salt
1 tablespoon chopped fresh parsley
½ teaspoon sea salt
2 cups dry white wine, preferably Spanish
6 pieces white bread, crusts removed, soaked
  in milk and squeezed
8 eggs separated (at room temperature)
1¼ cups cracker meal*
Olive oil for greasing casserole dish

GARNISH

Enough light mayonnaise to frost mold
¼ cup cooked baby green peas (petit pois)
¼ cup chopped fresh parsley
1 (4-ounce) jar red pimientos, drained and
  chopped
Cucumber slices

Using your hands, shred fish or crush into small pieces, then put in a large saucepot. Squeeze in the lime juice and add the thyme, bay leaves, and tarragon. Cover with tap water to the top of the fish. Bring to a boil, turn the heat to low, and simmer for 20 minutes. Drain fish in a colander, pressing on fish to remove excess water. Remove bay leaves and set aside.

Heat a large deep skillet and add the olive oil. When oil becomes fragrant, add onion, tomatoes, parsley, and salt. Pour in the wine and the shredded fish, stirring well. Add the bread and stir well to combine. Lower the heat to simmer for 5 minutes, then slowly add in the yolks, one at a time, stirring constantly to combine. Add 1 cup of the cracker meal, combine well, then remove mixture from heat and allow to cool for 15 to 20 minutes.

Preheat the oven to 350° F. Whip egg whites until stiff and refrigerate until fish mixture has cooled. Lightly grease a 3-quart mold with olive oil and coat lightly with remaining cracker meal by tilting bowl so that crumbs adhere well.

When the fish mixture has cooled, stir in stiff egg whites to combine, being careful not to deflate mixture, then pour mixture into the casserole. Place casserole in a large pan of water (bain-marie) and bake for 55 to 60 minutes, or until a toothpick comes out dry. Allow to cool.

When cooled, use a sharp knife and loosen around the rim, then place a flat plate on top and invert the custard onto a serving plate. Using a rubber spatula, cover with a light coating of mayonnaise and decorate with baby peas, fresh parsley, and chopped pimientos. Chill. Line cucumbers along the edge and place small pieces of pimiento on each slice.

*Available at most supermarkets, or make your own by processing saltine crackers in a food processor until finely ground—36 saltines make about 1 cup crumbs.

Paella Valenciana

Paella à la Valenciana

Paella, which contains chicken, seafood, rice, fresh vegetables, herbs, and spices, is the best known traditional main dish of Spain. The name of the dish comes from the circular, shallow double-handled pan in which it is cooked, called a *paellera*. In Spain, it is still often cooked outdoors over burning wood, which adds a spectacular aroma. At home I prepare this in a paella pan set atop a large steel ring I purchased on a visit to Spain. The ring is joined to a butane cylinder that distributes heat throughout the dish. But for most home cooks, the oven is the most practical.

The rice for this dish is similar to that used in making risotto. A short-grain hard rice is preferred, but Italian arborio rice is a good substitute. If overcooked, the rice tends to become mushy, so it is important to keep an eye on the dish and taste as you proceed. Medium-grain white rice will also work. **Serves 6 to 8**

½ cup olive oil
1 onion, chopped
1 green bell pepper, seeded and chopped
½ cup peeled and chopped ripe tomatoes
3 garlic cloves, peeled and minced
1 bay leaf
½ pound pork, cut into 1-inch chunks
½ fryer chicken, cut into 4 pieces
1 pound lobster, cut into chunks
½ pound shrimp, peeled
8 oysters in shell, cleaned and shells scrubbed
8 mussels in shell, cleaned and shells scrubbed
4 clams in shells, cleaned and scrubbed
4 stone crab claws or Alaskan stone claws
1 pound red snapper, cut into 1-inch chunks
3 cups fish stock (page 37), chicken stock (page 36), or bottled clam juice

Pinch of saffron or bijol*
1 teaspoon sea salt, or to taste
1½ cups short-grain pearl rice or Italian arborio rice
½ cup dry white wine
1 small can baby green peas (petit pois), for garnish
1 (10-ounce) can thin white asparagus, for garnish
1 (4-ounce) jar pimientos, for garnish

Preheat the oven to 350° F.

Pour olive oil into a paella pan or large heavy casserole. Add onion and pepper and fry until just limp. Add tomatoes, garlic, and bay leaf and cook 5 minutes. Add pork and chicken and sauté until tender, stirring to prevent sticking or burning. Add seafood, stock, saffron, and salt. When the stock boils, add rice by placing on top of mixture diagonally from top left to bottom right of the pan. Allow the rice to sit for a few minutes, then stir to combine with other ingredients and bring to a second boil. Cover and bake for about 20 minutes. To serve, sprinkle with wine and garnish with peas, asparagus, and pimiento.

*See page 6.

Pasta-Style Seafood Paella

Fideo de Mariscos

With the influx of the Cuban population to the United States, there has been much intermixing of cultures. In Tampa, for instance, there is a strong blend of Cuban and Spanish cuisine with elements of the Italian, such as in this modern-day paella, where linguine replaces the traditional rice.   **Serves 6**

2¼ cups canned plum tomatoes
2 tablespoons olive oil
⅔ cup diced green bell pepper
½ red bell pepper, seeded and diced
1 white onion, diced
¼ pound lean pork, cut into chunks
2 cups diced white chicken meat
4 garlic cloves, peeled
1 tablespoon chopped fresh parsley
1 tablespoon chopped fresh basil
1 teaspoon ground cumin
2 bay leaves, cracked
2 cups fish stock (page 37)
1 bottle (750 ml) dry white wine
Salt and pepper, to taste

SEAFOOD

2 dozen mussels, cleaned well
1½ dozen small clams, cleaned well
6 to 8 saffron threads or bijol*
2 dozen medium shrimp
½ pound medium stone crab claws (optional)
1 pound bay scallops
2 cups thin squid slices
1 chorizo sausage, cut into very thin slices
1 pound linguine, cooked according to
  package directions

GARNISH

1 (7-ounce) can baby green peas (petit pois)
1 (7-ounce) can thin green asparagus,
  drained
1 (4-ounce) jar pimientos, cut into thin strips

To prepare the sauce, drain the tomatoes and chop into small pieces. In a large heavy skillet, heat the olive oil. When the pan is heated and the oil begins to smell fragrant, sauté the peppers, onion, pork, and chicken. When onion turns translucent, add garlic, parsley, basil, and cumin. Sauté for a few minutes. Puree the mixture in the container of a food processor.

Put the fish stock in a large kettle and add the bay leaves, tomatoes, purée mixture, wine, salt, and pepper. Simmer sauce for 50 to 60 minutes.

To prepare the seafood, heat 1 cup of the sauce over medium-high heat in a shallow heavy skillet. Add mussels, clams, and saffron. Cover and steam until shells open, 3 to 4 minutes. Discard unopened shells. Add the shrimp, crab, scallops, chorizo, and another portion of the sauce. Cook shellfish until just done, stirring constantly. Do not overcook. Add squid and cook for an additional minute. Add remaining sauce. Mix in the cooked pasta and serve immediately. Garnish with peas, asparagus, and pimientos.

*See page 6.

Cuban-Style Lobster

Langosta à la Cubana

At Papa's restaurant in the Hemingway Marina in Havana, Candido Leva, the executive chef who was raised in the spice-oriented province of Oriente, serves some of the most enjoyed delicacies in the city. This sautéed stuffed lobster takes only a short time to prepare, and it can be made ahead and simply browned for a few minutes before serving. The more flavorful the rum, the better the dish.

Serves 4

    4 (1- to 1½-pound) lobsters, boiled or
      steamed
    ¼ pound plus 4 tablespoons butter
    3 garlic cloves, peeled and minced
    1¼ cups chopped onion
    6 ripe tomatoes, peeled, seeded, and chopped
    2 cups fine bread crumbs
    4 eggs, slightly beaten
    3 ounces white rum
    Sprinkling of Spanish paprika
    ⅔ cup clarified butter*
    Lemon and lime wedges
    Fresh parsley sprigs

Twist tails from the lobsters by grasping and turning until tail is released. Set aside remaining parts on individual large plates. With a sharp knife, cut each of the four tails in half lengthwise, opening center so that it can be stuffed. Remove all meat and dice. Put a shell on each plate.

Heat a large sauté pan and add the ¼ pound butter. When butter is melted, add garlic, onion, and tomatoes and cook for 5 to 7 minutes. Remove pan from heat. Add 1½ cups of the bread crumbs, eggs, and rum and combine well. Add the diced lobster and mix well. Fill the reserved shells with stuffing until overflowing. Dot with remaining 4 tablespoons butter. Sprinkle with remaining bread crumbs and the paprika. Brown under the broiler for 3 to 4 minutes.

Place each lobster on a separate plate, with claws and lobster chest at head of plate and stuffed tail at bottom, so that lobster looks whole again. Serve with individual cups of hot clarified butter, lemon and lime wedges, and fresh parsley sprigs.

*To clarify butter, melt over low heat, being careful that it does not brown. Remove from heat and allow to stand for 3 to 4 minutes until solids settle to bottom. Skim off the foam at top and discard sediment. One-half pound butter makes about ⅔ cup clarified.

Lobster and Stone Crab Creole

Enchilado de Langosta y Cangrejos Moros

Whenever I visit New York City, where I spent most of my youth, I stop in at Victor's. It's the city's most popular Cuban restaurant and is owned by Cuban-born Victor del Corral, who arrived from Guanabacoa in 1957.

Thirty-seven years later, his daughter, Sonia Zaldivar, oversees their second restaurant in Miami where, during stone crab season (starting in October), they prepare *enchilado* in large quantities. This Creole-style recipe combines the zesty spiciness of the hot pepper with the mildly delicate flavor of the stone crab and lobster.

Crack the claws well before serving so your guests have no struggle with the meat. It will also save the dining room carpet.   **Serves 6 to 8**

¼ cup olive oil
4 garlic cloves, peeled and finely chopped
1 medium onion, finely chopped
1 green bell pepper, seeded and finely
    chopped
1 jalapeño or serrano pepper, seeded and
    finely chopped
1 bay leaf, crushed
¼ teaspoon ground oregano
¼ teaspoon dried thyme
2 cups tomato sauce
1 cup beer
2 teaspoons sea salt, or to taste
6 (8-ounce) lobster tails, shelled and cut
    into 1-inch chunks
8 stone crab claws, slightly cracked, or
    lobster claws
2 tablespoons chopped fresh parsley, for
    garnish
2 red bell peppers, roasted, seeded, and
    sliced, for garnish

Heat a large skillet and add the olive oil. Add garlic and sauté until slightly golden. Add the onion, green pepper, jalapeño, bay leaf, oregano, and thyme. Cook for about 3 minutes.

Pour in tomato sauce and beer and season with salt. Mix well and simmer over medium heat for 10 minutes, or until sauce thickens slightly. Add lobster and stone crab claws and cook for 4 more minutes. Remove bay leaf and discard. Sprinkle with the chopped parsley and serve garnished with the slices of roasted peppers.

Serve with fried ripe plantains and a simple green salad with oil and vinegar.

Lump Crab with Crisp Plantains and Mango Vinaigrette

A Congrejo con Plátanos Tostados y

Vinagreta de Mango

Here's an elegant crab dish that is truly away from the mainstream, yet so easy and awe-inspiring you'll want to prepare it again and again. It's my variation on a dish created by Hubert Des Marais, of Palm Beach, one of my favorite chefs who is well known for his different combinations and outrageous taste sensations.

Take extra care when forming the plantain rings so they stay together while cooking.

Serves 4

½ cup olive oil
48 (⅛-inch) slices peeled green plantains
1 cup diced ripe avocado
¼ cup diced red onion
4 teaspoons fresh lime juice
1 Scotch bonnet pepper, seeded*
4 tablespoons chopped fresh chives
2 teaspoons chopped fresh cilantro leaves
Salt and pepper, to taste
2 cups jumbo lump crab, picked over
 and drained
1 cup puréed mango
2½ tablespoons tamarind juice†
4 teaspoons crème fraîche‡
2 teaspoons Sevruga or other caviar
¼ cup finely chopped zucchini and
 red and yellow bell peppers

Heat a large skillet and add ¼ cup of the olive oil.

Meanwhile, on a cutting board or plate, place 6 rounds together in a circle and press on sides to adhere. You should form 8 plantain rings with the 48 slices. When the pan is heated and the oil begins to grow fragrant, fry the plantains on both sides until crisp. Drain and set aside.

Mix avocado together with onion, half of the lime juice, half of the Scotch bonnet pepper, ½ tablespoon chives, and chopped cilantro. Season with salt and pepper. Set aside.

Combine the crabmeat with the remaining chives, remaining lime juice, and 1 tablespoon of the mango purée. Cover and set aside.

Mix the remaining mango purée, tamarind juice, remaining ¼ cup olive oil, and remaining Scotch bonnet pepper half. Purée in a blender.

Place avocado mixture in the middle of each of 4 plates. Place a plantain ring on top and then top with a portion of the crab mixture and another plantain round.

Ladle sauce around the stack and top with crème fraîche and caviar. Sprinkle with a confetti of the vegetables.

*Wear rubber gloves when seeding this pepper because it is very hot.
†To prepare 1 cup tamarind juice, combine 1 to 2 tablespoons of tamarind pulp (available in Asian and Indian markets) with ½ cup warm water in a small glass bowl. Knead the pulp to extract the flavor. The resulting juice will be brown and cloudy. Strain seeds. Remaining juice can be preserved in the refrigerator for several weeks.
‡To make crème fraîche, combine 1 cup whipping cream and 2 tablespoons buttermilk in a glass bowl. Cover and allow to stand for 8 to 24 hours, or until very thick. When ready, stir well, cover, and refrigerate. It will keep 7 to 10 days. Or purchase at a specialty store.

To prepare burgers, mix together the crab, celery, onion, bell pepper, milk, ½ cup of the cracker meal, Tabasco, Worcestershire, and salt. Form into 4 patties. Coat all sides of burgers in remaining cracker meal. Refrigerate for 1 to 2 hours.

Heat vegetable oil in a large skillet. Add burgers and cook until just soft. Do not overcook. Season to taste.

To prepare lime mustard sauce, mix all ingredients well. Serve alongside patties. Garnish with parsley, cilantro, or watercress, and fresh lime wedges.

*May substitute almost any other type of crab, including surimi, but be sure to flake well.

Moro Craburgers with Lime Mustard Sauce

Emparedado de Cangrejo Moro

This is my creation inspired by numerous Cuban friends. I like to serve these on fresh onion rolls or kaisers. Be sure to allow 1 to 2 hours for marination so the flavors of the celery, onion, and peppers permeate the crabmeat.

Serves 4

BURGERS

2 pounds jumbo lump crabmeat,* flaked
   and picked over
½ cup chopped celery
¼ cup chopped white onion
1 green bell pepper, seeded and chopped
6 tablespoons evaporated milk
1 cup cracker meal
½ teaspoon Tabasco sauce
1 teaspoon Worcestershire sauce
1 teaspoon salt
3 to 4 tablespoons vegetable oil, for frying
Fresh parsley, cilantro, or watercress, for
   garnish
1 lime, cut in wedges, for garnish

LIME MUSTARD SAUCE

1 cup light mayonnaise
⅛ cup fresh lime juice
¼ cup Dijon or other mustard

Cornmeal with Shrimp

Tamal en Cazuela con Camarónes

Typically this dish, particularly satisfying on a cold night, is made with pork, chicken, beef, or chorizo. Here I've used fresh shrimp, but other shellfish such as lobster and crab may be successfully substituted.

When the cornmeal is blended with the fresh seafood, tomatoes, peppers, and onions, a hearty yet savory dish emerges.   **Serves 4**

  **2 pounds medium shrimp, peeled and
     deveined**
  1½ cups stone-ground yellow cornmeal
  6 cups water
  1 teaspoon salt
  3 tablespoons olive oil
  3 garlic cloves, peeled
  1 white onion, finely chopped
  **½ green bell pepper, seeded and finely
     chopped**
  ½ red bell pepper, seeded and finely chopped
  **4 very ripe plum tomatoes, peeled, seeded,
     and chopped**
  2 fresh parsley sprigs
  1 bay leaf, cracked
  Few drops of Louisiana Hot Sauce
  Pinch of allspice
  ½ teaspoon dried thyme
  ½ teaspoon dried oregano
  2 tablespoons dry sherry

Cook shrimp by plunging into hot water to which a bay leaf has been added and cook just until they turn pink, 3 to 4 minutes. Do not overcook. Drain off water and set aside.

In the top of a double boiler, combine the cornmeal, water, and salt. Stir constantly over medium heat. Bring mixture to a full boil and continue to stir until it begins to thicken. Reduce heat and cover. Cook 25 to 30 minutes, until it becomes thickened and looks like mush. Cooking time may vary.

While cornmeal cooks, heat a large skillet and add the olive oil. When it is heated and the oil begins to smell fragrant, add garlic, onion, and peppers and sauté until tender, but be careful not to overcook. Add tomatoes, parsley, bay leaf, Louisiana Hot Sauce, allspice, thyme, and oregano. Sauté until the mixture looks like a well-cooked *sofrito,* or sauce.

Add the tomato mixture to the cornmeal mush and combine well. Cover pot and cook for 20 to 25 minutes. Add cooked shrimp, sherry, and more water if mixture becomes too thick.

Pour into an attractive tureen and ladle into large bowls. Serve with a leafy salad and Cuban bread.

Shrimp Creole

Camarónes à la Criollo

Many people new to Cuban cuisine are curious as to how the elements of Creole cooking became visible in a number of Cuban dishes. After the revolution in Haiti in the 1790s, slaves and planters fled to the nearby island of Cuba, to what was the province of Oriente, bringing with them the superior French Creole techniques of cooking and their use of favorite spices, such as thyme and allspice. The migration of these people reached a peak in the 1930s.

This recipe, which is most representative of that style of cooking, is fast and fail-proof. Salt pork and fresh vegetables combine magnificently with tomatoes and hot seasonings to produce a splendid sauce for the fresh shrimp. As with many sauces, this is even better the next day. You may want to prepare the sauce a day ahead and add the shrimp just a few minutes before serving.

Serves 6 to 8

1½ pounds medium shrimp, shelled and deveined
½ cup olive oil
½ cup diced salt pork
3 garlic cloves, peeled and finely chopped
2 large white onions, finely chopped
2 green bell peppers, seeded and finely chopped
1 teaspoon dried thyme
½ teaspoon allspice
2 bay leaves, cracked
1 (1-pound 12-ounce) can tomatoes with juice
1 (8-ounce) can tomato sauce
Salt to taste
½ to 1 teaspoon Tabasco sauce, or to taste
Dash of Worcestershire sauce
Salt and coarsely cracked black pepper, to taste
Fresh parsley sprigs, for garnish

Heat a 5-quart saucepot or a large deep skillet and add olive oil. When heated and the oil begins to smell fragrant, add salt pork, garlic, onions, bell peppers, thyme, allspice, and bay leaves and sauté until onion becomes translucent. Add the tomatoes and tomato sauce, salt, Tabasco, and Worcestershire and cook on medium-low heat 10 minutes. Add shrimp and cook 3 to 5 minutes, or until shrimp are pink. Season to taste with salt and cracked pepper. Do not overcook or shrimp will become tough. Remove salt pork, if desired. Garnish with fresh parsley sprigs and serve with cooked rice and fried ripe plantains.

Stewed Shrimp, Creole Style

Camarónes Estofados al Estilo Santiago de Cuba

Andres Revoredo, chef of Victor's Café in Miami, created this brilliant and flavorful dish that reflects the Creole-style cooking of his homeland, Santiago de Cuba province. If you prefer more heat, add additional hot peppers.

Serves 6 to 8

¼ cup olive oil

4 garlic cloves, peeled and finely chopped

1 large onion, finely chopped

1 green bell pepper, seeded and finely chopped

2 jalapeño or serrano peppers, seeded and finely chopped

¼ cup finely chopped fresh Italian parsley

1 bay leaf, cracked

1 teaspoon dried oregano leaves

¼ teaspoon dried thyme

2 cups tomato sauce

1 cup stale beer*

1 teaspoon salt

2 pounds large shrimp, peeled and deveined

½ teaspoon allspice

1 red bell pepper, roasted, seeded, and sliced†

Heat a large skillet or sauté pan and add the olive oil. When heated and fragrant, add garlic and sauté until slightly golden. Add onion, green pepper, jalapeño peppers, 3 tablespoons of parsley, the bay leaf, oregano, and thyme. Cook for about 5 minutes. Add tomato sauce, beer, and salt and stir to combine well. Simmer over medium heat for about 10 minutes, or until sauce thickens slightly. Add shrimp and allspice and cook for 4 to 5 more minutes, or until shrimp turn pink. Do not overcook. Remove from stove to a colorful serving bowl.

Sprinkle with remaining parsley and serve garnished with slices of roasted pepper. Serve with white rice, fried green plantains, and a garden salad.

*Allow beer to stand uncovered for several hours.
†See page 24 for how to roast peppers.

Shrimp with Mango and Papaya

Camarónes con Mango y Papaya

In today's evolving Cuban cuisine, inventive chefs are combining fresh island fruits, such as mangoes and papayas, with all sorts of fish and shellfish. Here is a New World entrée prepared with shrimp and these delicate fruits.
Serves 4

2 limes

½ red bell pepper, seeded and minced

½ yellow bell pepper, seeded and minced

1 teaspoon green peppercorns, brine drained, crushed

2 tablespoons light brown sugar

Juice of 1 orange

1 teaspoon salt

3 tablespoons olive oil

12 jumbo prawns, peeled, deveined, and butterflied

1 large ripe mango, peeled and diced,* about 1 cup

1 small papaya, peeled and diced,* about 1 cup

3 ounces 151-proof rum

Remove the zest from the limes and combine with red and yellow peppers, and peppercorns. Set aside. Combine the juice from the limes with the brown sugar and orange juice in a small saucepan and simmer until reduction measures 3 to 4 tablespoons. Add salt and zest mixture and cook for about 4 minutes. Remove from heat, then add 1 tablespoon of the olive oil and allow to cool for a few minutes. Set aside.

Sauté prawns in remaining 2 tablespoons oil for about 1 minute. Add the mango and papaya pieces and the rum and reduce for 2 to 4 minutes. Add to pepper-zest mixture. Serve with wild rice mixed with white rice and the eggplant boats on page 187.

*See page 23 for how to cut a mango and a papaya.

Baked Scallops with Pesto, Curried Black Bean Salad, and Mango Coulis

Vieiras al Pesto, Ensalada de Frijoles Negros, y Coulis de Mango

The black beans in this New World recipe, inspired by Lisa Petybridge, a talented young Miami chef, are prepared differently from other methods in this book, but simply and perfectly. The light olive oil is no less in caloric content, but lighter in flavor.

This variation on Lisa's recipe has more ingredients than most, but is easy to prepare.

Serves 8 as an appetizer

MACADAMIA NUT PESTO

½ pound macadamia nuts, lightly toasted
2 bunches fresh mint leaves (about 2 cups),
   stems removed, chopped
2 tablespoons grated Parmesan cheese
2 garlic cloves, peeled and chopped
3 tablespoons extra-virgin olive oil
Salt and pepper, to taste

BLACK BEAN SALAD

½ cup black beans, soaked overnight in water
   to cover
3 cups chicken stock (page 36) or defatted
   chicken broth*
½ cup olive oil
Juice of 2 limes
1 tablespoon chopped fresh cilantro
1 teaspoon medium spicy chili powder
Salt and pepper, to taste
1 medium mango, peeled and finely diced†

MANGO COULIS

2 medium mangoes, peeled and diced†
½ cup dry white wine
3 tablespoons light olive oil
Salt and pepper, to taste

SCALLOPS

2 pounds sea scallops
Salt and pepper, to taste
1 red bell pepper, seeded and sliced into rings
8 fresh cilantro sprigs, for garnish

To prepare the pesto sauce, place macadamia nuts in the container of a food processor. Pulse twice. Add the mint, cheese, and garlic. With motor running, add olive oil in a steady stream. Season with salt and pepper. Set aside.

To make the black bean salad, simmer drained black beans in chicken stock for 1 hour, or until tender. Drain and chill. In a bowl, whisk together olive oil, lime juice, cilantro, chili powder, salt, and pepper. Add to chilled beans along with diced mango. Set aside.

To prepare coulis, simmer mango slowly in wine until soft. Purée in the container of a blender or food processor and return to heat. Whisk in the light olive oil. Season with salt and pepper. Set aside and keep warm.

To prepare the scallops, preheat the oven to 375°F. Sprinkle scallops with salt and pepper. Place in a baking dish and bake for 8 to 10 minutes.

To assemble the dish, drizzle warm coulis over each of eight very large dinner plates in a decorative fashion. Spoon bean salad in center and arrange scallops around beans. Spoon pesto over scallops and garnish with red pepper rings and sprigs of cilantro.

*To defat canned broth, place can in refrigerator. Open can and skim off fat from the surface.
† See page 23 for how to cut a mango.

In a medium saucepan, combine shallots and wine and bring to a boil. Reduce heat and simmer until mixture is reduced by half. Carefully whisk in the cream and cilantro. Simmer until reduced by a third. The mixture should be slightly thick.

In a small bowl, mix the butter and cornstarch together to form a smooth paste. Whisk this mixture into the cream mixture and simmer for a few minutes. Season with salt and pepper.

To prepare the scallops, heat a medium sauté pan and add the olive oil. When hot, add the garlic and onion and sauté a few minutes, but do not brown. Add the scallops and cook a few minutes, until just done.

To serve, spoon the hot cilantro sauce onto a platter or individual plates and place scallops on top. Garnish with julienne of red pepper.

Sautéed Scallops with Cilantro Sauce

Vieiras Salteadas con Salsa de Cilantro

In my opinion, scallops are the ultimate fast-food treat, perfect for people on the run. They are easy to prepare, but it's important not to overcook, or they will turn into tough little balls. In this recipe, the creamy cilantro sauce acts as a bedding for the tender shellfish and brings out their delicate flavor without overpowering it.

Serves 4

6 shallots, peeled and finely minced
2 cups dry white wine
1½ cups heavy cream
1 teaspoon minced fresh cilantro
2 teaspoons butter or margarine,
   at room temperature
½ to 1 tablespoon cornstarch
Salt and cracked pepper, to taste
2 to 3 tablespoons olive oil
3 garlic cloves, peeled and finely minced
1 tablespoon finely minced Bermuda onion
1 pound bay or sea scallops
1 red bell pepper, seeded and julienned

Party Conch Chowder with Yuca and Boniato

Sopa de Cobo con Yuca y Boniato

You'll need some muscle and a heavy mallet because firm conch must be pounded thoroughly, or your guests will be chewing all night. Conch chowder is well known to many Cubans who live in the Florida Keys, but over the years it has become a standby at restaurants specializing in the *nuevo Cubano* style of cooking. This cuisine often takes the liberty of combining island ingredients, such as the fiery hot Scotch bonnet pepper added here. Add some crusty Cuban bread to this rich chowder and you'll have a complete meal.   **Serves 6 to 8**

6 cleaned conch* (about 3 pounds)
½ cup olive oil
1 large white onion, diced
1 large carrot, peeled and diced
1 large green pepper, seeded and diced
1 teaspoon dried thyme
1 teaspoon dried oregano
Salt and pepper, to taste
1 (28-ounce) can whole tomatoes
½ can tomato paste
½ Scotch bonnet pepper,† seeded and finely minced
1 quart fish stock (page 37)
1 medium yuca, peeled and diced
2 medium boniatos, peeled and diced
4 tablespoons butter or margarine
3 tablespoons all-purpose flour
¼ cup dry sherry

Using a heavy metal mallet, pound each conch 5 to 10 minutes, until very tender, then process in a food processor until the consistency of chopped clams.

Heat a 6-quart saucepot and add the olive oil. When oil becomes fragrant, add conch, onion, carrot, and green pepper. Sauté until green pepper and onion are limp, then add thyme, oregano, salt and pepper, tomatoes, tomato paste, and Scotch bonnet. Combine well, then add fish stock, yuca, and boniato. Combine well, bring to a boil, then lower heat and simmer until tubers are soft, about 40 minutes.

Melt butter in a saucepan, then whisk in flour to make a roux. Add a little stock from the hot chowder to smooth mixture, combine well, and pour into the chowder to thicken. Simmer soup another 30 minutes. When ready to serve, put a tablespoon of dry sherry in each bowl and ladle chowder over top.

*Available at most seafood markets, conch is usually frozen in 5-pound blocks. See page 25 for how to tenderize conch.
†Wear rubber gloves when seeding this pepper because it is very, very hot.

Poultry

Aves

Chicken is a staple in the diet of many Cubans, not only because it is so versatile, but also because it is very economical. Although pork is considered the most popular meat, chicken is enjoyed at least a few times a week.

Arroz con pollo, yellow rice and chicken, is the most famous dish in the Cuban repertoire. Even Theodore Roosevelt and his Rough Riders dined on this dish on their way to defend Cuba during the Spanish-American war. There are, however, numerous other Cuban recipes that perform wonders with poultry.

Whether in a marinade of sour orange juice and a sprinkling of herbs and seasonings, as done in Cuban-style fried chicken, or in an elegant turkey stuffed with rice, black beans, peppers, and spices, poultry dishes are prized by chefs and home cooks alike.

Yellow Rice and Chicken

Arroz con Pollo

Arroz con pollo is probably the most widely known Cuban-Spanish dish. Although Spanish saffron is generally more expensive than that of other countries, it emits an aroma like no other and its flavoring and coloring abilities are unsurpassed. When strands are immersed in hot liquid, an intense flavor is released into the ingredients. For maximum flavor, do not strain off the threads after steeping. If using *bijol* as a substitute for the saffron, add according to package directions.   **Serves 6 to 8**

½ teaspoon saffron threads or bijol*
¼ cup dry white wine
¼ cup olive oil
3 tablespoons butter or margarine
2 fryer chickens, about 2½ pounds each, cut into eighths
1 large white onion, finely chopped
1 green bell pepper, seeded and chopped
½ red bell pepper, seeded and chopped
4 garlic cloves, peeled and chopped
1 large red ripe tomato, peeled, seeded, and diced
2 bay leaves
1 teaspoon salt, or to taste
½ teaspoon Tabasco sauce
½ teaspoon freshly grated nutmeg
1 teaspoon ground cumin
1 teaspoon Spanish paprika
3 cups chicken stock (page 36) or defatted chicken broth†
1 cup beer, at room temperature
2 fresh parsley sprigs
2 cups short-grain Valencia rice or Italian arborio
1 (16-ounce) can white asparagus spears, drained
1 whole pimiento
1 cup baby green peas (petit pois), for garnish
1 pimiento, chopped, for garnish
Fresh parsley sprigs, for garnish

Steep saffron threads in ¼ cup warmed white wine for about 30 minutes.

Heat two large heavy skillets and add the olive oil and butter. When oil begins to smell fragrant, add the chicken pieces and sauté until golden brown, 20 to 25 minutes. With a slotted spoon, remove the chicken to a platter.

Add onion and green and red pepper to the skillet and cook until onion becomes translucent. Add garlic and tomato. Combine well and cook for about 5 minutes. Add bay leaves, saffron, salt, Tabasco, nutmeg, cumin, paprika, 1 cup of the chicken stock, and the beer. Mix well and bring to a boil. Add the parsley and return chicken pieces to skillet. Cover and cook until chicken is tender, 15 to 20 minutes, then transfer to a very large ovenproof casserole.

Preheat the oven to 325° F. Add the rice to the casserole and mix in well to distribute evenly. Add remaining 2 cups of chicken stock, bring to a boil, and remove to oven to bake for 15 to 20 minutes. Do not overcook. Five minutes before removing from the oven, uncover and arrange the asparagus artistically over the rice. Fill the whole pimiento with the tiny peas and place it in the center of the casserole. Scatter the chopped pimiento over all. Cover and return to the oven for 5 to 7 minutes longer. Garnish with fresh parsley sprigs.

*See page 6.
†To defat canned broth, place can in the refrigerator. When chilled, open can and skim fat from the surface.

Fried Chicken, Cuban Style

Pollo Frito, Estilo Cubano

Here's a very traditional recipe for fried chicken that can be found in Cuban restaurants and households all over the world.

It's important to allow 3 hours for the marinade to permeate the meat thoroughly. The tangy mixture of sour orange and garlic imparts a unique flavor to this favorite dish. **Serves 8**

4 to 4½ pounds chicken pieces, skin removed
3 garlic cloves, peeled and crushed
1 teaspoon ground cumin
1 lime, sliced, seeds removed
¾ cup sour orange juice*
1 large onion, very thinly sliced
¼ cup olive oil, for frying
¼ jar chopped pimiento pieces
1 teaspoon freshly ground black pepper
Salt, to taste

Wash and pat dry chicken pieces. Set aside.

Mix together garlic, cumin, lime slices, and sour orange juice. Pour over chicken pieces and mix well so that pieces are saturated. Cover with onion rings and allow to marinate for about 3 hours or longer.

Heat a large skillet and add the oil. When the skillet is heated and the oil begins to smell fragrant, sauté onion slices until golden brown. Add pimiento, pepper, and salt. Add chicken and marinade. Cook over medium-high heat for about 5 minutes, then turn over and cook on low heat for another 25 to 30 minutes, or until chicken is completely done.

*If sour orange juice is not available, combine ¼ cup fresh lime juice with ¾ cup fresh orange juice.

Creole-Style Chicken

Pollo Criollo

If you enjoy tender chicken, then you'll savor this recipe. Herbs meld splendidly with the sherry, effecting a fragrantly delectable feast. **Serves 6**

½ cup olive oil
2 tablespoons dry sherry
½ teaspoon salt
1 teaspoon ground oregano
½ teaspoon ground cumin
2 tablespoons minced onion
4 garlic cloves, peeled and minced
1 tablespoon Worcestershire sauce
6 skinless chicken breast halves, or
  12 chicken thighs

Preheat the oven to 300° F. In a large glass bowl, mix together all ingredients except chicken. Wash and pat chicken dry. Add chicken pieces to mixture and, using hands, coat each piece well. Allow to marinate for at least 1 hour, preferably 2 to 3.

Cook for about 45 minutes, basting the entire time, until chicken is cooked through. Place under broiler for about 5 minutes to turn golden brown. Serve with brown rice and fresh string beans.

Papaya Chicken with White Rice

Pollo con Papaya y Arroz

In this *nuevo Cubano* recipe, papaya joins with pineapple, fresh ginger, and orange marmalade to create a fruity sauce surrounding tender strips of chicken.   **Serves 4**

1 teaspoon plus 2 tablespoons cornstarch
½ teaspoon mild chili powder
½ teaspoon salt
½ teaspoon black pepper
½ teaspoon cayenne pepper
¼ cup granulated sugar
1 teaspoon plus 1 tablespoon light soy sauce
4 garlic cloves, peeled and minced
1 pound boneless chicken breasts, cut
   into ½-inch strips
1 (8-ounce) can pineapple chunks in heavy
   syrup, syrup reserved
¼ cup red wine vinegar
2 tablespoons olive oil
1 teaspoon butter or margarine
2 tablespoons chopped green pepper
¼ cup orange marmalade
1 tablespoon grated fresh ginger
½ cup light sour cream
1 cup fresh papaya, peeled, seeded, and cut
   into 1-inch chunks
2 cups cooked white rice
Edible flowers (optional)

In a medium glass bowl, mix together the 1 teaspoon cornstarch, chili powder, salt, pepper, cayenne, ¼ teaspoon of the sugar, 1 teaspoon of the soy sauce, and the garlic. Add the chicken strips and stir to coat. Cover and marinate, refrigerated, for about 30 minutes.

To the reserved pineapple juice, add enough water to make 1 cup. Add the remaining sugar and 2 tablespoons cornstarch, vinegar, and remaining 1 tablespoon soy sauce. Mix well and set aside.

Heat a large skillet and add the olive oil and butter. When the skillet is heated and the oil begins to smell fragrant, add green pepper and chicken slices to the pan and sauté for 5 to 7 minutes, or until the chicken is cooked through. Add the reserved juice mixture and bring to a boil, stirring constantly, until thick. Reduce heat to medium-low and stir in marmalade, ginger, and sour cream. Gently stir in reserved pineapple chunks and fresh papaya. Heat through, then serve over rice.

Garnish with fresh edible flowers for a special occasion; otherwise, fresh cilantro or parsley will do just fine.

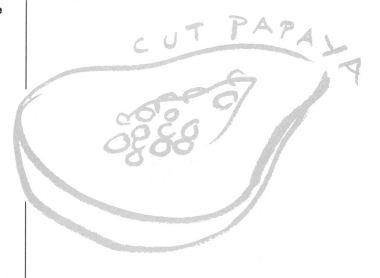

Rancho Luna Chicken

Pollo Rancho Luna

Here's a simple recipe for chicken that is moist and delicious—just make sure the chicken is young and tender. A marinade composed of olive oil and dry white wine blended with the tart orange and lime juices renders a delicate and moist baked chicken.   **Serves 4**

6 tablespoons olive oil
3 garlic cloves, chopped
1 (3- to 4-pound) chicken, quartered
3 tablespoons finely minced white onion
½ cup orange juice
½ cup lime juice
¼ cup dry white wine
Salt, to taste

Heat a medium sauté pan until hot and add 3 tablespoons olive oil. When oil is heated and begins to smell fragrant, add garlic and cook until soft, but not browned. Remove pan from heat.

In a medium nonmetallic bowl, whisk together the remaining olive oil, the onion, orange and lime juices, and white wine. Add the garlic and garlic-oil that has been set aside.

Preheat the oven to 325° F. Arrange chicken pieces in a rectangular Pyrex pan. Brush the chicken pieces generously with the mixture. Bake chicken for about 1 hour 15 minutes, or until cooked and marvelously browned. When done, mix pan juices with leftover marinade mixture, salt to taste, heat for a few minutes, and serve as a sauce. Serve with white rice.

Chicken Casserole

Pollo en Olla de Bodeguita del Medio

This recipe is a favorite at the Bodeguita del Medio, one of Havana's best eateries. The restaurant is famous for its typical Cuban cuisine and the home of the *mojito,* one of Ernest Hemingway's favorite rum libations. Here, potatoes and chicken are each sautéed before being combined in a savory wine and tomato sauce for baking.   **Serves 4 to 6**

3 tablespoons butter or margarine
2 tablespoons all-purpose flour
2 cups chicken stock (page 36) or defatted chicken broth*
½ cup dry white wine
½ cup tomato sauce
4 potatoes, peeled and cut into 1-inch squares
Olive oil or vegetable oil, for frying
1 (4- to 5-pound) chicken, boned, meat cut into small cubes (about 3 cups)
1 cup buttered bread crumbs

Preheat the oven to 350° F.

In a large heavy skillet, melt the butter or margarine. Make a roux by blending in flour. Gradually add chicken stock, a little at a time, and stir constantly over low heat until it begins to thicken. Add white wine and tomato sauce and continue cooking over low heat.

In a separate medium skillet, fry potatoes in olive oil until almost fully cooked. In a third skillet, fry chicken cubes in olive oil until golden brown. To assemble dish, mix potatoes and chicken together in a large Pyrex casserole dish, pour sauce over all, top with bread crumbs, and bake for 35 to 40 minutes.

*To defat canned broth, place can in the refrigerator. When chilled, open can and skim fat from the surface.

Hen with Herb-Cream Sauce

Gallina à la Yalodde

Santeria, which means "cult of the Gods" or *orishas,* is still a popular Afro-Caribbean religion that many Cuban people practice. Basically it combines ancient African beliefs with Catholicism.

Many dishes were created as a result of the rituals performed. The following was said to have resulted from an instance in which Orula, an old invalid man, was confined to a wheelchair. He was miraculously able to walk as a result of thunderbolts from the heavens that struck the house with fire where he lived with the beautiful and sexy but notoriously sinful Ochun, and Chango, her lover. So pleased that Orula was saved and remembered, the trio vowed eternal friendship. Said Orula, "You have sinned, but you remembered me at the most dangerous of times. From now on, you shall eat with me. We will share the adie, our favorite dish." This dish is believed to be similar to the one they shared.

Serves 4

¼ cup olive oil
1 (4 to 5-pound) hen or other fowl, cut into 4 pieces
1 tablespoon peeled and shredded fresh ginger
1 teaspoon ground allspice
2 garlic cloves, peeled and mashed
1 white onion, chopped
Salt and pepper, to taste
1 tablespoon cornstarch
2 egg yolks, well beaten with 2 tablespoons water
1 tablespoon finely chopped fresh parsley
1 teaspoon dried basil
1 teaspoon dried marjoram
Juice of 1 lime

Heat a large heavy skillet and add the oil. When it begins to emit a fragrance, add the hen pieces along with ginger, allspice, garlic, and onion. Combine well. Season with salt and pepper to taste. Sauté over medium heat until golden brown and hen is cooked through, about 1 to 1½ hours.

Meanwhile, prepare a sauce by whisking the cornstarch with the egg yolks and water mixture, parsley, basil, and marjoram. Pour sauce over the hen and cook on low heat for 2 minutes. Before serving, add the juice of a lime.

Chicken Breasts with Black Beans and Avocado Salsa

Pechugas de Pollo con Frijoles Negros

y Salsa de Aguacate

This recipe has become a classic of the *nuevo Cubano* cuisine since it was created several years ago by Oliver Saucy, the talented chef of Café Max in Pompano Beach, Florida.

The unusual flavor is achieved through the spicy black bean sauce with jalapeño and avocado salsa topped with sour cream and cilantro. The chicken is also good grilled.   **Serves 6**

CHICKEN

> **6 whole chicken breasts, skin removed**
> **¼ cup plus 3 tablespoons olive oil**
> **2 tablespoons white vinegar**
> **Salt and pepper, to taste**

BLACK BEAN SAUCE

> **3 ounces lean bacon**
> **1 tablespoon chopped onion**
> **2 garlic cloves, peeled and minced**
> **1 to 2 fresh jalapeño peppers, seeded and minced**
> **1 (12-ounce) package dried black beans, cooked and drained (page 88)**
> **1½ to 2 quarts chicken stock (page 36) or defatted canned broth***
> **1 tablespoon chopped fresh cilantro**
> **Juice of ½ lime**
> **½ teaspoon ground cumin**
> **Chili powder, to taste**
> **Salt and pepper, to taste**
> **¼ cup olive oil**

AVOCADO SALSA

> **2 ripe avocados, peeled and chopped**
> **1 large red ripe tomato**
> **½ fresh jalapeño pepper, seeded and minced**
> **2 tablespoons chopped onion**
> **Juice of ½ lime**

> **½ teaspoon ground cumin**
> **¼ cup olive oil**
> **1 tablespoon chopped fresh cilantro**
> **Salt and pepper, to taste**
> **Sour cream**
> **Fresh cilantro sprigs, for garnish**

Wash and pat chicken pieces dry. Prepare a mixture of ¼ cup olive oil, vinegar, and salt and pepper. Add chicken and marinate for 2 to 3 hours. Drain marinade from breasts and discard marinade. Heat a medium saucepan and add 2 to 3 tablespoons olive oil. When oil becomes fragrant, add breasts and sauté in oil until cooked through, 20 to 25 minutes.

In a large skillet, cook bacon until crisp. Add onion, garlic, and jalapeño and cook until translucent. Add cooked beans and chicken stock and cook for about 5 minutes longer. Add cilantro and lime juice and season with cumin, chili powder, and salt and pepper. Remove about a tenth of the beans and purée in the container of a food processor. Add back to bean sauce with olive oil and blend together well.

Combine all the salsa ingredients, being careful to mix together gently. Season with salt and pepper.

To finish, arrange black bean sauce in the inner circle of a dinner plate. Center chicken over sauce. Garnish with the salsa, dollops of sour cream, and fresh sprigs of cilantro.

*To defat canned broth, place can in the refrigerator. When chilled, open can and skim fat from the surface.

Savory Chicken with Cilantro-Lime Sauce

Pollo Sabroso con Salsa de

Cilantro y Limón Verde

These chicken thighs are especially savory with the addition of the cilantro-lime sauce. The jalapeño lends great flavor, but may not be favored by those who prefer a milder taste. If so, omit.   **Serves 6**

> 4 garlic cloves, peeled
> 1 fresh jalapeño pepper, seeded and minced
> ¾ cup fresh lime juice
> 2 tablespoons pure honey
> 1 teaspoon Spanish paprika
> ½ teaspoon Tabasco sauce
> 1 teaspoon cornstarch
> 1 tablespoon minced fresh cilantro
> 2 tablespoons olive oil
> 12 chicken thighs, skin removed
> 1 tablespoon chopped fresh parsley
> Fresh cilantro sprigs and lime, for garnish

In the container of a food processor, purée garlic, jalapeño, lime juice, honey, paprika, Tabasco, and cornstarch. Using a rubber spatula, empty mixture into a small saucepan and cook over medium-high heat for about 2 minutes. Remove from heat. Add the cilantro and parsley. Set aside and allow flavors to meld.

Heat a large sauté pan until hot. Add the olive oil and chicken thighs and cook over medium heat until cooked through and browned on the outside. Remove from pan. Place two thighs on each plate and pour sauce over all. Serve with white rice and fresh green beans. Garnish with fresh cilantro sprigs and slices of fresh lime cut lengthwise.

Baked Chicken Picadillo

Picadillo de Pollo al Horno

Picadillo is a favorite of many of Cuban heritage, and has been for centuries. Classically, it's made with beef, but here's a more contemporary variation, using chicken and a few added ingredients, including curry powder from the neighboring island of Jamaica. Be sure to use a flavorful curry that's mild to medium hot. It's an exceptional dish for a buffet dinner.
                                  Serves 6 to 8

> 1 (3- to 4-pound) chicken, cut into pieces, skin removed
> 4 tablespoons butter or margarine
> 2 tablespoons olive oil
> Salt and cracked pepper, to taste
> 1 cup chopped white onion
> 1 cup diced green bell pepper
> 1 cup diced red bell pepper
> 6 garlic cloves, peeled and crushed
> 1 cup cooked brown rice
> 1½ teaspoons mild curry powder
> ½ teaspoon ground cumin
> 1 teaspoon chopped fresh thyme
> ½ teaspoon cracked pepper
> ½ teaspoon granulated sugar
> ½ cup raisins
> 1 (16-ounce) can whole tomatoes, drained as needed
> 1 to 2 cups chicken stock (page 36) or defatted canned broth*

Preheat the oven to 350° F.

In a 3-quart casserole, melt butter in 1 tablespoon oil over moderate heat. Brown chicken pieces, sprinkling sparingly with salt and pepper. Set chicken aside.

In remaining 1 tablespoon oil, cook onion, peppers, and garlic until translucent. Add the rice, stirring to coat well. Add the curry, cumin, thyme, pepper, sugar, raisins, and tomatoes. Put the chicken back in the casserole and bake for about

1 hour, or until done. Add chicken broth as needed to keep casserole moist and cook the rice.

*To defat canned broth, place can in refrigerator. Open can and skim off fat from the surface.

Serve over white rice with fried plantains (page 195).

*If you do not have sour orange juice, substitute ⅓ cup fresh orange juice and ⅓ cup fresh lime juice.

Chicken with Mustard Yogurt Sauce

Pollo con Salsa de Mostaza y Yogur

In this recipe, the Dijon mustard and yogurt combine with cilantro and the fruit juice in a stimulating way that transforms these good ingredients into a great dish that will have you wanting more.   **Serves 4**

8 boneless, skinless chicken breast halves
⅔ cup sour orange juice*
2 teaspoons light olive oil
½ cup chicken broth (page 36)
¼ cup Dijon mustard
1 cup plain nonfat yogurt
1 teaspoon finely chopped scallions
1 tablespoon chopped fresh cilantro

Place chicken between sheets of wax paper or plastic wrap. Pound to a ¼-inch thickness with a heavy metal kitchen mallet.

Marinate in sour orange juice for about 1 hour. Drain off marinade and discard.

Heat a large skillet and add olive oil. When the oil begins to smell fragrant, add chicken and sauté over medium heat until browned on both sides, about 5 minutes per side. Transfer chicken to a plate and keep warm.

Pour off any excess fat. Add chicken broth to the pan and cook over high heat, stirring often, until reduced by half, about 5 minutes. Remove from heat. Whisk in mustard, yogurt, and scallions. Add cilantro. Return chicken to pan and coat with sauce.

Sofrito Chicken

Sofrito de Pollo

In this recipe, annatto oil and sherry are added to the *sofrito,* or seasoning sauce, to produce an aromatic marinade. You can also use it on pork and beef with good results.

If you don't feel up to making your own *sofrito,* you can purchase the commercial variety at most supermarkets. It has a long shelf life, but it isn't as good as homemade.   **Serves 8 to 10**

¾ cup annatto oil (page 5)
1 cup minced white onion
½ cup minced green bell pepper
4 garlic cloves, peeled and crushed
1 (8-ounce) can tomato sauce
¾ cup dry sherry
Salt, to taste
3 (3-pound) chickens, cut into small pieces, skin removed

Heat a heavy skillet and add annatto oil. When oil begins to smell fragrant, add onion, green pepper, and garlic and cook until lightly browned. Add tomato sauce and sherry. Season to taste. Cook over low heat for 30 minutes or more. Cool.

When cooled, put *sofrito* in a large bowl. Add chicken pieces and toss to coat well. Place pieces in a 13 × 9 × 2-inch rectangular pan or very large Pyrex dish. Cover and allow to marinate for 6 to 8 hours, or overnight.

Preheat the oven to 325° F. Bake chicken until thoroughly cooked, 1¼ to 1½ hours. Turn several times to coat with *sofrito* while chicken cooks.

Serve with white rice and ripe plantains.

Roasted Fresh Turkey with Rice and Black Bean Stuffing

Pavo Relleno de Congri

In this modern-day recipe I have used the popular rice and black bean combination to stuff the turkey instead of your typical bread stuffing. A fresh turkey rather than a frozen one makes a considerable difference in the taste.

I prepared this turkey for a farewell party of medical doctors from the University of Missouri in Columbia. Although they were used to a continental-style Midwest diet, they devoured the entire bird and could have eaten more.

Consider this creation an instant winner at any party. Nearly the whole meal is incorporated into one golden and eye-appealing dish. To complete the meal, add fresh snap beans and a salad of sliced red tomatoes and sweet onions with a sprinkling of extra-virgin olive oil and balsamic vinegar.

Serves 24 to 30

8 garlic cloves, peeled and crushed
1 teaspoon kosher salt
1 teaspoon coarsely ground black pepper
1 teaspoon poultry seasoning
1 tablespoon ground cumin
1 tablespoon ground oregano
1 cup sour orange juice*
1 white onion, minced
1 (12- to 16-pound) fresh turkey

CONGRI

8 thick slices slab bacon
½ cup chopped white onion
6 garlic cloves, peeled and minced
½ cup chopped green bell pepper
¼ cup minced red bell pepper
2 cups cooked black beans, or canned beans, rinsed
2 cups long-grain white rice, half cooked
2 bay leaves, cracked

1 teaspoon ground oregano
¾ cup dry white wine
Salt and pepper, to taste
Escarole or other greens and fresh edible flowers (optional)

In the container of a food processor, blend garlic with salt, pepper, poultry seasoning, cumin, and oregano. Add sour orange juice and onion and process into a purée for 5 to 10 seconds.

Using clean hands, or a pastry brush, spread mixture inside the turkey and out, coating well even into the recesses of the cavity. Continue to rub mixture over turkey while it marinates in the refrigerator for at least 2 hours, or overnight.

In a large skillet, fry 4 slices of the bacon until crisp. Remove and crumble. Add onion, garlic, and green and red pepper and sauté until soft and translucent. Add black beans, rice, bay leaves, oregano, wine, and salt and pepper to taste.

Preheat the oven to 325° F. Loosely stuff the turkey with the rice mixture, or *congri*. Close up turkey by sewing or other method to seal in stuffing. Place remaining uncooked slices of bacon on top of the skin, fastening with heavy round toothpicks to secure. Cover top loosely with aluminum foil. Roast for 4 to 5 hours, according to regular turkey roasting procedures.

When done, decorate bird on a huge platter laced with lots of frilly greens and colorful edible flowers.

*If you do not have sour orange juice, substitute ¾ cup fresh orange juice and ¼ cup fresh lime juice.

Guinea Hen, Creole Style

Etu (Gallina de Guinea) à la Criolla

This recipe was inspired by a legend rooted in the Santeria religion. It is prepared with guinea fowl, a delicious fowl with a vulture-like head that is usually raised on farms. It is gamier than turkey, tasting somewhat like pheasant with a smoky and strangely wild flavor. An exile from the African wilds, the fowl most likely first appeared in the New World in Haiti, probably brought in by slaves.

Because guinea fowl are considerably more expensive than chicken ($4 to $5 per pound) they are mostly found in gourmet shops or can be specially ordered through your butcher. They are smaller than most chickens, weighing 2 to 2½ pounds.   **Serves 2**

2 (2-pound) guinea fowl, cleaned
Lemon or lime juice, for washing fowl
1 teaspoon chopped fresh parsley
1 teaspoon dried rosemary
2 tablespoons butter or margarine, softened
¾ cup sour orange juice*
1 teaspoon dried marjoram
1 teaspoon dried basil
4 garlic cloves, peeled and chopped
1 cup finely minced onion
6 slices bacon, or 1 large piece pork fat
1 cup chopped carrots
2 cups diced skinned potatoes
1 cup finely chopped cabbage
1 bay leaf
1 cup chicken stock (page 36)
1 cup white vinegar
1 cup dry red wine
Salt, to taste

Wash hens inside and out with lemon juice and dry thoroughly. Mix the parsley, rosemary, and softened butter and insert under the skin where possible.

Prepare the marinade by thoroughly mixing together the sour orange juice, marjoram, basil, garlic, and onion. Place hens in a Pyrex baking pan. Pour marinade over the guinea hens and refrigerate covered for 24 hours, continuing to baste with marinade several times.

When hens are marinated, remove from refrigerator. Cook bacon in a large Dutch oven until fat is rendered. Add the marinated hens and brown, turning several times. Add carrots, potatoes, cabbage, and bay leaf. Cover and cook over low heat. When meat is half cooked, after about 30 minutes, add chicken broth and a cup of vinegar. Cover and simmer for another 45 minutes, basting constantly. When sauce begins to reduce, add the 1 cup red wine, or more if desired. Season with salt.

Serve with sauce poured over hen and also on the side.

*If you do not have sour orange juice, substitute ¾ cup fresh orange juice and ¼ cup fresh lime juice

Guinea Hen with Raisins and Hazelnuts

Guinea con Pasas

Partaking of the succulent guinea hen has been a favorite Cuban tradition, especially during holiday time. The birds are usually more plentiful during the fall. Here's a classic recipe with raisins and hazelnuts that's easy to prepare.

Serves 4 to 8

¾ cup lime juice
½ teaspoon white pepper
4 garlic cloves, peeled and crushed
3 tablespoons minced white onion
½ cup plus 1 tablespoon olive oil
4 guinea fowl, about 2 pounds each, cut into quarters
1 white onion, cut into rings
1½ cups dry red wine
2 tablespoons balsamic vinegar
Salt, to taste
1 cup seedless black raisins
⅔ cup peeled hazelnuts
Fresh parsley springs, for garnish

Make a marinade by combining lime juice, pepper, garlic, minced onion, and 1 tablespoon olive oil. Pour over guinea hens. Rub in well and allow to marinate in refrigerator for 2 to 3 hours. Turn hens several times to coat.

Heat two large heavy skillets and add ¼ cup olive oil to each. When oil begins to smell fragrant, add the onion rings and guinea hens, with their marinade. Cook until hens are browned on all sides.

Remove hens from pans and set aside. Add wine and vinegar to skillets, mixing with pan drippings, and season sauce with salt. Return hens to skillets, cover, and simmer on low heat for 50 to 60 minutes, until hens are tender. Uncover, add raisins and hazelnuts, and cook for 15 minutes longer, until sauce is reduced.

Serve hens topped with sauce and garnished with fresh parsley sprigs.

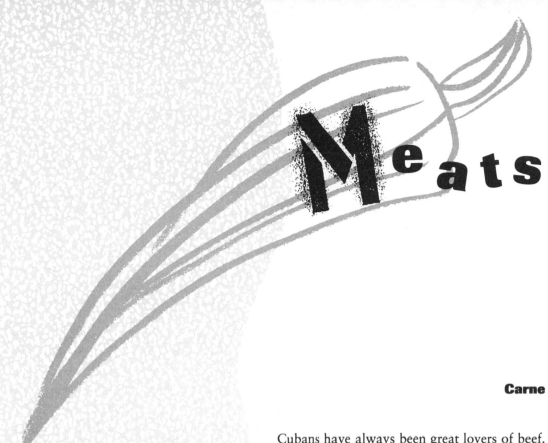

Meats

Carne

Cubans have always been great lovers of beef. At one time cattle raising was an integral part of the island's prosperity, but it is rare to see cattle in Cuba today and beef is considered a luxury, mostly available to tourists in the hotels. Pork is now the favorite meat of most Cubans, in the States, and it is 30 percent leaner than it was ten years ago.

Marination is the key to cooking any meat Cuban style. Even very tender cuts are so seasoned to coax out maximum flavors. Often the cuts are marinated for two to three days and are constantly turned so that the juices reach every recess. Garlic and sour orange juice are the ingredients used most prominently in these marinades.

Roast Beef

Carne Asada

Carne asada is a traditional Cuban dish of Spanish derivation. A sirloin tip roast, which is marginally tender, chunky, and quite lean, is used most often for this recipe, although other inexpensive cuts such as a rolled rump can be substituted. But if there is any doubt as to the tenderness, the marination process used here tenderizes the beef. Cubans take a great deal of care to season the roast to perfection. Add more garlic if you wish; that's what they would do.

Serves 6 to 8

4 garlic cloves, peeled and mashed
½ teaspoon salt
1½ teaspoons ground cumin
¾ cup red wine vinegar
1 teaspoon crushed dried oregano
1 (4- to 5-pound) sirloin tip roast
¼ cup olive oil
1 large white onion, chopped
2 tablespoons all-purpose flour
½ cup dry white wine
2 bay leaves
2 tablespoons Worcestershire sauce
1 (4-ounce) jar pimientos, drained and chopped
Fresh parsley sprigs, for garnish

In a mortar or small heavy bowl, mash garlic together with the salt, cumin, and oregano. Add the vinegar and mix well.

Make deep slashes across the beef in a diamond pattern (as if scoring a ham), rub the liquid mixture over the entire roast, and stuff into the cuts. Cover and marinate, refrigerated, for 3 to 4 hours. Drain meat, reserving marinade.

Preheat the oven to 350° F.

In a large roasting pan set on top of the stove, heat the olive oil and onions. Lightly dredge meat in the flour. When olive oil begins to smell fragrant, brown meat in oil. Add reserved marinade, white wine, bay leaves, Worcestershire sauce, and pimientos and cook a few minutes. Cover roasting pan and put in oven, but continue to baste until roast is tender, about 2 hours. Turn meat over several times. Remove from oven, slice, and return to the oven for about 20 minutes longer. Add additional water and wine as necessary to prevent meat from sticking to bottom of pan. Taste sauce for seasoning, then strain sauce and serve over sirloin slices.

Garnish with fresh parsley sprigs and serve with white or yellow rice and fried sweet plantains or boiled parsleyed potatoes.

Beefy Bayamo Casserole

Cacerola de Carne Bayamo

Bayamo, one of Cuba's oldest settlements, is located in the southwest corner, just west of Santiago de Cuba. It is known for its spicy Creole-style cooking. This casserole, although not nearly as fiery as the dishes of Santiago, will certainly add spice to any dinner party. The addition of the Tabasco sauce and the harmonious combination of beef, pork, beans, and vegetables produce a dish worthy of every compliment you receive. The *queso blanco* used for the topping is found in most Hispanic markets, but just about any mild white cheese will suffice.

Prepare this dish in the morning, then pop it in the oven just before serving; it takes only a half hour to cook. Serve with a juicy ripe avocado salad drizzled with olive oil and red wine vinegar.

Serves 6 to 8

2 tablespoons vegetable oil
2 pounds ground round or ground chuck
1 pound ground pork sausage
1 green bell pepper, seeded and thinly sliced
3 garlic cloves, peeled and minced
1 medium onion, thinly sliced
2 carrots, diced
1 cup diced celery
1 (16-ounce) can tomato sauce
2 bay leaves, cracked
1 teaspoon Tabasco, or to taste
1 cup chopped cured black olives
1 (15-ounce) can black beans, drained
  and rinsed
1 (17-ounce) can whole kernel corn
½ cup water
½ cup shredded sharp Cheddar cheese
¾ cup shredded queso blanco or Monterey
  Jack cheese
Spanish paprika

Heat a large skillet or sauté pan and add the oil. When oil is heated and begins to smell fragrant, add the ground round and pork sausage, then the green pepper, garlic, onion, carrots, and celery. Cook until meat is browned and cooked through. Drain off excess oil.

Preheat the oven to 350° F.

To the prepared mixture, add the tomato sauce, bay leaves, Tabasco, olives, black beans, corn, water, and Cheddar cheese and combine well. Top with *queso blanco*. Pour into a 2-quart ovenproof dish. Sprinkle with paprika and bake uncovered for about 30 minutes.

Boca Ciega Roast

Carne Asada Boca Ciega

Although beef has not always been in abundant supply on the Caribbean island, Cubans have treated it, and especially cuts of marginal quality, with great skill and imagination. The secret most often lies in the preparation of the sauce, often prepared with a base of sautéed vegetables that envelops the meat.

Nearly any other inexpensive cut, including rolled rump or top and eye round, is suitable.

Serves 4 to 6

1 (3-pound) boneless chuck roast,
   about 3 inches thick
2 thick slices wood-smoked bacon
4 garlic cloves, peeled and chopped
¾ cup chopped white onion
2 green bell peppers, roasted, peeled, seeded,
   and thinly sliced*
1 red bell pepper, roasted, peeled, seeded,
   and thinly sliced*
2 cups tomato sauce
½ cup dry white wine
2 cups dry red wine or dry sherry
2 tablespoons small capers, drained
1 teaspoon ground oregano
1 teaspoon ground cumin
1 tablespoon cider vinegar
1 teaspoon Worcestershire sauce
2 bay leaves
Salt, to taste

Heat a Dutch oven. Add bacon and cook until very crisp and brown. With a slotted spoon, remove bacon and set aside. In the same Dutch oven, brown roast well on both sides, then remove to a separate pan. Add garlic, onion, and green and red bell pepper to the pan and sauté until wilted. Put roast back in the sauté. Add tomato sauce, wine, capers, oregano, cumin, vinegar, Worcestershire, bay leaves, and salt. Blend sauce ingredients together well. Simmer over low heat until meat is very tender, about 3½ hours. Add water, if necessary, to keep a medium consistency to the sauce.

Serve by slicing roast into 2-inch-wide pieces. Crumble bacon and top each serving with a sprinkling. Serve with white rice and a separate bowl of sauce on the side.

*See page 24 for how to roast and peel peppers.

Cuban Stuffed Pot Roast

Boliche Asado

You won't find a one-pot dish that's more buffet-perfect than *boliche,* the name of the Spanish cut of beef used in this recipe. It takes some extra effort to prepare, but in addition to looking exquisite and very stylish, both the stuffed roast and wine sauce are delectable.

If you don't wish to cut the cavity yourself, have your butcher do it for you. Combined with the bacon, manzanilla olives, and wine, the chorizos lend a subtle spicy flavor to this very classic dish.

Serves 10 to 12

1 (4- to 5-pound) eye-of-round roast, about
   4 × 9 inches, excess fat trimmed
1 cup sour orange juice*
1 tablespoon chopped fresh cilantro
1 teaspoon chopped fresh oregano, or
   ½ teaspoon dried
4 garlic cloves, peeled and finely minced
½ pound smoked slab bacon
3 ounces chorizo sausage†
¼ cup pimiento-stuffed manzanilla olives
3 tablespoons olive oil
1½ cups chopped white onion
1 celery rib, finely chopped
¼ cup chopped green bell pepper
¼ cup chopped red bell pepper
1 cup peeled, seeded, and chopped plum
   tomatoes
1 cup Spanish sherry or dry red wine
1 teaspoon ground oregano
½ teaspoon Spanish paprika
Pinch of nutmeg
2 bay leaves
Salt and freshly ground black pepper, to taste
12 small new potatoes, cooked
5 carrots, peeled and cut diagonally into
   1-inch pieces, cooked
Chopped fresh parsley, for garnish

Cut a small lengthwise cavity in the heart of the roast, almost but not quite to the end of the meat. Mix together the sour orange juice, cilantro, oregano, and garlic, then rub mixture in the cavity and over the entire roast. Marinate, refrigerated, for 2 to 3 hours. Turn several times so that juices saturate all parts of the roast.

In the container of a food processor or blender, process the bacon, chorizos, and olives to a fine grind. Mix the contents with the marinade in a bowl. Loosely stuff mixture into the cavity of the roast by pressing it with a long-handled spoon as far into the cavity as possible.

Heat a large casserole that can be used on the stove as well as in the oven, then add olive oil. When olive oil is heated and begins to smell fragrant, add the roast and brown on all sides, turn-

ing with a large fork several times. Remove the roast to a separate pan and reserve drippings.

Preheat the oven to 325° F.

Add onion, celery, and the green and red peppers to the reserved drippings. Combine well and then sauté over medium-high heat until onions become translucent but not browned. Add plum tomatoes, sherry, oregano, paprika, nutmeg, bay leaves, and salt and pepper.

Return the browned roast to the casserole. Cover and bake for 2½ to 3 hours, basting constantly, until meat is fork tender. Do not turn off oven.

Remove the meat to a separate dish. Cool for at least 30 minutes. Place sauce in a bowl and refrigerate for a few hours.

Skim fat from surface of sauce with a large spoon, then place sauce in the container of a food processor or blender and process until liquefied. Pour into a 10-inch sauté pan. Adjust seasoning. Add the cooked potatoes and carrots, then cover and simmer for about 5 minutes.

Using a very sharp knife so that roast does not crumble, carefully slice the roast into 20 to 24 pieces, each about ¼ inch thick. Place slices overlapping on a large ovenproof platter so that center filling shows. Cover tightly with foil so that meat does not dry out. Heat until warmed, about 15 minutes, then raise temperature to 350° F and heat for another 10 minutes.

Arrange potatoes and carrots around the meat slices, then spoon sauce over meat and vegetables and serve remaining sauce in a covered heated gravy dish. Garnish meat with freshly chopped parsley. Serve immediately.

---

*If you don't have sour orange juice, substitute ¾ cup orange juice mixed with ¼ cup lime juice.
†You may substitute 3 ounces pepperoni, if necessary.

Cuban Cheeseburgers with Bacon

Fritas Cubana con Tocineta

On a recent trip to Havana, I was fascinated by a tiny bustling café just adjacent to a large tourist supermarket. The burgers looked so inviting that even though I had eaten lunch, I ordered one. Fernando Pereira, the manager of Rincón del Sabor Cerebral (which means "taste from the brain") told me that the bread, a Cuban-style crusty roll, was similar to one that his father made years ago at a bakery called Super Pané. The highly seasoned burgers are an unusual treat with the garnish of peppers and Canadian bacon.   **Serves 4**

    1 pound lean ground beef
    ½ cup bread crumbs soaked in ¼ cup milk
    1 egg, slightly beaten
    ½ cup chopped white onion
    1 tablespoon ketchup
    2 garlic cloves, peeled and minced
    1 teaspoon Spanish paprika
    ½ teaspoon salt
    2 tablespoons vegetable oil
    1 tablespoon soy sauce
    4 freshly baked kaiser or burger rolls
    4 thick slices Canadian bacon, grilled
    1 red bell pepper, seeded and thinly sliced
    2 carrots, julienned and marinated in olive oil
       and red wine vinegar
    Cornichons, for garnish

In a large mixing bowl, combine the ground beef with moistened bread crumbs. Add the egg, onion, ketchup, garlic, paprika, and salt and combine well. Form into four balls and refrigerate for about 3 hours.

To fry, flatten burgers with a pancake turner or with your hands, but form them smaller and thicker than you would most burgers. Put vegetable oil and soy sauce in a frying pan and combine well, then fry burgers over medium-high heat, or if you prefer, grill them.

Put on rolls and garnish with a slice of grilled Canadian bacon and thinly sliced red bell peppers. Garnish plates with tiny portions of the small julienne carrots and cornichons. Serve with thinly cut French fries, or add a few to the sandwich, if desired.

Cold Meat Loaf

Bollo de Carne Fría

This classic dish can be served hot or cold, although I prefer to serve it cold, as the title suggests. It is quicker to bake the beef roll, but some Cuban cooks prefer to tie the beef in cheesecloth and cook at a low temperature in a rich beef stock. Sometimes it is served as an appetizer, but is more commonly the main course for supper on a hot summer evening, or at picnics and buffets.

Serves 4 to 6, or 6 to 8 as an appetizer

½ **pound lean ground beef**
¾ **pound lean ground pork**
⅓ **cup chopped onion**
1 **teaspoon chopped fresh parsley**
½ **teaspoon cracked black pepper**
½ **teaspoon ground nutmeg**
1 **teaspoon Spanish paprika**
1 **teaspoon ground cumin**
½ **teaspoon thyme leaves**
3 **garlic cloves, peeled and minced**
Salt, to taste
3 **eggs, slightly beaten**
½ **cup cracker meal***
Olive oil, for coating beef
Fresh parsley sprigs, for garnish
12 **cherry tomatoes, for garnish**

Combine the meats in a large mixing bowl. Add the remaining ingredients except the eggs, cracker meal, olive oil, and garnishes. Place in the container of a food processor or blender and process until well blended and very smooth.

Form meat mixture by rolling by hand into two cylinders about 5 inches long and 3 inches wide. Dip each into egg mixture, then cracker meal.

Preheat the oven to 325° F.

Coat each cylinder of meat lightly with olive oil. Wrap each in a double wrapping of aluminum foil and bake for about 1 hour, or until meat is thoroughly cooked.

Remove and allow to cool. Thinly slice and arrange on a colorful platter garnished with parsley and cherry tomatoes.

*Available at most supermarkets, or make your own by processing saltine crackers in a food processor until finely ground—36 saltines make about 1 cup crumbs.

Pot Roast

Carne Mechada

Mechada is derived from the Spanish word *mechar,* which means to lard, or add strips of fat to the meat to make it more moist and tender. Larding consists of threading these thin strips of fat into a lean cut of meat that needs a little fat. You may choose to use that method, which I have included at the end, but I prefer to prepare this very classical dish in a simpler fashion.   **Serves 4 to 6**

> 1 (3- to 5-pound) boneless chuck roast, pot
>   roast, roast beef, or eye-of-round
> ¼ pound jamón de cocina,* or lean baked
>   Virginia ham, cut ½ inch thick and chopped
> 2 slices slab bacon, chopped

MARINADE

> ⅓ cup orange juice
> Juice of 2 limes
> ¼ cup olive oil
> 2 white onions, thinly sliced
> 3 garlic cloves, peeled and crushed
> 1 green bell pepper, seeded and cut into thin
>   strips
> 1 red bell pepper, seeded and cut into thin
>   strips
> 2 tablespoons chopped fresh cilantro, or 1
>   tablespoon dried coriander
> 2 bay leaves, cracked
> ⅓ cup dry sherry
> 1 teaspoon salt

> 3 tablespoons olive oil, for browning

With a very sharp knife, slice a pocket lengthwise deep into the center of the beef, but be careful not to cut through to the opposite end.

Prepare the filling by mixing ham and bacon together, then stuff loosely into the cavity of the roast. Secure open end with large toothpicks or small skewers.

Prepare the marinade in a large glass bowl by mixing together the orange juice, lime juice, and olive oil. Add the onions, garlic, peppers, cilantro, and bay leaves and mix once again. Add the stuffed roast to the marinade, rubbing marinade into the skin of beef and spreading mixture over entire roast. Cover and refrigerate for about 6 hours, being careful to turn occasionally.

Remove roast from the refrigerator, drain marinade, and reserve. Put oil in a large Dutch oven and when oil is heated and begins to smell fragrant, add roast and brown meat well on all sides. Add reserved marinade, bring to a boil, add sherry, reduce heat, cover, and braise over medium-low heat for 1 to 2 hours, or until tender. Add additional wine or water as necessary to prevent meat from sticking to pan.

Strain the sauce, taste and season with salt, then pour over the meat. Serve with potatoes or rice, black beans, and plantains.

Note: If you prefer to lard the roast, insert a long knife into the meat and twist in a rotating manner. Place a strip of pork fat into the larding pin and follow through the space prepared by the knife. Do this for the entire roast until all ham and bacon strips are incorporated. You can season the lardons with salt, pepper, and chopped fresh parsley if you desire.

Jamón de cocina is cooking ham that is sold in chunks at Hispanic markets. Virginia ham, country-cured, firm, and salty, is full of flavor and good, too.

Oxtail with Peppers and Capers

Rabo Alcaparrado

Here's an economical yet delicious dinner that originated with early Cuban emigrants trying to make more from less. The oxtails give a great deal of flavor and body to the dish, but look for those that are meaty and lean.

Rinse the capers first to remove excess salt. The peppers, spices, and tomato sauce combine with the vinegar and sherry for a smooth, piquant sauce.   **Serves 6**

> **2 pounds oxtails, excess fat removed,**
>   **cut into 2-inch pieces**
> **2 tablespoons plus ¼ cup olive oil**
> **2 cups chopped onion**
> **5 garlic cloves, peeled and chopped**
> **2 cups chopped green bell pepper**
> **1 cup chopped red bell pepper**
> **⅓ cup chopped fresh parsley**
> **1 (15-ounce) can tomato sauce**
> **2 cups dry red wine or sherry**
> **¾ cup capers, rinsed**
> **½ teaspoon ground cumin**
> **½ teaspoon dried thyme or sprig of fresh**
>   **thyme**
> **½ teaspoon dried oregano**
> **2 bay leaves**
> **1 tablespoon cider vinegar**
> **1 teaspoon salt, or to taste**
> **2 dashes of Tabasco sauce**
> **1 teaspoon coarsely ground black pepper**
> **Splash of dry sherry**

Wash meat well and dry thoroughly. Heat a Dutch oven, then add 2 tablespoons olive oil. When olive oil begins to smell fragrant, add oxtail pieces and brown on all sides. Using a slotted spoon, remove pieces to a bowl.

Add the ¼ cup of olive oil, onions, garlic, and peppers to the Dutch oven and sauté until onions and garlic are limp, then put the oxtail pieces back in. Add parsley, tomato sauce, wine, capers, cumin, thyme, oregano, bay leaves, cider vinegar, salt, and Tabasco. Combine ingredients well, then cook over medium heat until tender, about 3 hours. Season with salt and pepper. If necessary, add more wine to thin.

Add a splash of sherry just before serving to help flavors meld. Serve hot with rice and plantains.

Cuban Steak

Bistec de Palomilla

During the six years I lived in Miami, my teenage daughter, Julie, would tell me how her friend's mom made this steak at least four times a week. We experimented in our home with a few variations and came up with this one, which Julie said was even better than her friend's.

Many people of Cuban heritage in America and in Cuba still use pork lard to cook this steak, but because lard is so high in cholesterol, I prepare this one with a good olive oil, which imparts a lovely flavor. The succulent dish is typically served with white rice, black beans, and ripe golden-brown plantains.   **Serves 4 to 6**

    8 (¼-inch-thick) slices top butt steak or top
        round (about 2 pounds), butterflied*
    3 tablespoons olive oil or salted butter
    1 onion, thinly sliced
    1 lime, cut into 8 thin wedges
    ¼ cup chopped fresh parsley

MARINADE

    8 garlic cloves, peeled and crushed
    ½ teaspoon dried oregano
    1 teaspoon ground cumin
    ¾ cup sour orange juice†
    1 large onion, diced

Using a metal meat mallet, pound steaks on both sides to tenderize. Mix together marinade ingredients well and pour over steaks in a large glass bowl. Cover and marinate in refrigerator for 1 hour, turning frequently so all juices penetrate.

Heat a large heavy skillet and add olive oil. When heated and oil begins to smell fragrant, add steaks, onion, and enough marinade to make a light sauce. Cook until both sides are done and sliced onion is wilting, just a few minutes. Place steaks on a heated platter and pour sauce over.

Garnish with lime wedges and chopped parsley. Squeeze lime over steak when ready to eat.

*You can purchase steaks already butterflied, or do it yourself. To do so, split the steak down the center almost in half, but not quite through, so that the two halves can be opened flat, like butterfly wings.
†You may substitute ½ cup sweet orange juice and ¼ cup lime juice for the sour orange juice.

Havana Beef Hash

Picadillo Havana

This is the Latin version of the American sloppy joe, and is a mainstay in many Hispanic households. You can use regular ground chuck if you wish, but I prefer to use lean ground round. Freshly grated nutmeg melds the flavors and enhances this delightfully addictive dish. It's inexpensive, simple, heartwarming, yet robust. Don't let the number of ingredients stop you from trying this classic dish because, once assembled, it's a cinch to cook.   **Serves 6 to 8**

¼ cup olive oil

1 onion, finely chopped

4 garlic cloves, peeled and crushed

2 green bell peppers, seeded and finely
  chopped

2½ pounds lean ground round of beef

2 large ripe tomatoes, peeled, seeded,
  and finely chopped

2 bay leaves, crushed

1½ teaspoons dried oregano, crushed

¼ teaspoon crushed hot red pepper

½ cup seedless raisins

⅛ cup diced pimiento

¼ cup small capers, rinsed, drained,
  and crushed

⅓ cup pimiento-stuffed manzanilla olives,
  sliced or chopped

3 tablespoons red wine vinegar

1½ tablespoons white vinegar

¼ cup tomato sauce

¼ cup red wine, preferably Spanish

1½ teaspoons Tabasco or other pepper sauce
  (optional)

1 teaspoon dark brown sugar

¼ cup chicken stock (page 36) or defatted
  chicken broth*

¼ teaspoon freshly grated nutmeg

½ teaspoon salt, or to taste

Heat a 5-quart Dutch oven and add the olive oil. When medium hot, sauté the onion, garlic, and bell pepper until translucent. Add ground round and cook until just browned, then drain off excess oil.

In a bowl, combine tomatoes, bay leaves, oregano, chili pepper, raisins, and pimientos. Add to the meat mixture and cook, covered, over moderate heat for about 10 minutes. Add capers and cook another 5 minutes.

To the meat mixture add the olives, red and white vinegars, tomato sauce, wine, Tabasco sauce, brown sugar, chicken stock, nutmeg, and salt. Cover and simmer for 30 to 40 minutes, or until most of the liquid is absorbed.

Serve over white or yellow rice, with ripe plantains and an avocado salad.

*To defat canned broth, place can in refrigerator. When chilled, open can and skim fat from the surface.

Magnificent Beef Hash

Picadillo Magnífico

Here is another version of *picadillo*. I particularly like the addition of the potatoes and blanched almonds. The potatoes give the hash a sturdy texture, while the almonds add flavor to this very classic dish.   **Serves 6 to 8**

¾ pound lean ground beef

¼ pound lean ground pork

½ cup water

1 (14½-ounce) can whole tomatoes,
  including juice

1 cup finely chopped onion

3 medium potatoes, peeled and diced

1 (4-ounce) jar pimientos, drained and
  chopped

½ cup toasted blanched slivered almonds

3 garlic cloves, peeled and finely minced

1 (6-ounce) can tomato paste

2 jalapeño peppers, or ½ teaspoon Tabasco
  sauce

¾ cup seedless raisins

¼ cup pimiento-stuffed manzanilla olives

1 teaspoon chopped fresh oregano, or
  ½ teaspoon dried

1 teaspoon ground cumin

1 tablespoon chopped fresh parsley

Salt and pepper, to taste

Sauté beef and pork over medium heat and break up well so that there are few chunks, then carefully pour off excess oil. Add the water and allow meat to simmer for about 30 minutes.

Add tomatoes, onion, potatoes, pimientos, almonds, garlic, tomato paste, jalapeños, raisins, olives, oregano, cumin, and fresh parsley and combine well. Season with salt and pepper. Cook until potatoes are cooked through. Serve with plantains and a tropical fruit salad.

Rancha Luna Beef

Carne Rancha Luna

Here's a classic treatment for a relatively inexpensive cut of steak, with a Jamaican twist. The Pickapeppa Sauce is a full-flavored pepper sauce containing the sour-sweet tamarind juice that tends to tease out the best flavors of the beef. I named this recipe after an outdoor barbecue-style restaurant I visited in Havana, but it is very much the Cuban version of our beef stew. This dish can also be cooked with diced potatoes (about 3 large) and served in hearty stew bowls. **Serves 4**

⅛ cup olive oil
2 pounds beef round steak, cut into 1-inch
    pieces, most fat trimmed off
1 teaspoon Spanish paprika
1 teaspoon ground cumin
½ teaspoon ground oregano
2 bay leaves, crushed
1 cup chopped white onion
4 garlic cloves, peeled and chopped
1 green bell pepper, seeded and chopped
1 (10-ounce) can tomato sauce
2 tablespoons red wine vinegar
1 tablespoon Pickapeppa Sauce
1½ cups dry red wine, such as Burgundy,
    or a dry Spanish
1 tablespoon chopped fresh parsley
Salt and coarsely ground pepper, to taste
1 cup canned baby green peas (petit pois), for
    garnish
Fresh parsley sprigs, for garnish

Heat a large Dutch oven and add olive oil. When it begins to smell fragrant, add the round steak pieces. Sauté until browned on all sides, then add paprika, cumin, oregano, and bay leaves. Combine well, then add onion, garlic, and green pepper and cook for about 5 minutes. Add tomato sauce, vinegar, Pickapeppa Sauce, wine, parsley, and salt and pepper. Cover and simmer over low heat for about 1½ hours, or until meat chunks are tender.

Serve over white rice or yellow rice with fresh green beans. Garnish with peas and fresh parsley sprigs.

Shredded Beef in Tomato Sauce

Ropa Vieja

Literally translated, *ropa vieja* means "old clothes," a reference to the fact that the meat eventually becomes shredded. It differs from *tasajo*, which is also shredded, in that it is prepared with fresh meat rather than dried.

This entrée uses *sofrito* as a base, as do many of the Cuban meat and poultry dishes. In this variation (and there are many of this popular recipe), the *sofrito* includes tomatoes, peppers, onions, and garlic, but no meat. If you prefer, you can substitute a *sofrito* that includes ham from the basic sauce section of this cookbook. The addition of ham will add another dimension to the already savory stew.

This is one of those meat dishes that tastes better the longer the flavors blend, so I always like to serve it the day after it's prepared.   **Serves 4**

1½ pounds flank steak
1 large onion, peeled
2 large carrots
2 bay leaves
2 cups sofrito (page 14)
1 tablespoon dry sherry
1 (8½-ounce) can baby green peas
  (petit pois)
2 tablespoons finely chopped celery
1 (4-ounce) jar pimientos, finely chopped
1 (8-ounce) can tomato sauce
Salt and pepper, to taste

Put 2 quarts of water in a heavy 4-quart kettle. Add flank steak, onion, carrots, and bay leaves and bring to a rolling boil. Reduce heat to medium-low, then cook for about 2½ hours, or until meat is tender and easy to shred. Pull a few strands of meat off with your hands. If it tears easily, it's done. Set aside to cool.

Strain the liquid and reserve broth. Discard the bay leaves, but reserve the vegetables and then chop carrots and onion and set aside.

When meat has cooled, using hands or a fork, shred the meat fibers until they are threadlike strips.

Heat a large skillet or sauté pan and add the *sofrito*, ½ cup reserved beef broth, the sherry, peas, celery, reserved carrots and onions, and shredded beef. Consistency of sauce should be light, a little thicker than soup. Add more stock, if necessary, and cook 7 to 8 minutes. Add the pimientos, tomato sauce, salt, and pepper, then stir and cook for another 2 to 5 minutes, or until heated through. Serve with fluffy white or yellow rice, sweet plantains, and black beans.

Sautéed Steak Fillets

Bistec Salteado

In this recipe borrowed from Spanish ancestors, soft tenderloin is combined with specially seasoned pork sausages (chorizos) to achieve a delicate yet robust dish.

Frying the potatoes first instills flavor and keeps them from getting soggy. Ripe plum tomatoes are used here for more pronounced flavor.

Serves 4

½ cup olive oil
2 pounds tenderloin steak fillets
5 garlic cloves, peeled and mashed
1 large red onion, chopped
1 red bell pepper, seeded and chopped
1 green bell pepper, seeded and chopped
2 chorizo sausages, thinly sliced
24 small button mushrooms
2 white Idaho potatoes, diced and deep-fried
2 pinches of white pepper
1 teaspoon chopped fresh thyme, or
   ½ teaspoon dried
⅔ cup dry red Spanish wine
Salt and pepper, to taste
3 ripe plum tomatoes, diced, for garnish
Chopped fresh parsley and lime slices, for
   garnish

Heat a large skillet or sauté pan and add olive oil. When olive oil begins to smell fragrant, sauté the fillets until cooked as desired. Add the garlic, onion, and bell peppers and cook until onion is translucent. Add the chorizo, mushrooms, potatoes, white pepper, and thyme and cook until sausage is browned. Add wine and reduce for 5 to 10 minutes. Season with salt and pepper. Garnish with ripe tomato, fresh parsley, and lime slices. Serve with ripe plantains and a fresh green vegetable.

Salt-Cured Beef with Sofrito Sauce

Tasajo "La Rueta"

Tasajo, a favorite of many Cubans, is salt-dried beef that is desalted then cooked until tender. In this recipe, the *sofrito* is added to season the beef.

Salt-dried beef can be purchased at most Hispanic supermarkets.

Serves 8

3 pounds salt-dried beef
2 bay leaves
2 cups sofrito (page 14), or purchased sofrito*

Soak the salt-dried beef overnight (at least 6 hours) in a large glass bowl in enough water to cover, changing water two to three times. It's not necessary to refrigerate during this process.

Drain the beef and discard the water. Place beef in a Dutch oven. Cover with fresh cold water. Add 1 bay leaf and cook on medium-high heat until tender, about 45 minutes. Remove from pan with a large fork and allow to cool at room temperature. Finely shred beef into fibers. There should be no more than 3 to 4 strands together in each fiber section. Set aside.

In a separate saucepan, heat the prepared *sofrito*. Add the shredded meat with about ½ cup of water and 1 bay leaf and combine well. Add 1 tablespoon olive oil, if necessary. Cook on low heat for about 40 minutes.

Serve with black beans and rice on page 92 and fried sweet potatoes on page 190.

*Available in the dairy section of most Hispanic markets.

Heat a Dutch oven and add ¼ cup of the olive oil. When the oil begins to smell fragrant, add pressed garlic and 1 sliced onion. Add the whole piece of meat and the lime and lemon juices. Constantly turn meat to coat with juice, onion, and garlic. Season with salt and pepper. Cover and braise until meat tenderizes, about 2 hours, adding a little water if necessary. Cool and then shred meat by hand into threads. Put back in marinade in a covered glass bowl and cool in refrigerator for 1 to 2 hours, or overnight.

Remove the shredded meat from the marinade. Using your hands, squeeze out any excess marinade.

Heat a large skillet and add the remaining ¼ cup olive oil. When oil begins to smell fragrant, add a whole garlic clove. When it begins to brown, remove and discard. Add the second sliced onion. Add the shredded meat to the pan and stir-fry at a low temperature. When coated and hot, serve immediately with rice and golden fried plantains. Garnish with lime wedges.

*This recipe also works well with sour orange juice. To substitute, use ½ cup sour orange juice instead of lemon and lime juices.

Stir-Fried Shredded Beef

Vaca Frita

This delicious classic recipe translates as "fried cow." The beef is fried, shredded, marinated in lemon and lime juices or sour orange juice and seasonings, then refried just before serving. Allow at least 1 hour for marinating, or preferably overnight.

I use a point cut of brisket for this recipe because it has more flavor and more fat than flank steak.

Serves 4 to 6

- ½ cup olive oil
- 3 garlic cloves, peeled and pressed
- 2 medium onions, thinly sliced, each placed in separate bowls
- 2 to 2½ pounds beef brisket or flank steak, rubbed with ½ teaspoon salt
- ¼ cup lime juice*
- ¼ cup lemon juice*
- Salt and cracked pepper, to taste
- 1 whole garlic clove, peeled
- 1 lime, cut into thin wedges, for garnish

Fried Pork Chunks

Masas de Puerco Fritas

Be sure to leave time for the pork chunks to marinate. The sour orange juice, available today at most Hispanic markets, imparts a one-of-a-kind flavor to the meat. Many look just like an orange, although some varieties have a pocked skin. But beware, these are not for eating! A friend of mine tried them once and it took a long time to eradicate the sourness from her mouth.   **Serves 4 to 6**

16 garlic cloves, peeled and crushed
½ large onion, peeled and chopped
½ cup sour orange juice*
⅓ cup olive oil
Salt and cracked black pepper, to taste
1 (2½- to 3-pound) fresh pork loin, most fat removed
Vegetable oil, for deep-frying
½ large red onion, sliced into thin rings, for garnish
Lime wedges, for garnish

Combine the garlic, chopped onion, sour orange juice, olive oil, and salt and pepper.

Cut the loin into 1- to 2-inch chunks, being careful to remove most of the fat. Pour marinade over the pork chunks and marinate in the refrigerator for several hours, or overnight.

Heat the oil, remove the pork from the marinade, and deep-fry until done. Serve with plenty of fluffy white rice and black beans. Garnish with onion slices and lime wedges.

*If you have no sour orange juice, combine ¼ cup orange juice and ¼ cup lime juice to duplicate the flavor.

Pork with Yellow Rice and Okra

Cerdo con Arroz Amarillo y Quimbombó

This dish probably traces its ancestry to Africa, where okra is a well-loved vegetable. The saffron enhances the flavors of the peppers and okra, but if this most expensive spice in the world is too heavy on the budget, try *bijol* or *bija bekal,* yellow coloring and flavor enhancers that will do just fine.

This is an eye-catching dish, easy to prepare and delicious too. Slice your own meat from a budget cut, or ask the butcher to do it for you.   **Serves 6 to 8**

¼ cup olive oil
3 pounds lean pork, cut into ½-inch cubes
½ cup chopped white onion
½ green bell pepper, seeded and chopped
½ red bell pepper, seeded and chopped
½ yellow bell pepper, seeded and chopped
1 large ripe tomato, seeded and diced
2 to 3 garlic cloves, peeled and crushed
⅓ pound fresh okra, ends trimmed and cut into ½-inch rings
2½ cups water
A few threads of saffron, or ¼ teaspoon bijol*
2 cups long-grain rice
2 tablespoons cider vinegar

Heat a large skillet and add the olive oil. When oil begins to become fragrant, sauté pork chunks for about 10 minutes, or until golden. Add onion, bell peppers, tomato, and garlic. Fry until onion becomes browned and vegetables are soft. Add okra, water, and saffron. Turn up heat and boil about 5 minutes. Add rice and boil for about 5 more minutes. Lower heat to a simmer, cover tightly, and simmer for 20 to 25 minutes, or until rice is cooked.

Add cider vinegar, stir, and serve steaming hot.

*See page 6.

Loin of Pork Cuba Libre

Lomo de Puerco Mentirita

The first time I prepared this classic pork loin it was an experiment for about two dozen friends. They thought it was one of the most unusual and delicious roasts they ever tasted. The fruity stuffing combined with the herbal marinated pork made the evening a memorable experience.

Have your butcher prepare and butterfly the loins for you—it makes the recipe very easy from there.   **Serves 10 to 12**

> 2 cups sour orange juice*
> 8 garlic cloves, peeled and crushed
> 4 bay leaves, crushed
> 1 tablespoon Spanish paprika
> 1 (6- to 7-pound) center-cut boneless pork
>   loin, cut lengthwise into 2 pieces, then
>   butterflied open lengthwise
> 8 ounces baked Virginia country ham, thinly
>   sliced
> 4 hard-boiled eggs, peeled and sliced
> 1 cup dried pitted prunes
> ½ cup chopped red bell pepper
> 1 cup chopped leeks
> 1 cup sliced carrots
> 1 tablespoon chopped fresh parsley
> 9 slices lean bacon
> 2 cups dark brown sugar
> 1 cup dry red wine, or 1 (12-ounce) bottle
>   Hatuey malta†

APPLE-ORANGE SAUCE

> 2 Granny Smith apples, peeled and chopped
> 1 cup fresh orange juice
> ¾ cup sugar
> 1 teaspoon lime juice

Blend together the sour orange juice, garlic, bay leaves, and paprika. Score and pierce loin and remove excess fat. Place pork in a large glass bowl or Pyrex baking pan. Pour marinade over meat and place in refrigerator. Allow to marinate overnight, or at least 4 hours. Turn several times, piercing roast with the tines of a fork so that both loin halves are well marinated. Remove loins and discard marinade.

Place one half of loin in a large rectangular baking pan. Spread ham slices evenly on top, then egg slices, then prunes, red peppers, leeks, and carrots. Sprinkle with parsley. Place the remaining loin half on top. Wrap the bacon around the whole sandwich-style loin, firmly securing with string or wooden skewers so that filling does not fall out.

Preheat the oven to 325° F.

In a small bowl, blend brown sugar with wine or malta. Pour mixture over loins and bake for about 1 hour, or until meat is cooked, constantly basting with wine-sugar sauce.

Meanwhile prepare the apple-orange sauce by combining in a small saucepan the apples, orange juice, sugar, and lime juice. Heat, stirring, until thickened.

Remove roast when done and cool for about 20 minutes. Using a very sharp knife, cut into thin slices and serve with apple-orange sauce.

---

*If you don't have sour orange juice, substitute 1 cup orange juice mixed with 1 cup lime juice.
†Malta, a nonalcoholic grain-based beverage, is available in Hispanic supermarkets. Brewed from water, malt, sugar, corn, caramel malt, malt syrup, and hops, it imparts a nice flavor to roasted meats, but is also widely consumed as a beverage.

Pork Tenderloins in Wine Sauce

Filetillos de Cerdo en Salsa de Vino

These lightly sautéed tenderloins are baked in a savory sauce of Chardonnay and chicken stock, creating a mouth-watering robust entrée.   **Serves 4 to 6**

2 (2-pound) pork tenderloins
½ cup cracker meal*
Salt, to taste
½ teaspoon ground cumin
2 tablespoons olive oil
5 garlic cloves, peeled and minced
1 white onion, minced
1 cup chicken stock (page 36) or defatted
   chicken broth†
½ cup white wine (preferably Chardonnay)
4 tablespoons sofrito (page 14)

Preheat the oven to 325° F.

Dredge tenderloins in the cracker meal seasoned with salt and cumin.

Heat olive oil in a Dutch oven over medium-high heat. Add tenderloins and thoroughly brown on each side. Add garlic, onion, chicken stock, and white wine and bake for about 1 hour, until just done.

Remove from oven and drain juices into a sauté pan. Add *sofrito* to drippings. Blend well and heat.

Slice tenderloins and pour sauce over, or serve separately.

---

*Available at most supermarkets, or make your own by processing saltine crackers in a food processor until finely ground—36 saltines make about 1 cup crumbs.
†To defat canned broth, place can in refrigerator. When chilled, open can and skim fat from the surface.

Ginger Sherried Roasted Pork

Cerdo Asado Sazonado
con Jengibre y Jerez

Having lived in Miami, where cooking pork is a true art, I found many seasoning combinations to be outstanding. But none quite as good as this ginger-roasted version.

The perfect combination of tart sour orange juice together with fragrant ginger, pungent allspice berries, and dry sherry gives the tenderloin a magnificent texture and aroma.   **Serves 4 to 6**

3 garlic cloves, peeled and minced
1 (4-inch) slice of fresh ginger, peeled and
   mashed
4 whole allspice berries, smashed
2 teaspoons light brown sugar
2 tablespoons dry sherry
¼ cup sour orange juice*
2 teaspoons honey
2 tablespoons Worcestershire sauce
1 teaspoon ground cumin
1 teaspoon kosher salt
2 pounds pork tenderloin, trimmed

Combine all ingredients except the pork. Pour over meat and coat thoroughly, using your hands. Marinate, refrigerated, for 2 to 3 hours, turning several times to assure even marination.

Preheat the oven to 325° F.

Remove meat from marinade and roast for 1½ hours, basting with marinade and drippings. Serve with black beans and plantains.

---

*If you don't have sour orange juice, substitute ¼ cup sweet orange juice mixed with ⅛ cup lime juice.

Orange-Pineapple-Honey-Glazed Roast Pork

Cerdo Asado Glaceado con Naranja, Piña, y Miel

I prepare this with an inexpensive cut of pork and save the skin to make pork rinds. You may wish to use a more expensive boneless pork loin or a few large tenderloins, which will be fantabulous, too.

Be sure to allow time for the marinade to permeate the meat.

Serves 4 to 6

¾ cup orange juice
¼ cup lime juice
½ cup pineapple juice
1 canned pineapple ring
2 tablespoons orange zest
5 garlic cloves, peeled
1 teaspoon ground cumin
1 teaspoon ground oregano
2 tablespoons olive oil
1 (5- to 6-pound) pork shoulder (picnic), trimmed, excess fat removed
¼ cup pure honey

Put ¼ cup of the orange juice, the lime juice, and pineapple juice in a food processor. Add pineapple ring and orange zest and process a few seconds. Add another ¼ cup of the orange juice and the garlic, cumin, oregano, and olive oil. Process to combine.

Using the tines of a fork, puncture pork shoulder all over so that juices will penetrate. Place shoulder in a large bowl and pour fruit mixture over all. Turn shoulder several times so that juices penetrate well. Rub mixture into shoulder. Refrigerate and marinate for 1 to 2 hours, turning in marinade several times.

Preheat the oven to 325° F. Remove roast from the marinade and place on a rack in the middle of a roasting pan. Roast for about 1½ hours, or until internal thermometer reads 137 to 165° F. About 20 minutes before you think roast will be done, blend remaining ¼ cup orange juice with honey and baste several times until a glaze appears.

When done, remove from oven and cool for about 20 minutes before slicing.

Serve with plantain pie (page 197), white rice, and black beans.

Stir-Fried Pork and Bok Choy

Cerdo y Bok Choy Frito-Revuelto

T he Chinese, or *Chinos de Manila* as the Chinese population in Cuba was referred to, did not really contribute many recipes to Cuba's popular cooking repertoire, but many Asian fishermen and farmers helped supply products to the local food markets.

One vegetable that was popular was the Chinese white cabbage, or bok choy. It was included in a number of dishes that were accompanied by plantains and served alongside numerous Cantonese creations. This practice still continues in many Cuban-Chinese restaurants in the United States.

Serves 4

SAUCE

> 2 tablespoons medium hot chili paste†
> ½ cup soy sauce
> 1 tablespoon plus 1 teaspoon white vinegar
>
> 1 tablespoon olive oil
> 2 teaspoons minced garlic
> 2 tablespoons chopped fresh ginger
> 1 small head bok choy, sliced diagonally into 1½-inch pieces
> 6 scallions, sliced diagonally
> 2 cups sliced green bell pepper
> 1 pound pork tenderloin, cut into ½-inch strips
> 1 cup chicken stock (page 36) or defatted chicken broth*
> 1 tablespoon plus 1 teaspoon cornstarch

In a small mixing bowl, combine all sauce ingredients and mix well.

Heat a wok and add the olive oil. Add garlic and ginger and fry until light golden, 25 to 30 seconds. Add bok choy, scallions, and green pepper. Stir-fry until slightly wilted but still crunchy.

Remove to a heated plate. Add pork and stir-fry 2 to 3 minutes. Remove to plate with vegetables.

Mix chicken stock with cornstarch until smoothly incorporated. Add to wok with sauce. Heat a few minutes, turning, then add vegetables and pork and toss and stir until thickened. Serve over white rice with black beans on the side.

*To defat canned broth, place can in the refrigerator. When chilled, open can and skim fat from the surface.
†Available in Asian markets.

Grilled Palma Pork Chops

Parrillada de Chuletas de Cerdo Palma

T hese moist and mouth-watering grilled pork chops are great for entertaining. Begin the evening with a glass of dry, fine sherry before placing the marinated chops on the grill.

Serves 4

> 4 (2-inch-thick) center-cut pork chops, about ½ pound each

MARINADE

> ¼ cup dry white wine
> 8 garlic cloves, pressed
> 1 teaspoon ground cumin
> 1 tablespoon fresh lime juice
> ¼ cup olive oil
> ½ cup orange juice
> 1 teaspoon chopped fresh cilantro

In a medium-size flat glass baking dish, mix together all marinade ingredients. Pierce chops all over with the tines of a fork and add to baking dish. Turn a few times so marinade penetrates all parts of the chops. Marinate overnight in refrigerator, or at least 6 hours.

Drain marinade and grill chops over hot coals. Serve with fried apples and snow peas drizzled with extra-virgin olive oil.

Preheat the oven to 425° F.

To prepare the pork, brush with olive oil. Using your hands, coat well with herbs, pepper, and salt. Make slits in several places in the tenderloins and insert garlic pieces. Place on a rack sprayed with olive oil and put in a roasting pan. Roast about 12 minutes, then reduce heat to 325° F. Roast 15 to 20 minutes longer, or until internal temperature registers 160° F. Turn roast and cook another 5 to 10 minutes. Transfer to a carving board and allow to stand for about 10 minutes to cool.

To prepare mango-ginger sauce, purée the mangoes in the container of a food processor or blender. Pour into a medium saucepan. Add the brown sugar, vinegars, sherry, and ginger. Heat over medium heat until sugar dissolves. Remove from heat.

Carve loins into thin slices. Spoon sauce over and garnish with sprigs of fresh herbs. Serve with yuca with Creole Seasoning Sauce (page 183) and fresh green beans.

*See page 23 for how to cut a mango.

Pork Tenderloin with Mango-Ginger Sauce

Filetillos de Cerdo con

Salsa de Mango y Jengibre

The sauce for this recipe can be made ahead and kept in the refrigerator for a couple of days, or frozen and kept for up to 2 months.

Be sure to choose mangoes that are soft to the touch and smell aromatic at the ends. The flavor is similar to a combination of peach and pineapple.   **Serves 6**

    2 (1-pound) pork tenderloins
    2 tablespoons olive oil
    2 teaspoons fresh rosemary, or 1 teaspoon
       dried
    2 teaspoons fresh thyme, or 1 teaspoon dried
    1 teaspoon freshly cracked pepper
    Salt, to taste
    4 garlic cloves, peeled and cut in half
       lengthwise

SAUCE

    3 pounds mangoes, peeled and cut
       into chunks*
    ½ cup brown sugar
    ⅛ cup red wine vinegar
    ⅛ cup cider vinegar
    ¼ cup dry sherry
    3 tablespoons grated fresh ginger

Grilled Pork Tenderloin Medallions with Yuca and Mojo

Medallónes de Solomillo de Cerdo à la Parrilla con Yuca y Mojo

This succulent pork dish blends the flavors of the citrus marinade with the potatolike yuca in a sharp and zesty garlic *mojo*.

Serves 6 to 8

MARINADE

½ cup fresh orange juice
¼ cup fresh lime juice
½ cup coarsely chopped onion
3 tablespoons chopped fresh oregano
2 tablespoons chopped fresh cilantro,
   or 1 tablespoon dried
2½ teaspoons ground cumin
1 teaspoon orange zest
1 teaspoon lemon zest
Salt and freshly ground pepper, to taste
½ cup olive oil

2 pounds trimmed pork tenderloin, sliced and
   pounded into 12 thin medallions*
Yuca with Creole Seasoning Sauce (page 183)

GARNISH

½ red onion, chopped
1 Valencia orange, seeded and diced
1 lime, seeded and diced
Chopped fresh oregano
Chopped fresh parsley
2 green plantains, sliced lengthwise into 4
   strips and fried in olive oil
6 scallions, thinly sliced lengthwise
1 red bell pepper, seeded and julienned

Place orange and lime juice, onion, oregano, cilantro, cumin, orange and lemon zests, and salt and pepper in the container of a food processor. Process until combined and, with motor running, add olive oil a few drops at a time through feed tube to finish the marinade.

Place pork in a glass dish. Pour marinade over pork, cover, and refrigerate overnight.

Grill or broil the pork medallions about 1 minute per side.

To serve, divide the yuca among 6 oversized dinner plates. Arrange 2 pork medallions, slightly overlapping, on top of the yuca.

Garnish pork with chopped red onion and parsley. Garnish the rim of plates with diced orange, lime, and chopped oregano and parsley. Stand thin slices of fried plantains on end, using a portion of the yuca to support them. Garnish with scallion spears and red pepper strips.

*To prepare medallions, place pork tenderloin slices between two sheets of wax paper and pound until thin.

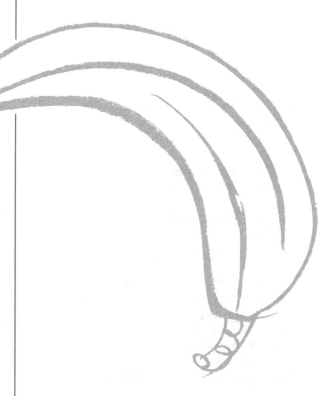

Calle Ocho Chops

Chuletas de Cerdo Calle Ocho

This marinade, which combines maple syrup, wine vinegar, and mustard, imparts a lovely flavor and delicate juiciness to the chops. Serve the chops with a side dish of sautéed fresh vegetables, tiny new potatoes, and a salad of mixed lettuces. **Serves 4**

¼ cup pure maple syrup
¼ cup lime juice
¼ cup red wine vinegar
¼ cup Dijon mustard
¾ cup tomato sauce
3 garlic cloves, peeled and finely minced
1 teaspoon fresh thyme, or ½ teaspoon dried
1 teaspoon chopped fresh cilantro
1 tablespoon finely minced onion
½ teaspoon grated nutmeg
4 whole cloves
1 teaspoon grated fresh ginger
1 teaspoon Worcestershire sauce
4 (2-inch-thick) loin pork chops, about
  ½ pound each
Sprigs of fresh thyme or parsley, for garnish

Combine all ingredients except chops and garnish ingredients in a medium glass mixing bowl.

Trim any excess fat off chops, leaving a little for flavor. Dip chops into marinade to coat well. Place chops in a shallow glass baking dish and pour remaining marinade over all. Allow to marinate, refrigerated, overnight, or for at least 6 hours. Turn chops several times.

When ready to cook, preheat broiler. Remove chops from marinade and broil about 6 inches from the heat source. Discard remaining marinade. When done, garnish with sprigs of fresh thyme or parsley.

Veal Scallops with Cilantro Pesto

Filetas de Ternera con Cilantro

It is important to prepare the scallops as thin as possible. To do this, place scallops between two sheets of heavy wax paper and beat with a metal mallet until very thin. Do this ahead and assemble recipe at last minute. **Serves 4**

4 garlic cloves, peeled
2 tablespoons chopped fresh parsley
½ cup chopped fresh cilantro
Salt and coarsely ground pepper, to taste
2 tablespoons water
2 tablespoons olive oil
1 pound veal scallops, pounded very thin

To prepare the cilantro mixture, put the garlic in the container of a food processor. Process until minced, 8 to 10 seconds. Add the parsley, cilantro, salt, and pepper and process until minced. Add the water and the olive oil through the food tube while processor is running. Blend well, occasionally scraping sides with a rubber spatula to mix well.

Heat the broiler. Spread the cilantro mixture over both sides of veal pieces. Place on a rack coated with olive oil spray and set in a shallow roasting pan about 6 inches from heat. Broil for 2 to 3 minutes, turning several times, or until scallops turn white and are cooked through.

To serve, garnish veal with fresh sprigs of cilantro. Serve with a crispy watercress salad and grilled tomatoes.

Roast Suckling Pig #1

Lechón Asado #1

The proper way to prepare this very Cuban dish, traditionally eaten during the Christmas season, is to roast the pig on a spit over green mangrove wood. The pig is typically laid on a stretcher device fashioned from wood poles so it can be moved up and down according to the temperature of the fire. It is cooked upside down and carefully watched throughout the roasting, which takes 6 to 7 hours for a 100-pound pig.

Today, of course, roast pig, whole or in pieces, is most often prepared in an oven. The pig should always be evenly browned and very, very crisp.

Chances are you may wish to tackle only a small suckling pig, or half of one for this recipe. In that case, adjust the ingredients accordingly. If you cannot find suckling, you can use pork shoulders or a number of large tenderloins.

This first recipe is for serious pig roasters. The second, also delectable but not as time consuming, is ideal for a smaller crowd. The types of stuffings can easily be interchanged, but be sure to adjust the amount to the size of the pig.

Serves 24 to 30

1 (25- to 30-pound) suckling pig
3 whole heads garlic, cloves separated, peeled, and crushed
1 cup chopped fresh parsley
2 tablespoons chopped fresh thyme, or 1 tablespoon dried
3 tablespoons oregano leaves, or ½ tablespoon dried
2 tablespoons ground cumin
8 bay leaves
2 tablespoons salt
2 teaspoons coarsely ground black pepper
1 quart sour orange juice*
4 cups sliced onion
2 cups dry red wine
½ cup olive oil mixed with 1 tablespoon lard or butter
Seasoned rice stuffing (see following recipe)

Have your butcher prepare the pig for roasting by cleaning it inside and out, removing the eyeballs, and placing several cuts on the pig's skin on each side of the backbone so that it doesn't burst during cooking. Have him prop the mouth open with aluminum foil or a piece of wood, or do this yourself.

If you purchase the pig in advance, store it back side down on a very large tray in a commercial refrigerator.

In a medium bowl, crush the garlic with a pestle. Add ½ cup of the parsley, thyme, 2 tablespoons of the oregano, cumin, bay leaves, 1 tablespoon salt, and pepper. Add the sour orange juice, onions, wine, and the remaining ½ cup parsley. Combine well. Using your hands, rub marinade into the skin and cavity. Place in the refrigerator and allow to marinate for at least 12 hours.

Remove pig from the marinade and blot dry with paper towels. Combine the remaining oregano and salt and rub into the skin of the pig. Smear the oil onto the outer skin and into the cavity.

To stuff, lay the pig on one side and pack stuffing in loosely. Wrap any extra in foil to heat later. Close the cavity with skewers and lace to close. Wrap the feet, tail, and ears with aluminum foil.

Cook the pig on a large outdoor barbecue grill, specially dug ground pit, or on a spit that is strong enough to hold a large size pig.

If cooking in a pit, as Cubans still do on the island and for holidays in the States, spread and secure the pig between large holding racks. Truss the pigs' legs to the body in a kneeling position. Insert spit lengthwise through the center of the pig. Racks are usually centered on a large metal container that has about 1 inch of water in the bottom, which keeps the internal temperature below 212° F. A cover is usually placed on the top and a charcoal fire built on the cover, then the charcoal is spread evenly over the cover and the pig is located centrally inside the container. It is slowly roasted and turned many times so that the skin becomes crisp and golden and the juices run clear.

To roast in a large commercial oven, position the pig with legs down on a large roasting tray. Preheat the oven and bake at 325° F until the skin is a lovely dark brown and very crisp. (The internal temperature, when done, should register 190° F.) Baste constantly with marinade ingredients. Add water if juice evaporates. Remove foil from the ears, feet, and tail during the last half hour to assure browning.

Carefully remove pig from pit, spit, or oven to a large foil-covered tray. Allow to cool for about 30 minutes. Remove any skewers, lacing, and foil from pig. Place a shiny apple or lemon in mouth and cherry tomatoes secured with toothpicks in eye sockets, if desired.

Garnish pig in tropical fashion with fresh fruits such as pineapple, orange, and mango on a bed of watercress. Edible flowers add nice touches.

To carve the pig, start on the ham section at the back of the pig and work toward the head area. Remove hams and forelegs. Divide the flesh down the center of pig's back. Separate the ribs and be sure to serve a portion of the crackling skin

to each person. Serve with black beans and white rice, guava paste, Edam cheese, oranges, Amontillado sherry or red wine.

*If you cannot find sour orange juice, substitute 2 parts orange juice mixed with 1 part lime juice.

SEASONED RICE STUFFING FOR ROAST PIG
RELLENO DE ARROZ SAZONADO PARA LECHÓN ASADO
Enough for a 30-pound suckling pig

- ¼ pound plus 4 tablespoons butter or margarine
- 6 garlic cloves, peeled and crushed
- 3 cups chopped white onion
- 3 cups peeled and sliced celery
- 1 cup chopped celery leaves
- 9 cups cooked white rice
- 1 teaspoon ground thyme
- 1 teaspoon ground cumin
- 1 teaspoon ground sage
- Salt and pepper, to taste
- Mango nectar or apple juice, to moisten

In a large Dutch oven, melt the butter. When hot, sauté garlic, onion, celery, and celery leaves until translucent. Add the cooked rice, thyme, cumin, sage, and salt and pepper and mix well. Add mango nectar to moisten.

Roast Suckling Pig #2

Lechón Asado #2

Stuffings for roast pig vary considerably all over the Caribbean islands, although the method of cooking is often much the same. Here's a simple way to cook a small stuffed pig.

Serves 10 to 12

1 (10- to 15-pound) suckling pig
Vegetable oil
Salt and pepper, to taste
Dried thyme leaves, to taste

STUFFING

1 pound lean ground pork
1 pound lean ground beef
2 white onions, chopped
1 green bell pepper, seeded and chopped
6 garlic cloves, peeled and chopped
5 to 6 scallions, sliced
3 large sweet potatoes or yams, peeled and chopped
1 apple, peeled and chopped
2 bay leaves, cracked

Have your butcher clean the pig. Ask him to remove the eyeballs, as they will pop during roasting.

Rinse the pig well inside and out, then pat dry. Using your hands, coat with vegetable oil inside and out, then mix salt and pepper together and coat well inside and out. Rub thoroughly with thyme.

Mix stuffing ingredients together in a very large mixing bowl. Loosely stuff cavity, then with a kitchen needle and thread, sew up the pig's cavity. Tie front legs together and then back legs. Place a large peeled yam or aluminum foil in the pig's mouth and then place pig on a large rack inside a large roasting pan (you may need a commercial oven depending on pig size). Cover the ears and tail with heavy aluminum foil.

Bake at 350° F for about 4 hours, allowing about 20 minutes per pound. When meat temperature reaches 185° F, thigh meat is tender, and juices run clear when pricked at thickest part, the feast is ready.

Place pig on a very large serving platter or wooden plank covered in heavy foil. Allow pig to cool for about 20 minutes. Remove yam or foil and replace with a nice shiny apple and make a flower garland around pig's neck. Garnish around sides with beautiful edible flowers.

When ready to serve, snip thread and slice into large pieces, being certain to include a portion of the crispy skin.

Baby Back Ribs with Guava Sauce

Costillitas de Cerdito al Horno con Salsa de Guayaba

The aromatic guava fruit lends a wonderful flavor to these succulent pork ribs. The cider vinegar helps to tenderize and flavor them.

You can also prepare this dish with beef, but most Cubans prefer pork ribs.

Serves 4 to 6

1 tablespoon chopped fresh rosemary
1 tablespoon chopped fresh thyme
2 tablespoons minced white onion
4 garlic cloves, peeled and minced
Salt, to taste
1 teaspoon cracked black pepper
3½ to 4 pounds baby back ribs, cut into
   individual ribs
½ cup cider vinegar
1 (16-ounce) can guavas*
Juice of 1 lime
2 tablespoons guava jelly
1 tablespoon pure honey
2 tablespoons dark molasses
Fresh cilantro or parsley sprigs, for garnish

Preheat the oven to 250° F.

In a very large nonmetallic bowl, combine the rosemary, thyme, onion, garlic, salt, and pepper. Using your hands, rub seasonings into ribs so that each rib is nicely coated. Place in one layer on a shallow baking sheet with sides. Carefully pour the vinegar onto the sheet and turn each rib so that it is coated with vinegar. Bake for about 1 hour 30 minutes, until tender.

Pour guavas, including juice, into the container of a blender or food processor. Purée for 15 seconds.

Combine lime juice, guava jelly, and honey in a medium saucepan. Cook over low heat, stirring with a wire whisk, until the jelly has melted, 2 to 3 minutes. Add guava purée and molasses and blend well. Cook about 5 minutes. Sauce should be the consistency of a thick barbecue sauce. If too thick, add a little water.

When ribs are tender, brush with guava sauce, turn oven heat to 325° F and cook 10 to 15 minutes, or until golden brown. Baste several times.

Garnish ribs with fresh cilantro or parsley sprigs. Serve with white rice, plantains, and Erasmo's black beans (page 90).

*When puréed, the guavas (usually about 6 per can), including can juice, equal about 1¼ cups.

Spicy Goat Stew

Chilindrón de Chivo

Goat is a favorite meat of many Cubans, and when it is under 6 years, its flavor is delicate and the meat is tender, somewhat similar to lamb, but a lot less expensive. Most stores have several grades; the better grade is usually younger (a kid) and more lean. You can find it in most Hispanic and Jamaican specialty stores.

This very delicious spicy stew is a typical *guajiro*, or peasant dish, one specially prepared to celebrate feasts with friends and family. Lamb, of course, can be substituted.   **Serves 4 to 6**

4 pounds goat meat, cut into 2-inch cubes
Juice of 3 limes
2 onions, chopped
3 ají cachucha peppers, or other hot peppers, such as Scotch bonnet, seeded and chopped
1 tablespoon chopped fresh cilantro
3 bay leaves
1 tablespoon dried oregano
⅛ cup chopped fresh parsley
3½ quarts water
½ cup olive oil
1 onion, sliced
1 green bell pepper, seeded and chopped
1½ whole heads of garlic, cloves peeled and chopped
1 pound ripe tomatoes, seeded and chopped
¼ cup tomato paste
3 ounces dark rum
2 ripe plantains, peeled and cut into 2-inch slices*
4 green plantains, peeled and cut into 2-inch slices*
2 pounds namé or white potatoes, peeled and sliced
1 pound malangas, peeled and sliced
1 pound calabaza or Hubbard squash
2 tablespoons cider vinegar

Place the goat meat in a very large nonmetallic bowl. Add the lime juice, chopped onions, and 1 hot pepper. Using clean hands, mix thoroughly so that all surfaces are coated. Marinate, covered, for at least 8 hours or overnight.

When meat has marinated sufficiently, place it in a large Dutch oven. Add 1 hot pepper, cilantro, bay leaves, oregano, parsley, and water. Bring to a boil, then reduce heat and simmer for about 2 hours, or until meat becomes tender. Skim the surface occasionally to remove scum.

Remove the meat from the Dutch oven. Strain and reserve the liquid. Wash Dutch oven, then heat. When pan is heated, add the oil. When the oil is heated and begins to smell fragrant, add the sliced onion, green peppers, garlic, and the remaining hot pepper and cook until vegetables become translucent. Add the chopped tomatoes, tomato paste, and rum and blend well. Cook for about 5 minutes, then return the meat to the Dutch oven and add 1 quart of the reserved liquid. Bring to a boil, then reduce to a simmer.

Add the plantains, namé, malangas, and calabaza. Cover with a tight lid and simmer for 40 to 45 minutes, or until the vegetables are tender and the calabaza has nearly dissolved, thickening the stew. Season with salt. Just before serving, add the vinegar and cook another 3 to 4 minutes. Serve over white rice in large bowls.

*See page 23 for how to slice plantains.

Country-Style Rabbit

Conejo al Estilo Campesino

Here's a variation on a dish that I had at La Rueta, a country-style restaurant outside Havana.

In the United States, most rabbit available in markets is farm-raised for a standard quality. Here the Burgundy-garlic sauce adds a continental flavor to this Cuban favorite.

When preparing small game like rabbit, it is always advisable to wear gloves and to make sure the meat is sufficiently cooked.

Serves 4 to 6, depending on size of rabbit

1 whole head garlic, cloves peeled and minced
¼ cup white vinegar
½ cup plus 2 tablespoons olive oil
1 teaspoon salt
1 teaspoon dried oregano
1 teaspoon Spanish paprika
1 rabbit, cleaned and cut into small pieces
½ cup red Burgundy wine
2 tablespoons butter or margarine
½ cup red bell pepper strips
½ cup toasted blanched slivered almonds, for garnish
Fresh parsley, for garnish

In a large 13 × 9 × 2-inch Pyrex baking dish, combine the garlic, vinegar, ½ cup olive oil, salt, oregano, and paprika. Add pieces of rabbit. Sprinkle wine over all and allow to marinate, refrigerated, overnight, or for about 8 hours.

Heat a large heavy skillet and add the 2 tablespoons olive oil and butter. When butter has melted and fat has reached the point of fragrance, add the red pepper strips and sauté until tender. Next add the rabbit pieces from the marinade mixture. Reduce heat and continue to cook on low heat for 45 minutes or more, according to the amount of rabbit in the skillet. Cook until tender. Garnish with toasted almonds and fresh parsley. Serve immediately while piping hot.

Sausage Stew with Annatto

Guiso de Salchichas con Achiote

Annatto, sometimes called *achiote*, was once used by Caribbean Indians to decorate their bodies. Today it is a flavor enhancer and colorant for food.

Ground annatto seed is widely used throughout many Latin-speaking countries and by many chefs experimenting in the world of *nuevo Cubano* cuisine.

Serves 4 to 6

¼ cup olive oil
4 garlic cloves, peeled and minced
½ cup chopped white onion
½ cup chopped green bell pepper
½ cup tomato purée
¼ cup dry Burgundy or other dry red wine
1 teaspoon cider vinegar
¼ teaspoon annatto (achiote) seed, ground into powder*
2 cups water
½ teaspoon ground cumin
Salt, to taste
2 pounds small new potatoes, well scrubbed
½ pound lean pork link sausage, browned, drained, and cut into 1-inch pieces
½ cup baby green peas (petit pois)
Chopped fresh parsley

Heat a large Dutch oven and add olive oil. When the oil is heated and begins to smell fragrant, add garlic, onion, and bell pepper and cook until translucent or slightly limp. Add the remaining ingredients except the peas, parsley, and sausage. When potatoes are tender, add cooked sausage to the dish and cook for 15 to 20 minutes. Add peas and cook 5 minutes longer. Serve garnished with parsley and with boniato on the side.

*Process the *achiote* for a few seconds in a coffee grinder to make powder.

Fruits and Vegetables

Frutas y Legumbres

The island of Cuba is rich with many varieties of tropical fruits and vegetables. Exotic fruits such as the papaya, called *fruta de bomba,* and the delectable peachlike mango perhaps head the list, but there are also the more unusual mamey sapote and avocado, guava, and plantain.

Plantains, rapidly gaining acceptance in kitchens throughout the United States, are native to Africa and were brought to Cuba by slaves. Today, there is no question as to the popularity of these *plátanos,* which appear at most meals. The flavor is a mix of potato and banana.

There are many unusual vegetables now common in modern Cuban cuisine, such as the boniato, the tropical sweet potato (and a personal favorite because of its beguiling flavor and sweetness), namé, the true yam, and calabaza, often called the Cuban or West Indian pumpkin. Yuca, also called cassava, is one of the most popular tuber vegetables. These root vegetables, or tubers, are often eaten daily at lunch and dinner and are a necessity to create a truly island-style meal.

Baked Yuca

Yuca al Horno

Pronounced YOO-ka, never yukka, this tuber appears daily on some Cuban tables. The addition of butter or extra-virgin olive oil will make a decided difference in the taste.

Coating the tuber skin with olive oil keeps the moisture in and helps it to cook faster.

Serves 4 to 6

2 pounds yuca (2 large or 4 small)
¼ cup vegetable oil
4 tablespoons butter or extra-virgin olive oil
Salt and pepper, to taste

Preheat the oven to 325° F. Wash and scrub yuca tubers well with a vegetable brush to remove any impurities, then place in very cold water with a few ice cubes for about 30 minutes, or until ready to cook.

Dry yuca and rub outer surfaces with oil. Bake in a heavy iron or other baking pan until tender. You will know it's done when fork slides in easily. It will take 40 minutes or longer, depending on the size of the tuber.

Split open lengthwise, add a tablespoon of butter or oil to each tuber (2 tablespoons to each if using 2 large). Serve in shell or remove from shell. Season with salt and pepper.

Fresh Parsleyed Yuca

Yuca Fresca con Perejil

Here's a simple preparation of the popular yuca where the innate blandness of the vegetable is awakened by the fresh parsley and the acidity of the lime juice.   **Serves 4**

3 to 4 pounds yuca, peeled, fibers removed,
**   cut into 3-inch strips about 1 inch wide**
2 to 3 tablespoons butter or margarine
¼ cup finely chopped fresh parsley
1 tablespoon fresh lime juice
Salt, to taste

Place yuca in a saucepan, cover with water, and bring to a boil. Add a little cold water and continue to cook about 35 minutes, or until tender. If the water begins to boil, add a little salt and more cold water each time to keep it at a simmer. Be careful not to overcook or to undercook, as texture is important. Remove, drain, and add butter, parsley, and fresh lime juice. Serve steaming hot.

Yuca with Creole Seasoning Sauce

Yuca con Mojo Criollo

When boiled, yuca has a pleasant flavor that is propelled to greater heights by the addition of the savory *mojo criollo,* or Creole seasoning sauce.   **Serves 4 to 6**

2 pounds yuca, peeled and cooked*
¾ cup Creole seasoning sauce (page 30)

In a saucepan, pour seasoning sauce over yuca and cook over low heat until heated throughout. Serve steaming hot.

*See page 24 for how to cook yuca.

Baked Calabaza Squash with Apples and Cheeses

Calabaza Horneada con

Manzanas y Queso

Calabaza, or West Indian pumpkin, was once a staple of Florida's early Indians. Now it is in demand by Hispanics living throughout the United States. The squash melds beautifully with the tropical spices of the Caribbean, and particularly well with cinnamon and nutmeg.

If you have difficulty finding calabaza, you may substitute pumpkin or acorn or other winter squash.   **Serves 6**

3 to 4 pounds calabaza squash, peeled, seeded, and cut into small pieces
1 teaspoon salt
6 Granny Smith apples, peeled and cored
½ cup firmly packed light brown sugar
½ cup grated extra-sharp Cheddar cheese
½ cup grated queso blanco or Monterey Jack cheese
2 tablespoons lime juice
1 teaspoon ground cinnamon
1 teaspoon grated nutmeg
3 tablespoons butter or margarine

Put squash in a large saucepan and fill with water to cover. Add salt and bring to a boil. Cook until squash is fork-tender, 20 to 25 minutes.

Preheat the oven to 350° F.

Drain squash well to remove excess water, then mix together with the apples, sugar, cheeses, lime juice, cinnamon, and nutmeg. Pour into a medium casserole and dot the top with butter.

Cover with foil and bake for about 45 minutes, or until heated through. Serve immediately.

Calabaza Soufflé

Suflé de Calabaza

In this recipe, the sweetness of the coconut and the raisins helps develop the pleasant pumpkin flavor of the squash. It's always a hit at covered dish events.   **Serves 6 to 8**

        3 to 4 pounds calabaza squash
    ½ teaspoon salt
    1 cup granulated sugar
    1 cup cream of coconut*
    1½ to 2 cups heavy whipping cream
    ¼ cup raisins

Boil calabaza in a large kettle of salted water until soft, about 25 minutes. Cool and peel skin.

Preheat the oven to 350° F.

Put squash pulp in the container of a food processor or blender and process until well mashed, then slowly add the sugar and coconut cream. Add the whipping cream until a medium thick consistency is reached and the mixture is very smooth. Fold in raisins by hand, then pour into a greased ovenproof casserole dish and bake for 30 minutes.

*You can purchase cream of coconut in a 15-ounce can in supermarkets.

Sharply Stuffed Chayote

Chayotes Rellenos con Queso y Nuez

Moscada

Hispanic newcomers to our continent are responsible for the recent popularity of the chayote. In this updated gratin recipe, the delicate cucumber-zucchini flavor of the chayote is maintained, but not overruled by the delectable cheese sauce.   **Serves 6 to 8**

    4 medium chayotes, halved lengthwise and
        seeds removed*
    ½ pound lean ground beef
    ½ pound lean ground veal
    ⅔ cup tomato sauce
    ½ cup bread crumbs
    ½ cup whole milk
    1 egg, slightly beaten
    1 cup minced onion
    2 garlic cloves, peeled and pressed
    ½ teaspoon dried thyme
    Salt and pepper, to taste
    1½ cups grated sharp Cheddar cheese
    ¼ cup sliced pimiento-stuffed manzanilla
        olives

Heat a 4-quart saucepan filled with water. Trim any brown or bad spots off chayotes. When water comes to a rolling boil, add the chayotes and cook until flesh is tender, 30 minutes or more, depending on size. Remove with a slotted spoon and allow to cool.

Meanwhile, sauté beef and veal in a skillet until cooked through. Drain and set aside.

Using a tablespoon or fruit scoop, scoop out the inside of the chayotes, leaving about ¼ inch of peel and skin as a shell. In a medium bowl, mash the chayote pulp with a fork or potato masher. Add the cooked beef and veal, tomato sauce, bread crumbs, milk, egg, onion, garlic, thyme, and salt and pepper. Combine well, then fill the shells with the mixture.

Preheat the oven to 350° F.

Place shells in an ovenproof dish and bake for about 30 minutes. Remove from oven and drain off any excess liquid. Pile cheese onto each chayote, then add sliced olives. Place under the broiler until cheese is melted and golden brown.

*Reserve the almondlike seeds to cook with squash; they will enhance the flavor.

Chayotes Stuffed with Vegetables

Chayote Santa Clara

Chayote is a delicate fruit that tastes like a combination of zucchini and cucumber. In this recipe I have re-created a Cuban classic, but with the addition of fresh white mushrooms for extra flavor. When baked, the marvelous flavors of the chayote join with the vegetables, olive oil, and cheese to produce an outrageously different vegetable dish.

Although this recipe takes some work, it is not difficult. To save time, you may cook the chayotes a day or two before. Reserve the pulp and shells separately, covered with plastic, then stuff when ready to serve.

Double the recipe if you prefer to serve it as a main course.   **Serves 6**

3 medium chayotes
¼ cup olive oil
2 garlic cloves, peeled and minced
¼ cup chopped onion
½ cup thinly sliced fresh mushrooms
½ red bell pepper, seeded and finely chopped
3 medium-size very ripe tomatoes, diced*
1 tablespoon chopped fresh parsley
½ teaspoon granulated sugar
½ teaspoon salt
Cracked black pepper, to taste
1 cup shredded low-fat Cheddar cheese
   or queso blanco
1 teaspoon Spanish paprika

Heat a 4-quart saucepan filled with water. Using a sharp paring knife, trim any brown or bad spots off chayotes. When water comes to a rolling boil, add chayotes, turn heat to medium, and continue to cook until flesh is tender, 30 minutes or more, depending on size. Carefully remove with a slotted spoon and allow to cool. When cool, use a teaspoon or melon scooper to remove the flesh and place in a small bowl, leaving about ¼ inch of peel and skin as a shell. Dice the chayote flesh.

Heat a large sauté pan or skillet and add the olive oil. When the oil begins to smell fragrant, add the garlic and onion and sauté until translucent. Add mushrooms, red bell pepper, tomatoes, diced chayote pulp, and fresh parsley. Combine vegetables well and sauté until cooked and lightly browned. Drain off excess liquid. Add the sugar, salt, and black pepper.

Preheat the broiler with shelf positioned about 8 inches from the heat element.

Lay out chayote shells on a lined cookie sheet or large baking pan. With a tablespoon, heap each boat with vegetable mixture, then sprinkle cheese generously on top of each to cover vegetables. Sprinkle with paprika. Place under preheated broiler and broil until cheese is melted and golden brown. Serve on a large platter surrounding entrée.

*It is not necessary but if you prefer, peel and seed tomatoes before dicing.

Chayotes in Cheese Sauce with Nutmeg

Chayotes Rellenos con Nuez Moscada

This is another recipe that brings out the wonderful cucumber and zucchini flavor of chayotes. If you haven't tried this vegetable, don't put it off any longer. **Serves 4**

4 fresh chayotes, halved
2 tablespoons butter or margarine
⅓ cup all-purpose flour
2 cups whole milk
½ teaspoon grated nutmeg
Salt, to taste
½ teaspoon white pepper
½ cup grated Cheddar or other cheese
Bread crumbs
Butter or margarine

Cut blemishes or brown spots off the vegetables before cooking. Add to a large pan of boiling water. Cook until soft, about 40 minutes, depending on size.

Prepare a béchamel sauce by melting the butter or margarine over low heat in a heavy saucepan. Add the flour and stir briskly with a wire whisk until the mixture is smooth, not changing color. Slowly add the milk, whisking well to prevent any lumps from forming. Season with the nutmeg, salt, and pepper. Cook slowly, stirring from time to time so that it does not get a film on the surface, until mixture thickens.

Preheat the oven to 325° F.

Coat a Pyrex dish with a film of pure olive oil. Add the chayote halves and cover thoroughly with the béchamel sauce. Sprinkle the cheese over the top. Sprinkle with bread crumbs and dot with butter or margarine. Bake for 30 to 40 minutes, depending on size of chayote.

Broiled Tomatoes with Fresh Herbs

Tomates Asados à la Parrilla con Hierbas Aromáticas Frescas

I often serve these broiled beauties with a simple fish dish and a side of steamed green beans. The herbs meld beautifully and enhance the sweetness of the tomatoes. **Serves 4**

4 medium-size ripe tomatoes
½ teaspoon ground cumin
½ teaspoon salt
1 teaspoon freshly cracked black pepper
½ cup fresh bread crumbs
3 scallions, finely chopped
2 large garlic cloves, peeled and finely chopped
1 tablespoon finely chopped fresh cilantro
1 teaspoon finely chopped fresh basil leaves
1 tablespoon olive oil
¼ cup grated queso blanco or other mild white cheese
Chopped fresh parsley, for garnish

Preheat the broiler. Cut away the core and halve the tomatoes. Combine the cumin, salt, and black pepper and sprinkle over the tomato halves. In a small bowl, combine the bread crumbs, scallions, garlic, cilantro, basil, and olive oil. Mix together well.

Top each tomato half with mixture, being sure to cover tomato completely. Place halves in a baking dish and sprinkle the grated cheese over the tops. Place under broiler about 6 inches from the heat. Broil until tomatoes are browned, about 5 minutes, but watch carefully so as not to burn. Sprinkle with chopped parsley.

Put salt in a large bowl of cold water, add eggplant, and soak for 1 hour, making sure that water covers all pieces.

Place bread crumbs in a large bowl, add milk and egg yolks, and combine well. Allow to soak a few minutes so that consistency is like oatmeal.

Pour water into large skillet and heat until the water boils.

With a slotted spoon, remove eggplant, place in boiling water, and cook until tender, about 20 minutes. Remove, drain, and set aside to cool.

With a thin-edged spoon or fruit scoop, remove the flesh of the eggplant, being careful that skin stays intact.

Heat a large sauté pan or skillet and add olive oil. When the oil is heated and begins to smell fragrant, add onion, garlic, and green pepper and sauté until tender. Add tomatoes, cumin, salt, and raisins. Sauté for a few minutes longer.

Add bread crumb mixture to eggplant flesh and mash together well. Add onion-garlic mixture and combine well.

Preheat the oven to 350° F. Prepare a 13 × 9 × 2-inch baking pan, or larger depending on eggplant size. Fill eggplant shells and place in pan. Top each with bread crumbs and shredded cheese and bake for 15 to 20 minutes. Remove from oven and place under broiler until cheese melts and is golden brown.

Stuffed Eggplant

Berenjena Rellena Casera

This classic stuffed eggplant is prepared by many Cuban cooks, and I have added a few flavors of my own—the cumin and the bell pepper, which give added dimension to the dish. It takes a little time to prepare, but is a show stopper and can be prepared a few hours ahead. Vegetarians enjoy it as main course, but used as a side dish it complements any meat or fowl.

There are a variety of new types of eggplant on the market, in all sizes, shapes, and colors. I often prepare this dish using white eggplant, which I feel is one of the most flavorful varieties.

Serves 8

1 teaspoon salt
4 medium eggplants, sliced in half lengthwise
½ cup bread crumbs
½ cup milk
2 egg yolks
2 tablespoons olive oil
2 cups chopped white onion
1 tablespoon minced garlic
1 cup chopped green bell pepper
2 cups diced ripe tomatoes
1 teaspoon ground cumin
Salt, to taste
⅛ cup raisins
½ cup fresh bread crumbs
½ cup grated soft white cheese, such as
   queso blanco or Monterey Jack

Snow Peas in Olive Oil Sauce

Vainitas Chinas en Salsa de Aceite de Oliva

Snow peas, not typically Cuban, are enjoyed today in many Cuban-American homes. Mint leaves, still widely used in Cuba today, add the crowning touch to this simple sauté prepared in olive oil.　**Serves 4**

¼ cup olive oil
1 medium yellow onion, chopped
2 garlic cloves, peeled and pressed
1 large ripe tomato, seeded and diced
1 pound bright green snow peas, stems and
　strings removed
½ teaspoon chopped fresh parsley
½ teaspoon chopped fresh cilantro
¼ cup water
Salt and pepper, to taste
Fresh mint leaves

Heat a large saucepan and add olive oil. When oil is heated and begins to smell fragrant, sauté onion and garlic until translucent. Add the diced tomato and simmer for about 5 minutes, then add the snow peas, parsley, cilantro, water, and salt and pepper. Cover and cook until peas are slightly tender, about 2 minutes. Serve hot with mint for garnish.

OKRA

Sautéed Green and Red Peppers

Ajíes Verdes y Rojos Salteados

Bell pepper is frequently used by Cubans to flavor black beans, but it's delicious as a side vegetable paired with roasted meats or grilled fish.　**Serves 4**

2 green bell peppers, roasted,* peeled,
　seeded, and sliced into thin strips
2 red bell peppers, peeled,* seeded, and
　sliced into thin strips
3 to 4 tablespoons olive oil
2 garlic cloves, peeled and chopped

Halve pepper strips crosswise. Put oil into a large skillet or sauté pan and heat. Add garlic and when oil becomes fragrant, add bell peppers and cook over medium heat until peppers are cooked and slightly blackened. Serve hot.

*See page 24 for how to roast and peel peppers.

Okra with Creole Seasoning Sauce

Quimbombo con Mojo Criollo

Okra is known as *quimbombo* to Cubans and its use is a reminder of the strong African influence in so much of island cooking. In this recipe, the combined acidity of the lime juice and the Creole seasoning sauce work harmoniously with the lovely qualities of the vegetable.

Serves 8

    2 pounds small young okra
    1 lime
    2 tablespoons olive oil
    1 slice lean bacon
    1 medium onion, thinly sliced
    3 garlic cloves, peeled and chopped
    4 medium-sized ripe tomatoes, finely chopped
    1 red bell pepper, seeded and finely chopped
    3 whole cloves
    1 bay leaf
    ½ pound coarsely ground fresh pork or ham
    2 cups chicken stock (page 36) or defatted
      chicken broth*
    Salt and pepper, to taste

Prepare okra by rinsing carefully. Dry pods, then cut off the stem and top of the caps. Slice pods diagonally into thin slices. Squeeze lime into a large bowl of cold water. Add sliced okra and allow to soak while preparing the sauce.

Heat the olive oil in a large skillet or sauté pan. Add the bacon and cook until crisp. Remove to drain, then add the onion and garlic and sauté until tender. Add the tomatoes, red pepper, cloves, and bay leaf and cook until tomatoes and red pepper are softened. Add the ground pork and cook until meat turns brown, then add the chicken stock and simmer for about 30 minutes.

Drain the okra and add to the sauce, stirring gently. Cover the saucepan and cook until okra is just done, about 15 minutes. Add salt, pepper and crumbled bacon.

Serve with steaming hot white rice and plantains.

*To defat canned broth, place can in refrigerator. When chilled, open can and skim fat from the surface.

Old-Style Tropical Sweet Potatoes

Boniatos Asados

Also called white sweet potato, *camote*, and *batata*, the boniato is similar to a regular white potato, yet more delicate, with a nutlike flavor and creaminess. This vegetable is available now year-round at most Hispanic markets. When choosing, be sure to select firm smooth-skinned tubers with no mold.

Boniatos are delicious served with *tasajo*, salt-dried beef. Here they are baked and served with a cinnamon-sugar topping.

Serves 4

    4 large boniatos
    2 tablespoons granulated sugar
    2 tablespoons cinnamon
    2 tablespoons butter or margarine

Preheat the oven to 400° F. Wash and scrub boniatos well, as you would any potato. Poke each several times with the tines of a fork. Bake 55 to 60 minutes, depending on size, then split each lengthwise and sprinkle with sugar and cinnamon. Add a chunk of butter to each. Serve steaming hot.

Fried Sweet Potatoes

Boniatos Fritos

The cream-colored flesh of the boniato lends itself to deep frying, much like our sweet potato. Be sure to serve these right away as the flavor diminishes as the light rounds cool.   **Serves 4 to 6**

 2 pounds boniatos, peeled and sliced into
   ⅛-inch rounds
 Pure vegetable oil, for frying
 Salt, to taste

Heat oil in a heavy large skillet or sauté pan. Add potatoes and fry until they turn light brown. Drain on brown paper bags or paper toweling. When ready to serve, fry once again on high heat until golden brown. Serve piping hot. Sprinkle with salt. They're also good served with the cilantro dipping sauce on page 34.

Sweet Potato Pudding

Pudín de Boniato

If you have a sweet tooth you will devour this dish made with the Cuban sweet potato, sugar, and island spice. Pineapple preserves qualify it to double as a dessert, if desired.   **Serves 4 to 6**

 5 medium boniatos, baked, peeled,
   and mashed
 ¼ pound unsalted butter or margarine,
   softened
 ¼ cup light cream
 3 tablespoons light brown sugar
 ½ teaspoon cinnamon
 ½ teaspoon nutmeg
 Salt and pepper, to taste
 1 cup pineapple preserves
 3 eggs, separated, at room temperature

Preheat the oven to 325° F.

Blend potatoes in the container of a food processor until very smooth. Add the butter, cream, sugar, cinnamon, nutmeg, and salt and pepper. Scrape mixture into a large glass bowl, then add the pineapple preserves. Mix well with a wooden spoon. Beat the egg yolks and blend in well.

In a separate bowl, beat the egg whites until stiff and then fold into the mixture. Pour into a 2-quart ovenproof casserole and bake for 45 to 55 minutes.

Sweet Potatoes Bodeguita

Boniatillo Bodeguita

This recipe is still prepared, as it has been for years, at the famous Bodeguita del Medio in Havana. The potatoes are flavored with star anise, a Chinese fruit that for centuries has been touted as an aid to digestion, and imparts a licorice flavor.   **Serves 4 to 6**

½ teaspoon salt
2 dried star anise fruits
2 pounds medium boniato, peeled and
   cut into fourths
½ cup granulated sugar
1 teaspoon lime peel
¼ pound unsalted butter

Place salt and anise in water and bring to a boil. Add the boniato. In a separate heavy saucepan, dissolve the sugar and flavor with lime peel.

When potatoes are cooked, remove anise, drain well, then mash and place them in the prepared syrup and cook slowly over low heat until the mixture is thoroughly blended. Add butter and stir until melted. Serve in custard dishes.

Cheese-Stuffed Boniatos

Boniatos Rellenos con Queso

The red skin of the boniato is much more tender than that of the Irish potato, so be careful when removing the flesh.
          Serves 4 to 8

4 baked boniatos, cooled
2 cups low-fat cottage cheese
1 cup shredded low-fat part-skim mozzarella
   cheese, plus ⅓ cup for topping
2 tablespoons chopped fresh chives
½ teaspoon Spanish paprika
Freshly cracked black pepper, to taste
2 tablespoons chopped fresh parsley

Preheat the broiler.

Cut baked boniatos in half. Carefully remove the potato fillings to a large bowl. Add the cottage cheese, 1 cup mozzarella, chives, paprika, and black pepper. Mix well to an almost creamy consistency. With a spatula or spoon, place filling in potato shells and top with the ⅓ cup cheese. Sprinkle with parsley. Place potato boats under the broiler about 6 inches from the heat source until cheese melts and is browned.

Malanga with Mojo

Malanga con Mojo

You can prepare malangas just about any way you've ever prepared white potatoes. The taste of this tuber is starchier, more nutlike than our variety, and more digestible.

Serves 4

2 pounds malangas, peeled, scrubbed, and
   cut into 1-inch cubes

MOJO

¼ pound butter or margarine
3 to 4 garlic cloves, peeled
1 tablespoon olive oil
1 tablespoon finely chopped fresh parsley
Salt and coarsely ground pepper, to taste
Juice of ½ lime or lemon

In a medium saucepan, boil the malangas in water to cover for 20 to 25 minutes, or until tender. Meanwhile, prepare the *mojo* in a small sauté pan by melting the butter, then adding the garlic, olive oil, parsley, salt, pepper, and lime juice. Combine well and cook for 1 to 2 minutes.

Drain the malanga and serve with *mojo* generously poured over.

Caribbean Yam

Namé Asado à la Plancha

Namé is often cooked in soups or stews because it absorbs the distinctive flavors of the meats and fish. Its texture becomes much like a white potato and it contributes a heartiness to the dish in question.

Many Cubans, however, prefer this simple preparation with garlic and butter, which brings out the nutty flavor of the namé.   **Serves 4**

2 pounds namé, scrubbed, peeled, and
   cut into 1-inch chunks
2 tablespoons butter or margarine
5 to 6 garlic cloves, peeled and crushed
Salt, to taste

In a medium saucepan, boil the namé in water to cover until soft—when the tines of a fork are inserted into the tuber.

Drain and season with butter, garlic, and salt.

Sautéed Potatoes with Fresh Parsley

Papas Salteadas con Perejil

Cubans often prefer their vegetables relatively unadorned. This very modest preparation of pan-fried potatoes, which I enjoyed in many homes in Miami, is good served alongside *palomilla* steak, a thinly sliced marinated steak that is a mainstay in many Cuban homes.   **Serves 4**

> **4 tablespoons butter or olive oil**
> **3 pounds tiny white potatoes**
> **3 tablespoons chopped fresh parsley**
> **Salt, to taste**

Melt butter in a large skillet or sauté pan. Add potatoes and fry until tender, about 15 minutes. Add parsley, season to taste, and cook another 5 minutes.

Thin Fried Potatoes

Papas Fritas

For these deep-fried potatoes, which are often served as an integral part of the Cuban hamburger, choose firm potatoes that are smooth to the touch. The thinness of the potato sticks makes a lovely difference in their crispness.   **Serves 4 to 6**

> **4 Idaho potatoes**
> **Vegetable oil, for frying**
> **Salt, to taste**

Peel and grate potatoes with a food processor, a mandoline equipped with a julienne blade, a Mouli grater, or slice by hand. To slice by hand, cut potatoes lengthwise into very thin slices, then stack a few slices and cut into matchstick strips. Dry between paper toweling.

Heat enough vegetable oil (to 350° to 360° F) to completely submerge the potatoes in a deep-fat fryer. Place one quarter of the potatoes into the basket of the deep-fryer. Lower potatoes in basket fryer and cook until very crisp, 1 to 2 minutes. Remove and drain on brown paper bags or paper toweling. Repeat with remaining batches, keeping cooked potatoes warm in a 200° F oven. Season with salt and serve immediately.

Papaya au Gratin

Papaya con Queso al Horno

Papaya, also called pawpaw, is available year-round. The fruit varies in size, shape, and color, from golden pink-orange to pale yellow. The flesh has a smooth, moist texture with a delectable sweetness.

Papaya with tomato? It may seem an unlikely combination, but together with fresh herbs and the rich, sharp flavor of the Pecorino, this papaya-with-cheese recipe is a revelation to those seeking outstanding casserole dishes.

Ask your produce man to help you pick out a good unripe papaya. Signs of ripening include gentle yellow speckling on the skin and a fruity fragrance when sniffed.

Serves 4

2 tablespoons olive oil
1 tablespoon butter or margarine
1 large onion, chopped
2 large unripe papayas, seeds removed, peeled and diced
3 plum tomatoes, peeled, seeded, and chopped
1 teaspoon chopped fresh thyme, or ½ teaspoon dried
1 teaspoon chopped fresh basil, or ½ teaspoon dried
½ cup fresh bread crumbs
¾ cup grated Pecorino or Parmesan cheese

Preheat the oven to 350° F.

Heat a large skillet and add the olive oil and butter. When butter melts and oil begins to smell fragrant, add onion and sauté until golden brown. Add the papayas, tomatoes, thyme, and basil and mix well. Cook for about 10 minutes over medium heat, stirring constantly.

Pour mixture into a 9 × 9 × 2-inch pan. Sprinkle with bread crumbs and cheese. Bake until the topping is golden brown and crunchy, 10 to 12 minutes.

Potato Plantains

Papas Plataneras

The secret to this modern-day mock plantain recipe is flattening the potatoes, as you would when preparing *tostónes*, then sautéing until golden brown. Combined with the garlicky zip of the *mojo* sauce, it is a very addictive side dish.

These are also exceptional seasoned simply with salt and freshly cracked black pepper.

Serves 4

12 small new potatoes
2 tablespoons olive oil
Mojo agrio (page 31)

Peel and boil new potatoes until done. Cool and pat dry. Heat a large skillet and add the olive oil. When oil is heated and begins to smell fragrant, add potatoes and fry for about 7 minutes. Drain on brown paper bags or paper towels.

Using the same technique as you would to fry green plantains, place each fried potato between 2 sheets of wax paper and mash with a wooden mallet or your fist. Return to oil and fry again until potatoes are nicely browned. Drain. Pour *mojo* sauce over potatoes and serve piping hot.

Fried Sweet Plantains

Maduros Fritos

This preparation is my favorite, a simple sauté with olive oil and butter and just a little lime juice. The fried plantains are typically served with black beans and rice and an entrée of fish, pork, or beef.

The owner of a popular restaurant in Miami, called La Esquina de Tejas, told me the secret to preparing these is to choose very ripe fruit that is completely black. You will need to slice carefully since the fruit at this stage is very soft. The butter is not necessary and often not used in Cuban homes, but I feel it adds richness to the dish.

Serves 4

4 ripe plantains, peeled and cut diagonally
   into ¾-inch pieces*
2 tablespoons olive or vegetable oil
2 tablespoons butter or margarine
Juice of ½ lime
Salt, to taste

Heat a large skillet and add the olive oil and butter. When the oil is heated and begins to smell fragrant, carefully add plantain slices. Fry 3 to 4 minutes on each side, turning with a pancake turner or spatula to prevent pieces from clinging to pan. Add more oil, if necessary.

Remove from skillet with a slotted spoon and drain on brown paper bags or paper towels. Place on a serving platter and sprinkle with lime juice and salt. Serve hot.

*See page 23 for how to peel plantains.

Twice-Fried Green Plantains

Tostónes

In this classic recipe, green plantains are twice fried to crispy perfection. Also called *plátanos al puñetazo, aplastados,* or *chatinos,* the plantains function like a bread and are a favorite side dish.   **Serves 6 to 8**

Vegetable oil, for frying
2 large green plantains, peeled and cut into
   1-inch diagonal slices*
Salt, to taste

Fill a deep-fryer about halfway full with light vegetable oil, or a large skillet one-third full. Heat over medium-high heat to about 375° F.

Deep-fry the plantain slices for 2 to 3 minutes, or until they begin to turn golden brown. If using a skillet, fry the slices for 2 to 3 minutes on each side.

Remove plantains with a slotted spoon. Allow to drain on paper towels or brown paper bags for a few minutes. When cooled, place a piece of paper toweling or brown bag paper on top. Using the palm of your hand, push down and flatten the slices to look like pancakes, about ⅛ inch thick.

Return smashed plantains to the oil, or store at room temperature until mealtime. Then fry again until golden brown, 3 to 4 minutes, depending on the thickness. Remove with a slotted spoon and allow to drain again. Sprinkle with salt and serve warm. If you wish to cook a large amount, keep cooked plantains warm in a 225° F oven until ready to serve.

*See page 23 for how to peel plantains.

Plantain Balls

Fufu

This dish originated in West Africa and has been passed down from generation to generation. Originally the natives would pound cassava and yams into small balls that would be served with souplike dishes and stews. In this recipe, plantains are boiled and then combined with butter and seasoned before adding to a soup or stew. Fufu is delicious when served with the *ajiaco* recipe on page 76.   **Serves 6**

4 green plantains, unpeeled
2 tablespoons butter or margarine
Salt and freshly ground black pepper, to taste

Put unpeeled plantains in a large kettle with enough cold water to cover. Bring to a boil over medium heat. Lower heat and simmer about 30 minutes, until plantains are soft and skins have started to split. Drain plantains and, when cool enough, peel and mash well. Pound with a pestle for about 20 minutes, or until the flesh forms a smooth ball. Dip the pestle into cold water to keep from sticking. Add butter and salt and pepper and, with wet hands, form into balls. Drop into soups, stews, or vegetable dishes and let simmer a few minutes before serving.

Grilled Plantains

Plátanos à la Parrilla

Memories of a fantastic lawn party at Viscaya Gardens in Coconut Grove inspired me to create this recipe for grilled plantains. I usually serve this as a vegetable with grilled fish, but it also makes a novel dessert.   **Serves 4**

4 ripe plantains, unpeeled
Olive oil, for coating
4 ounces mozzarella cheese
Extra-virgin olive oil, for drizzling

Coat plantains lightly with olive oil. Grill with peel on for 15 to 20 minutes over a low heat, turning frequently. Cut off ½ inch from both ends. Slice into each plantain as you would when cutting into a baked potato and stuff with mozzarella cheese. Drizzle extra-virgin olive oil over all.

Plantain Pie

Pastel de Plátano

Plantains become black and rather unattractive when ripening, but when cooked they have a fragrant sweetness. Choose the blackest plantains you can find; green or unripe fruit is not sweet enough.   **Serves 6**

    2 tablespoons olive oil
    3 ripe plantains, peeled*
    ¼ pound shredded Monterey Jack cheese
    ¼ pound shredded Colby or yellow Cheddar
    ¼ pound mango jelly†

Preheat the oven to 350° F. Grease a shallow 1-quart mold. Slice plantains diagonally.

Heat a medium sauté pan and add olive oil. When oil begins to smell fragrant, add plantains and fry over medium heat until softened, carefully turning a few times. Remove with a slotted spoon and allow to drain on paper towels or a brown paper bag.

Mix cheeses together in a small bowl. Place a flat layer of plantains on the bottom of the prepared mold. Cover with a layer of shredded cheese and a thin layer of mango jelly, then a second layer of plantain slices. Top with the remaining shredded cheeses. Bake for about 20 minutes, or until cheese is bubbly and melted.

*See page 23 for how to peel plantains.
†Available at most Hispanic markets.

Salsas

Salsas, chopped vegetable and fruit relishes, are an integral part of Cuban cuisine. They have hit a peak of popularity in the United States as a stroll through almost any supermarket will testify. In restaurants specializing in *nuevo Cubano*, they are served with increasing popularity as appetizers, as dips for crudités or tortilla chips, and as dressings for grilled meats and fish. Often they are served as side dishes to embellish the flavors of the meal.

When preparing salsas, use the best ingredients. Uncooked salsas should be made with the freshest vegetables available for the crispiest texture. Juicy ripe tomatoes, fresh peppers, herbs, and good red onions add an extra punch to these fresh dishes.

Simmer cooked salsas in a large open sauté pan over moderately high heat so the contents reduce quickly and the ingredients stay crisp. Remove excess juice from fresh tomatoes before use; the salsa will taste better.

All of these condiments complement a range of dishes and can be blended in many ways using a variety of ingredients. Let your own taste be the guide.

Black Bean, Jícama, and Corn Salsa

Salsa de Frijoles Negros, Maíz, y Jícama

The serrano seco pepper is orange-red and measures about 2 inches long. It adds real zip to this crunchy salsa.

Makes about 4 cups

½ cup cooked or canned black beans
1 cup peeled and diced jícama
Kernels from 4 ears of charcoal roasted corn,*
    or use 2 cups canned corn, drained
1 cup minced red onion
1 serrano seco,† diced
2 garlic cloves, peeled and minced
½ cup extra-virgin olive oil
2 tablespoons fresh lime juice
Salt, to taste

Combine all ingredients in a glass bowl. Allow to marinate overnight so that flavors meld.

*To roast corn ears over charcoal, prepare a moderately hot charcoal fire. Pull back the husks on each ear to expose the kernels; do not remove. Carefully remove the silk, then smooth the husks back over the ears and secure and tie at tips. Turn ears frequently to ensure even heat.
To roast in the oven, preheat oven to 400° F. Wrap each ear in foil and then place on lower rack. Roast for 55 to 60 minutes, or until corn is soft.
†Also known as *chile seco*, it is a very intense pepper and can also be found in powdered form. Use any hot pepper as a substitute, or if you prefer a mild sauce, use 2 tablespoons chopped green bell pepper.

Tomato-Chile Salsa

Salsa de Tomate y Chile

Most Cuban cooking is performed with a minimum of hotness, except for an occasional dalliance with the jalapeño pepper or a few other hot varieties. If you prefer a mild salsa, leave out the jalapeños or replace them with a mild pepper. This sauce can be stored in the refrigerator or can be frozen for future use.

Makes 2 cups

4 fresh jalapeño peppers, seeded and minced
    (set aside ½ teaspoon seeds)
⅓ cup water
½ cup chopped green bell pepper
2 large ripe tomatoes, chopped
2 garlic cloves, peeled and mashed
½ cup minced red onion
½ cup peeled and minced celery
½ cup finely chopped fresh cilantro
Salt, to taste

Put all the ingredients except the seeds in a medium saucepan. Combine well, bring to a boil, then reduce heat and simmer for about 2½ hours. Add reserved seeds to mixture and simmer for 30 minutes. Serve as an accompaniment to pork, beef, and fish dishes.

Pineapple-Citrus Chutney

Chutney de Piña y Frutas Cítricas

Y ou'll love this chutney, because it is easy to make and can be prepared ahead. Its sweet and sour flavor is especially good with grilled seafood. Try it with plantain-coated fish.   **Makes about 2½ cups**

1 tablespoon olive oil
1 tablespoon butter or margarine
½ cup diced red onion
½ cup diced green bell pepper
3 tablespoons grated fresh ginger
3 garlic cloves, peeled and finely minced
¾ cup dark brown sugar
⅓ cup red wine vinegar
1 pineapple, peeled, cut into ½-inch slices, and broiled or grilled on both sides
1½ cups mango chunks*

Heat a medium sauté pan and add olive oil, then the butter. When sizzling, add onion, green pepper, ginger, and garlic. Cook about 2 minutes on medium-high heat. Add brown sugar and wine vinegar and bring to a boil.

Cut the broiled or grilled pineapple in ½-inch pieces. Add to the mixture along with the mango chunks. Cook about 5 minutes, until flavors meld.

*See page 23 for how to cut a mango.

Mango, Papaya, and Black Bean Salsa

Salsa de Mango, Papaya, y Frijoles Negros

P apaya and mango combine better than one might expect with the black beans to produce a lightly fragrant and flavorful salsa. Mild cubanella peppers add flavor but no heat, as do the hot peppers in so many other salsas.   **Makes about 4½ cups**

1 cup peeled and diced mango*
1 cup diced papaya
¼ cup finely diced white onion
¼ cup finely diced red onion
2 cups cooked or canned black beans
2 tablespoons minced cubanella pepper†
2 tablespoons chopped fresh cilantro
1 teaspoon minced garlic
1½ tablespoons extra-virgin olive oil
2 tablespoons freshly squeezed lime juice
1 teaspoon cracked black pepper

Gently mix all ingredients together. Refrigerate until time to serve. Serve very cold as a topping on seafood or pork dishes, or as a separate garnish.

*See page 23 for how to cut a mango.
†This is a mild pepper found in most Hispanic markets. You may substitute green bell pepper.

Pepper Salsa

Salsa de Ajíes

This is a good accompaniment to the potato and black bean pancakes on page 94. Both are quick and easy to make. The yellow pepper is a colorful addition in this salsa.

Makes about 1 cup

1 green bell pepper, seeded and finely chopped
1 red bell pepper, seeded and finely chopped
1 yellow bell pepper, seeded and finely chopped
2 tablespoons red wine vinegar
1½ tablespoons chopped fresh cilantro
2 scallions, minced
1 tablespoon fresh lime juice
½ teaspoon freshly ground black pepper

Mix all ingredients together and allow to marinate for a few hours. Chill.

Simply Salsa

Simplemente Salsa

Here's a very simple salsa. I use plum tomatoes, which seem to have much more flavor than most commercial tomatoes.

Makes 3 cups

2 cups chopped very red plum or farm tomatoes
¼ cup chopped red onion
2 tablespoons red wine vinegar
1 medium green bell pepper, seeded and chopped
1 tablespoon chopped fresh cilantro
½ teaspoon salt

Combine all the ingredients in a glass bowl. Allow to stand at room temperature for about 30 minutes before serving. Chill to store.

Cilantro Salsa

Salsa de Cilantro

This salsa is great with tortilla chips! The fresh cilantro brings it all together.

Makes 2 cups

2 large ripe tomatoes, chopped
2 tablespoons chopped red onion
3 tablespoons chopped green bell pepper
3 tablespoons chopped red bell pepper
2 tablespoons chopped fresh cilantro, or 1 tablespoon dried
2 tablespoons red wine vinegar
½ teaspoon salt
1 teaspoon freshly cracked black pepper
2 tablespoons extra-virgin olive oil

In a large glass mixing bowl, combine tomatoes, onion, peppers, cilantro, wine vinegar, salt, and pepper. Stir in olive oil. Allow to marinate for a few hours before serving. Serve on the side or with toasted tortilla chips.

Hot Peppery Salsa Santiago

Salsa Pimentosa Caliente Santiago

Cuban food is typically not spicy, but I often see many Cubans at the very popular Miami restaurant, La Esquina de Tejas, reaching for the hot sauce and applying it with a very heavy hand.

Here's an easy-to-prepare *salsa fresca* with that extra peppery taste that many love. This salsa is delicious with a tender pork loin or a juicy red fillet; but if you're not a big pepper fan, leave out the jalapeños.   **Makes 2½ cups**

2 cups diced very red plum or farm tomatoes
¼ cup chopped red onion
½ cup diced green bell pepper
½ cup diced red bell pepper
2 jalapeño peppers, minced
2 tablespoons red wine vinegar
Juice of ½ lime
1 tablespoon finely chopped fresh cilantro
1 tablespoon finely chopped fresh flat-leaf
  parsley
½ teaspoon salt
1 teaspoon coarsely ground black pepper

In a glass bowl, combine the tomatoes, red onion, green, red, and jalapeño peppers, vinegar, lime juice, cilantro, parsley, and salt. Mix well. Add the black pepper and mix well again. Allow to stand at room temperature for about 1 hour before serving. Chill to store.

Avocado Salsa

Salsa de Aguacate

Often nicknamed the "alligator pear," the buttery avocado is rich in Vitamin A and potassium. The red onion adds a nice measure of sweetness. Serve with any kind of firm white broiled fish.   **Makes 1 cup**

1 avocado, peeled, seeded, and mashed
2 very ripe plum tomatoes, peeled and
  chopped
¼ cup seeded and minced cubanella pepper,*
  or 1 small jalapeño, seeded and minced
1 tablespoon fresh lime juice
1 tablespoon chopped fresh cilantro
½ teaspoon ground cumin
Dollop of sour cream
1 tablespoon minced red onion

Combine all ingredients except sour cream and red onion in a medium glass mixing bowl. Mix well but keep chunky. Sprinkle a little lime juice over salsa to keep avocado from discoloring. Chill.

Serve as soon as possible, adding a dollop of sour cream and the onion as garnish.

*A lemony-yellow rather mild pepper available at most Hispanic markets. They are grown almost to the size of a green bell pepper.

Papaya Salsa

Salsa de Papaya

This is pleasant as a topping on grilled chicken, as a side dish, with grilled or whole baked fish or skewers of shrimp.

Makes about 3 cups

1 tablespoon olive oil
1 red onion, minced
1 fresh jalapeño pepper, seeded and minced
½ cup chopped red bell pepper
2 tablespoons fresh lime juice
3 garlic cloves, peeled and crushed
2 cups seeded and diced fresh ripe papaya
½ ripe tomato, seeded and chopped
2 tablespoons chopped fresh cilantro
1 teaspoon chopped fresh parsley

Heat a large sauté pan or skillet and add the oil. When the oil begins to smell fragrant, add onion and cook until transparent. Add the peppers and cook about 5 minutes longer. Reduce to medium heat. Add the lime juice, garlic cloves, papaya, tomato, cilantro, and the parsley. Reduce to low heat and simmer for about 5 minutes. Cool.

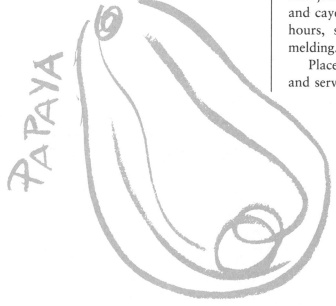

Papaya-Onion Salsa

Salsa de Papaya y Cebolla

The honey and vinegar blend with the red onion, papaya, and hot pepper in this sweet and sour salsa. It makes an exotic presentation when served in the papaya shell. Serve with grilled fish, such as grouper or red snapper. Allow at least 1 hour to marinate.

Makes about 2 pints

2 medium papayas
1 tablespoon minced green bell pepper
1 cup minced red onion
¼ cup chopped fresh cilantro
1 tablespoon fresh lime juice
¼ cup red wine vinegar
½ teaspoon honey
¼ cup extra-virgin olive oil
½ jalapeño pepper, seeded and diced
Salt, to taste
½ teaspoon cayenne pepper

Scoop out the papaya, reserving shells for serving. Dice the papaya flesh.

In a large glass bowl, combine the papaya chunks with the green pepper, red onion, cilantro, lime juice, vinegar, honey, olive oil, jalapeño, salt, and cayenne. Mix well and refrigerate for 1 to 2 hours, stirring several times while flavors are melding.

Place mixture back into reserved papaya shells and serve.

Easy Corn Salsa

Salsa de Maíz Fácil

This flavorful salsa is usually made with charred corn fresh off the cob, but that takes a lot of time. This easy recipe is exceptional if made with a good canned corn that retains its crunchiness.

Serves 4 to 6 as a side dish

2 tablespoons olive oil
1 cup minced red onion
½ cup diced yellow bell pepper
½ cup diced red bell pepper
2 garlic cloves, peeled and minced
1 (17-ounce) can whole kernel corn
1½ tablespoons finely chopped fresh cilantro
1 teaspoon finely chopped fresh parsley
1 tablespoon extra-virgin olive oil
1 teaspoon red wine vinegar

Heat a medium sauté pan and add the olive oil. When oil is hot, add the onion, peppers, and garlic, coating well with the oil. Cook about 1 minute on medium heat so that vegetables remain crisp. Drain the corn and rinse with water to remove excess salt. Add corn to sauté pan and cook until heated through. Remove from stove to a serving bowl. Cool. Mix in the cilantro, parsley, extra-virgin olive oil, and vinegar. Serve at room temperature, but keep refrigerated if serving the next day.

Black Bean Salsa Relish

Aderezo de Salsa de Frijoles Negros

Chorizo sausage and ham are added to this black bean salsa. It's a hearty spicy dip, great for winter entertainment. In a pinch, canned black beans will work fine. Be sure to rinse them to remove any excess salt. **Makes 2 cups**

1 tablespoon olive oil
¼ cup finely chopped celery
½ cup minced red onion
¼ cup finely chopped carrot
4 garlic cloves, peeled and minced
1 red bell pepper, seeded and minced
1 very ripe plum tomato, chopped
1 teaspoon ground cumin
2 cups black beans, or 1 (15-ounce) can, drained and rinsed
1 (3-inch) piece chorizo sausage, thinly sliced
¼ cup chopped lean ham
2 tablespoons chopped fresh cilantro
1 teaspoon chopped fresh oregano, or ½ teaspoon dried
2 tablespoons water
½ teaspoon salt
2 tablespoons red wine vinegar

Heat the oil in a medium saucepan and sauté the celery, onion, carrot, garlic, red pepper, tomato, and cumin until onion is translucent and tender. Add the beans, chorizo, ham, cilantro, oregano, water, and salt and bring to a boil. Reduce heat and simmer uncovered for about 15 minutes. Add 2 tablespoons red wine vinegar. Serve hot as a side dish or with tortilla chips as an appetizer.

Mango–Black Bean Relish

Aderezo de Mango y Frijoles Negros

Here's a delicious salsa relish developed by Hubert Des Marais, a talented young chef who specializes in what he calls Floribbean-Cuban cuisine. Marais joins tropical fruits with crunchy jícama, hot pepper, and black beans to achieve a full-bodied salsa with an unusual spicy-sweet flavor.

Makes about 4 cups

2 limes, seeded and halved
Juice of 1 fresh lime
1 cup puréed mango*
½ cup diced mango*
½ cup diced pink papaya
½ cup cooked and drained black beans
½ cup peeled and diced jícama
¼ cup finely chopped cucumber peel
¼ cup diced red bell pepper
¼ cup diced yellow bell pepper
¼ cup diced red onion
½ bunch fresh cilantro, finely chopped
½ Scotch bonnet pepper,† seeded and minced
1½ teaspoons extra-virgin olive oil
Salt and freshly ground black pepper, to taste

Place limes in a nonreactive saucepan and cover with water. Bring to a boil and reduce heat to a simmer. Cook limes until soft, about 20 minutes. Cool and dice. Combine with all other ingredients. Store in refrigerator. Serve at room temperature.

*See page 23 for how to cut a mango.
†Scotch bonnet is a very hot Jamaican pepper with a fruity and smokelike flavor.

Rum, Mango, and Pineapple Relish

Aderezo de Ron Sazonado, Piña, y Mango

This is an appetite-stimulating salsa prepared with rum, mango, and pineapple. Spiced rum, available in most liquor stores, can also be used for a uniquely spicy substitute.

Makes about 4 cups, depending on size of pineapple

1 tablespoon granulated sugar
2 tablespoons sherry vinegar
1 ripe pineapple, peeled and cut into small pieces
1 cup peeled and chopped mango*
½ cup finely chopped yellow onion
1 red bell pepper, seeded and finely diced
¼ cup finely diced scallions
¼ cup golden rum

Heat sugar and vinegar in a medium saucepan over low heat. Add pineapple, mango, onion, and pepper and allow to simmer for about 3 minutes. Add the scallions and rum; combine well. Cook for another 3 to 4 minutes. Serve warm or cold.

*See page 23 for how to cut a mango.

In a very large canning pot, combine the peppers, vinegar, salt, and light brown sugar and cook until sugar dissolves. Add remaining ingredients. Mix well and bring to a boil. Turn heat off, cover, and allow mixture to sit for 2 hours. Turn heat on again and simmer for 4 to 5 hours, or until a nice chutney consistency is achieved (thin but solid) and mangoes are well cooked. Cool and pour into sterilized canning jars.

*See page 9.
†You may use canned tamarind, if available, or prepare your own by soaking 1 cup fresh tamarinds, shells removed, in ½ cup cider vinegar. When pulp has softened off the seeds, press through a sieve or colander to remove the seeds. Pulp will be a rich brown color.
‡See page 23 for how to cut a mango.

Mango Chutney

Salsa de Mango Verdes

There is nothing quite like cooking with the fresh juice of the exotic tamarind, a popular fruit throughout the Caribbean. It lends a sour, fruity taste that enhances poultry and fish. The tamarind, a tree originally from the Far East, was brought to the Caribbean by Spanish conquistadores in the 1600s. This chutney has an unusual tartness to it that goes extremely well with roast pork or chicken.

When choosing tamarinds be sure that the flesh of the pod is ripe with a rich tan color, not green. Crack and pull away the thin skin from the pod to reach the flesh. The aroma is haunting.

Makes about six 6-ounce jars

1 large cubanella pepper,* or 3 chile peppers, seeded and minced
1 quart cider vinegar
2 tablespoons salt
6 cups firmly packed light brown sugar
½ cup tamarind pulp†
10 cups peeled and diced ripe mangoes‡
4 cups chopped onion
1 (15-ounce) box golden seedless raisins
1 teaspoon celery seed
¼ cup sliced almonds
4 garlic cloves, peeled and minced
2 tablespoons finely grated fresh ginger
½ cup fresh or bottled lime juice
1½ cups whole cloves
1 tablespoon cinnamon
1 tablespoon whole mustard seeds
2 cinnamon sticks

Breads and Sandwiches

Panes y Bocaditos

Cubans seldom use sliced bread as we know it here in the United States. Instead, they prefer crusty yard-long loaves topped with laurel leaves.

These hearty breads derive from the intermingling food styles that passed between slave and master in the early days when Africans were brought to the island to work the sugar plantations.

Cuban bread is good cut into long thin strips, toasted, buttered, and eaten for breakfast, along with steaming hot coffee with milk. It also marries perfectly with thick slices of oven-roasted pork, Virginia ham, and imported cheese. The Cuban sandwich has hundreds of variations and is rapidly becoming one of the most popular urban lunchtime offerings in the States.

Cubans also treasure their dessert breads, made with tropical fruits and native island tubers.

All these breads round out any Cuban meal and can stand alone as snacks that can be savored anytime.

Yuca Bread

Pan de Yuca

This recipe was given to me by my dear friend Lucy Cooper, a food journalist who has been writing about Florida and Caribbean cuisine for many years. Its flavor is very similar to potato breads and is at its finest when toasted. As a matter of fact you can substitute mashed potatoes if yuca isn't available. However, Lucy maintains that yuca creates a denser, more flavorful loaf. I often vary the results by forming the dough into rolls before cooking and then baking for 15 to 20 minutes.   **Makes 1 large loaf**

1 cup cooked and mashed yuca*
3 cups all-purpose flour
1 teaspoon kosher salt
2 (¼-ounce) envelopes active dry yeast
1 tablespoon granulated sugar
½ cup warm water (110° F)
¼ cup vegetable oil

Place yuca, flour, and salt in the container of a food processor.

Meanwhile, place yeast, sugar, and water in a cup and allow to sit for about 5 minutes.

Turn on the food processor and mix ingredients well. With the motor running, slowly add yeast mixture and oil through the feed tube. Process until dough forms a ball, adding more warm water, a tablespoon at a time, as needed. If dough becomes too soft, add more flour, about ¼ cup at a time. When dough has formed a ball and is pliable, remove from processor and knead into a round ball. Place in a covered greased bowl and allow to rise until doubled in bulk, about 1 hour.

Punch down dough and form into a rectangle long enough to fit an 8½ × 4½ × 2½-inch greased (loaf) pan. Place in pan and allow to rise until doubled in bulk, 30 to 45 minutes.

Preheat the oven to 400° F.

Bake bread for 10 minutes. Reduce heat to 350° F and bake another 30 minutes. If crust browns too quickly, cover with foil for last 15 minutes. Remove from bread pan and allow to cool.

*See page 24 for how to cook yuca.

Calabaza Bread

Pan de Calabaza

This is a very rich bread, enhanced by a combination of spices and almonds that impart a delightfully aromatic flavor. The resulting fragrance in the kitchen is well worth the effort. Calabaza is a fleshy vegetable much like a pumpkin, often weighing as much as 20 pounds. However, some greengrocers cut and wrap it in smaller pieces.   **Makes 2 loaves**

2 cups cooked and puréed calabaza or
   pumpkin (2 to 2½ pounds)
¼ pound butter or margarine, melted
2 cups granulated sugar
1 cup whole milk
4 eggs, slightly beaten
4 cups all-purpose flour
1 tablespoon plus 1 teaspoon baking powder
1 teaspoon baking soda
1½ teaspoons salt
1 teaspoon nutmeg
2 teaspoons ground cinnamon
½ teaspoon allspice
½ cup blanched slivered almonds, chopped

Preheat the oven to 350° F.

In a large bowl, combine puréed calabaza, melted butter, sugar, milk, and eggs. Mix well.

In a separate bowl, combine flour, baking powder, baking soda, salt, nutmeg, cinnamon, and allspice. Add almonds and mix well. Add to calabaza mixture.

Generously grease two 9 × 5 × 3-inch loaf pans. Pour mixture equally into pans. Bake for 45 to 50 minutes, or until firm when touched.

Cuban Bread

Pan Cubano

This basic recipe is as close as Cuban bread gets to the French version. The essential difference is that the Cuban rendering is lighter and crispier. This recipe omits the traditional proofing stage of the yeast, unnecessary because of the dramatic changes in the product found in stores today. "Active" or "fast-rising" dry yeast usually requires less quantity than called for in standard bread recipes using cake yeast.

Many Cuban bakeries make loaves 3 feet and longer. **Makes 2 large loaves**

2 (¼-ounce) packages fast-rising yeast
1 tablespoon granulated sugar
1½ to 2 cups or more lukewarm water
1 teaspoon salt
6 cups all-purpose flour
2 tablespoons cornmeal, for baking sheet
6 to 8 bay leaves, for tops of loaves

In a small bowl, dissolve the yeast and sugar in ½ cup of warm water (110 degrees F). In a separate large mixing bowl, to be used with an electric mixer with a dough hook, combine flour and salt and mix thoroughly.

Add yeast mixture to flour mixture and blend with the dough hook at low speed. Add additional water, ½ cup at a time, until mixed thoroughly and dough is smooth. The amount of water you need will vary with the mixture's ability to absorb water. Cover dough with a clean cloth and place in a warm area (85° to 90° F) where there are no cold drafts. Note the size of the dough at this point.

Allow dough to rise until doubled in volume, about 1 hour when using the fast-rising yeast, about 2 hours if you use regular yeast. When doubled, deflate the dough by punching it two or three times.

When dough has risen, turn out onto a lightly floured wooden board. Divide into two equal balls. Shape by stretching and rolling each piece of dough into a long sausage shape about 2 inches in diameter and about a foot long.

Sprinkle cornmeal heavily onto an ungreased baking sheet. Arrange loaves with considerable space between. Cover with cloth and allow to rise 5 to 7 minutes.

With a sharp knife, slash the tops of the loaves in five or six places and place bay leaves in slits. Brush loaves with water and place in an unheated oven.

Turn on the oven to 400° F. Add a pan of boiling water to the oven. Bake until bread is crusty and browned, 40 to 45 minutes. When done, loaves will sound rather hollow when tapped lightly on top. Remove loaves and cool on wire racks.

To serve, cut in half lengthwise. Butter liberally. Serve immediately or reheat and serve hot and crispy.

Coconut Bread

Pan de Coco

Cubans use the sweet meat of the coconut in many native dishes. In this recipe it produces a rich sweet bread that is almost a dessert cake.   **Makes 1 loaf**

**2¼ cups all-purpose flour
1 cup granulated sugar
1 tablespoon baking powder
¼ pound butter or margarine
1⅓ cups grated fresh coconut* meat or flaked
    unsweetened coconut
2 eggs, slightly beaten
½ teaspoon vanilla extract
2 cups heavy cream**

In a large bowl, combine flour, sugar, and baking powder. Mix well. Using a pastry blender, work in the butter. Add coconut meat and mix well.

In a separate bowl, beat the eggs, vanilla extract, and cream and add to the flour mixture. Pour into a greased loaf pan and bake for 40 to 45 minutes. Serve hot.

*See page 24 for how to open a coconut.

Squash Bread

Pan de Calabazine

This *nuevo Cubano* recipe is the perfect solution for the bumper crop of zucchini home gardeners harvest every year. The taste is an enchanting combination of sweet and spice that is accentuated when toasted.

Makes 1 loaf

**1½ cups all-purpose flour
1 tablespoon ground cinnamon
½ teaspoon baking soda
1 teaspoon baking powder
¼ teaspoon salt
2 eggs
¾ cup granulated sugar
½ cup vegetable oil
1½ teaspoons vanilla extract
1½ cups lightly packed shredded zucchini
    or other summer squash
½ cup chopped nuts**

Preheat the oven to 350° F. Generously grease a 9 × 5 × 3-inch loaf pan.

Mix flour, cinnamon, baking soda, baking powder, and salt together well. Set aside.

Beat eggs until frothy in a separate bowl. Add sugar, vegetable oil, and vanilla and beat until mixture becomes lemon colored, about 3 minutes. Stir in squash.

Add dry mixture and nuts. Pour into loaf pan and bake about 40 minutes, or until a toothpick inserted in center comes out clean. Cool. Serve warm or cold in thick slices, with or without butter.

Mango Sour Cream Nut Bread

Pan de Mango de Nueces y Crema Agría

The mango in the following recipe not only provides a golden color and texture to the finished loaf, it also serves as a framework, bringing together all of the other ingredients. This aromatic bread can be refrigerated or frozen, then toasted to bring back the full fruit flavor.

The addition of sour cream makes for a very moist and cakelike bread. **Makes 1 loaf**

    1½ cups sifted all-purpose flour
    2 teaspoons baking powder
    ¼ teaspoon baking soda
    ½ teaspoon salt
    5⅓ tablespoons butter or margarine
    ⅔ cup granulated sugar
    ½ cup sour cream
    2 eggs
    1 cup mashed ripe mango pulp*
    ¾ cup chopped pecans
    ½ cup raisins

Preheat the oven to 350° F. Grease an 8½ × 4½ × 2½-inch loaf pan.

Sift together the flour, baking powder, baking soda, and salt. Set aside.

Place the butter, sugar, and sour cream in a mixing bowl. Beat the mixture at medium speed or by hand until creamy. Add the eggs and beat until fluffy and light. Blend in the flour mixture alternately with the mango just until smooth. Add the nuts and raisins and pour into the greased loaf pan. Bake for about 1 hour, or until a toothpick inserted comes out clean or with a dry crumb. Cool in the pan on a wire rack for 15 to 20 minutes. Carefully run a sharp thin knife around the inside edge of the pan, then carefully shake the loaf onto the rack. Finish cooling. Serve slightly warm.

*See page 23 for how to cut a mango.

Pepper Corn Muffins

Ají Cachucha de Bagatela

These spicy muffins are light years removed from the sweet staple found in American bakeries and coffee shops. They can be served with fish or salads, or are ideal to accompany *ajiaco*, the classic Cuban stew. I love the way they sop up the gravy. **Makes 6 large muffins**

    ¼ cup granulated sugar
    1 cup all-purpose flour
    2 tablespoons baking powder
    ½ teaspoon salt
    1 cup yellow cornmeal
    2 eggs
    1 cup whole milk
    4 tablespoons butter or margarine
    2 ají cachucha peppers, seeded and chopped*
    1 cup corn kernels, fresh or frozen

Preheat the oven to 425° F. Grease a large 6-muffin tin.

Combine sugar with flour, baking powder, and salt. Add cornmeal, eggs, milk, and butter. Beat with an electric mixer just until smooth, about 1 minute. Fold in hot peppers and corn. Pour batter into muffin tins and bake for about 20 minutes, or until a toothpick inserted comes out clean or with a dry crumb. Serve with whipped butter.

*See page 5.

Buttered Rum Biscuits

Bizcochillos de Ron

These are a particular favorite of mine and guests love their savory tasty. A combination of golden rum blended with Spanish brandy produces a very tasty biscuit. The alcohol in both evaporate during the baking process, leaving behind the tang of both beverages.

Makes about 10 biscuits

¼ pound butter or margarine
1 cup sifted all-purpose flour
½ teaspoon salt
2 tablespoons golden rum
1 tablespoon Spanish brandy
3 egg yolks

Cut the butter into the flour until the granules are pea-sized. In a separate bowl, combine the salt, rum, brandy, and 2 of the egg yolks. Stir combination into the flour mixture. Knead lightly (10 to 12 strokes), then chill very well.

When dough is chilled, roll out to about ¼-inch thickness. Beat remaining egg yolk slightly.

Preheat the oven to 350° F.

Cut dough with a biscuit cutter and place on an ungreased baking sheet. Brush with the reserved egg yolk. Bake for 10 to 12 minutes, until golden brown.

Cornmeal Muffins

Panecillos de Maíz

Cornmeal bread has a long history in Cuba, dating to the time when slaves were brought from Africa. Although native to the New World, corn and the process of grinding it into meal was introduced by slaves who were more familiar with the vegetable than their Spanish masters. Cornmeal comes in three textures: fine, medium, or coarse. For this recipe I find the medium texture is best because the grinding process retains some of the hull and germ of the corn. It makes for more nutritious muffins.

Makes 8 large or 12 to 16 small muffins

2 eggs
¾ cup whole milk
1 tablespoon granulated sugar
2 teaspoons baking powder
1 teaspoon salt
2 cups white cornmeal
1 cup cold water
2 tablespoons vegetable oil

Preheat the oven to 450° F. Butter 8 large or 12 to 16 small muffin tins.

Beat eggs until frothy and add milk. Set aside. Mix sugar, baking powder, and salt with cornmeal. Add cold water to the mixture. Blend egg mixture with the cornmeal mixture. Add the oil. Combine well until smooth. Fill greased muffin tins two-thirds full. Bake for about 20 minutes, or until a toothpick inserted comes out clean or with a dry crumb.

Cuban Special Sandwich

Cubano Especial

This sandwich is a meal in itself, especially when accompanied by a chilled bottle of beer, called *cerveza*.

In my travels in search of the perfect Cuban sandwich, I have tasted over 75 varieties. Most restaurants have a special sandwich press to flatten them, but you can use a waffle iron. Here is my all-time favorite. **Serves 1**

Olive oil or butter
1 (9 × 4-inch) slice freshly baked Cuban bread
4 to 6 thick slices very lean roasted pork
4 to 6 thick slices Virginia ham
4 slices imported Swiss cheese
4 to 8 thin dill pickle slices

Slice a 9-inch piece from a long loaf of Cuban bread, or use a 9-inch Cuban roll. Brush insides lightly with olive oil or butter. Add pork, ham, cheese, and some of the pickle slices. Place whole sandwich in a waffle iron or toasting element that browns bread top and flattens sandwich. Slice diagonally to serve. Garnish with remaining pickle slices.

Cuban Sandwich, Tampa Style

Sandwich de Tampa

Restaurants in the Tampa area, particularly Ybor City, feature an Americanized version of the Cuban special sandwich. This one is like our grinder or submarine with its many garnishes, particularly the heavy layer of mayonnaise, which you would never find in South Florida. **Serves 6**

1½ loaves Cuban bread
Butter or margarine
Prepared yellow mustard
1 pound baked Virginia ham, thinly sliced
1 pound barbecued or roast pork, thinly sliced
¾ pound hard salami
½ pound Swiss cheese, thinly sliced and cut into thin strips
Lengthwise slices of dill pickle
Iceberg lettuce, shredded (optional)
Very ripe tomatoes, thinly sliced (optional)
Mayonnaise

Cut bread into 6 pieces, each 8 inches long. Slice open lengthwise and spread butter on one side, mustard on the other. Divide ham, pork, and salami along one half of the bread. Spread Swiss cheese strips along the length of the sandwich and top with pickle slices. Add lettuce and tomato and spread mayonnaise over all. Close sandwich and wrap in a paper napkin or piece of wax paper and secure with a toothpick. To further improve flavor, warm in the oven or grill before serving.

Midnight Sandwich

Media Noche

If you're able to make your own soft egg buns for this recipe, all the better. But they are available at most bakeries and are a necessity for creating this sandwich, which is famous in Hispanic communities throughout the world. Made with garlic mayonnaise, it's a very special treat. Extra butter or olive oil is often spread on the inside of the sliced bread.

Serves 4

4 soft egg buns, halved
4 teaspoons prepared yellow mustard
2 tablespoons garlic mayonnaise (page 32)
1 pound thinly sliced roast pork
1 pound thinly sliced baked ham
12 thin slices imported Swiss cheese
8 thin slices dill pickle, plus more for garnish
Salt and pepper (optional)

Preheat the oven to 350° F. Spread mustard on top side of the buns and mayonnaise on the bottom. On the mayonnaise-coated side of the roll, pile on the meat slices, then the cheese, and 2 pickle slices per sandwich. Season with salt and pepper, then put tops on each sandwich and place on a well-greased baking pan. Place a heavy weight, such as a cast iron skillet, on top of the sandwiches. Bake until cheese melts and sandwiches are piping hot, 15 to 18 minutes. Serve with extra pickle garnish.

Elena Ruz Sandwich

Pida un Elena Ruz

When Elena Ruz Ulacia of Miami was young, she and her proper Cuban lady friends would spend afternoons on the porches of the old *casonas,* or large houses in Havana, gathering for gossip and tea. But often Elena and friends would go to Alvarez's Place, then known as El Carmilo, in the Vedado neighborhood.

El Carmilo prepared the following sandwich to Elena's specifications and it's been famous ever since, appearing on the menus of many casual Cuban restaurants. The combination, although it sounds a little strange, is surprisingly good.

Serves 1

1 egg bread roll, about the size of a 6-inch hero, sliced lengthwise
2 to 3 ounces strawberry preserves
3 ounces cream cheese
¼ pound roast breast of turkey

Toast both sides of split roll on the inside. Spread one side with cream cheese, the other side with strawberry preserves. Carefully place the turkey on the cream cheese side so that meat is equally distributed. Top with the strawberry side. Eat as is, or heat by placing sandwich inside a hot sandwich press or waffle iron.

Combine all marinade ingredients except pineapple and blend well with a fork or whisk. Add pineapple slices. Place chicken breasts in marinade, cover tightly, then refrigerate for about 2 hours. Drain and discard marinade, reserving pineapple slices.

Pan-grill breasts in olive oil for about 4 minutes on each side, or until cooked through, then remove from pan and set aside. Discard remaining oil. In the same pan, sauté pineapple slices until golden brown.

To assemble the sandwich, spread honey mustard on both sides of the Cuban bread. Add chicken breasts to bottom half. Top with mushrooms and slices of Monterey Jack cheese. Place top on and slice into 6 sandwiches.

Island-Grilled Chicken Sandwich

Pollo Isleño à la Parrilla con Pan Cubano

This chicken sandwich, which combines some of the best touches of the new Cuban cuisine, can be served for lunch or dinner. In smaller portions, it is an ideal appetizer. It is best to start the marination process early since the secret of this tangy dish lies in the melding of the flavors. **Serves 6**

MARINADE

1 cup vegetable oil
½ cup pineapple juice
Salt, to taste
½ teaspoon ground cumin
1 tablespoon chopped fresh cilantro
6 slices canned pineapple

SANDWICH

6 boneless skinned chicken breast halves
3 to 4 tablespoons olive oil
¾ cup honey mustard
1 loaf Cuban bread, sliced in half lengthwise and toasted
¾ cup sliced marinated mushrooms
12 thin slices Monterey Jack cheese

Desserts

Considering that much of the island's land has been devoted to raising sugar cane and the manufacture of sugar, it is no surprise that Cubans enjoy extra sweetening in the pot. Sugar is everywhere—the cane grows in backyards and is also sold in stick form in the markets. It was once common to see children nibbling on the bits of cane, sucking out the sweet sugar as they would an all-day sucker.

Cubans are famous for creating puddings, cakes, flans, and other items of decadent delight. But as in many European cultures, dessert can be a simple affair. Fresh fruits, especially yellow and pink guavas, are often eaten as a starter and a finish to a fine meal.

Rum Custard

Natilla al Ron

Here's an uncomplicated and very light custard. A good rum is essential when preparing this dessert; the better the flavor of the rum, or *ron,* the better the flavor of the custard. Use country-style heavy custard cups or a fancier demitasse style for a special occasion.

Serves 6

4 large egg yolks
½ cup granulated sugar
2 tablespoons cornstarch
2¾ cups whole milk
1 teaspoon vanilla extract
⅛ cup white rum
⅛ cup dark aged rum
3 maraschino cherries, stems removed,
 for garnish
Ground cinnamon, for garnish

In a mixing bowl, beat egg yolks vigorously until lemon colored. Add sugar and cornstarch and combine well. Set aside.

In a heavy saucepan, scald the milk. Add vanilla and both rums. Remove from heat and allow to cool for 10 to 15 minutes.

Slowly add egg yolk mixture to milk mixture, constantly stirring with a wire whisk. Cook slowly over very low heat until mixture begins to thicken; continue to stir constantly. Mixture should coat the back of a wooden spoon when ready.

Carefully pour mixture into small 4-ounce porcelain custard cups. Halve maraschino cherries and add one to the top of each. Sprinkle with cinnamon. Chill.

Bacon from Heaven

Tocino del Cielo

The name of this very classic Cuban dessert is highly misleading since bacon is found only in the title. Actually, aside from the fact that the dish itself is divine, the bacon reference comes from the crisp dark brown appearance of the caramel.

Serves 6

1 cup granulated sugar
½ cup water
9 egg yolks
1 teaspoon vanilla extract

Caramel-line 6 custard cups according to directions on page 25. Preheat the oven to 325° F.

Put sugar and water in a small saucepan and bring to a boil for a few minutes until sugar is fully dissolved.

Beat egg yolks in a bowl. Add sugar syrup and vanilla and stir to combine. Pour mixture into caramelized cups.

Set in a large rectangular pan filled with water to come halfway up sides of cups. Bake for about 35 minutes. Remove cups from water and let cool, then refrigerate. When ready to serve, invert cups on dessert dishes that have been lightly greased with butter.

Diplomatic Pudding

Pudín Diplomatico

This pudding transforms stale Cuban bread into a magnificent nutty, fruity dessert. Using fresh fruit cocktail will make all the difference in the world, whether the pudding is served warm or, as is more common, chilled and topped with whipped cream and a maraschino cherry. If you wish, prepare individual servings in small porcelain cups. **Serves 8**

CARAMELIZED SUGAR

½ cup granulated sugar
1 tablespoon unsalted butter or margarine
2 tablespoons water

PUDDING

3 slices stale white Cuban bread, crusts removed
1 (14-ounce) can sweetened condensed milk
¾ cup water
¼ teaspoon baking powder
3 egg yolks, beaten
1 tablespoon sweet vermouth
1 tablespoon all-purpose flour
1 teaspoon vanilla extract
1 cup fruit cocktail (preferably fresh), drained
Fresh whipped cream
Maraschino cherry

To prepare the caramelized sugar, preheat oven to 350° F. Place a 9-inch pie pan or other baking dish in the oven to preheat.

Mix the sugar, butter, and water in a small nonmetallic saucepan. Cook on medium to medium-high heat, stirring constantly until the mixture begins to bubble and turns a caramel brown. Be careful not to burn the mixture; this will take some practice.

Pour the caramelized sugar into the warm baking dish. Carefully and quickly, holding the dish with potholders, roll the caramel around the inside of the dish to coat its bottom and sides evenly. Set aside to cool.

To prepare the pudding, crumble the bread into a large mixing bowl and add the condensed milk, water, baking powder, egg yolks, vermouth, flour, and vanilla. Stir in the fruit cocktail. Pour mixture into the dish. Set baking dish in a pan. Fill with water until it comes about halfway up the side of the baking dish. Bake for about 50 minutes, or until a fork, when inserted in the pudding, comes out clean.

Remove dish from the pan of water and chill pudding. When cool, invert onto a platter and slice. Serve with dollops of fresh whipped cream and a maraschino cherry.

Rice Pudding with Raspberries and Toasted Almonds

Pudín de Arroz con Frambuesa y

Almendras Tostadas

This baked version of rice pudding is an example of how a basic Island classic has been transformed by the addition of a few ingredients, in this case the raspberries and almonds. **Serves 6**

¾ cup long-grain rice, cooked
1⅓ cups scalded milk
¼ cup granulated sugar
¼ teaspoon salt
2 eggs, beaten
1 teaspoon almond extract
1 (10-ounce) package frozen sweetened
    raspberries, thawed
2 teaspoons cornstarch
1 tablespoon granulated sugar
1 cup fresh raspberries, for garnish
1 cup toasted blanched slivered almonds,
    for garnish
Mint leaves, for garnish

Preheat the oven to 325° F.

Combine the cooked rice, milk, sugar, and salt. Whisk in the eggs and almond extract. Pour mixture into 6 small greased molds. Place molds in a large baking pan filled with hot water to come halfway up sides of cups. Bake about 30 minutes, or until a knife inserted in center comes out clean. Allow to cool.

To prepare sauce, combine the thawed raspberries, including their syrup, cornstarch, and sugar in a small heavy saucepan. Cook over medium heat, stirring constantly but gently for 5 to 7 minutes, or until sauce thickens. Strain mixture and cool.

To serve, pour equal amounts of raspberry sauce on individual serving plates. Invert molds onto sauce and garnish each serving with fresh raspberries, toasted almonds, and mint leaves.

Calabaza Pudding

Pudín de Calabaza

Cubans boil calabaza, steam it, and use it in myriad ways, but one of my favorites is in this delicious spicy pudding. Although this recipe calls for calabaza, butternut or orange winter squash can be substituted. Be sure to accompany with a respectable ice cream. **Serves 6 to 8**

2 tablespoons butter or margarine
⅓ cup all-purpose flour
2 cups whole milk
4 eggs, beaten
2 teaspoons ground cinnamon
1 teaspoon freshly grated nutmeg
½ teaspoon ground allspice
½ cup black seedless raisins
⅓ cup granulated sugar
2 cups cooked and mashed calabaza
1 quart vanilla ice cream

Preheat the oven to 400° F. Grease a 2-quart Pyrex dish.

In a saucepan, mix together the butter, flour, and milk until blended. Add the eggs, cinnamon, nutmeg, allspice, raisins, sugar, and calabaza and combine well. Pour into the prepared dish. Bake for 50 to 60 minutes, or until a knife inserted comes out clean.

Serve hot over vanilla ice cream.

In a large glass bowl, soak the bread in milk until saturated, 10 to 15 minutes. Using a large spoon, press down any floating bread into the milk.

In a separate large glass bowl, beat together the eggs, sugar, butter, lime zest, cinnamon, nutmeg, vanilla, and salt.

Sprinkle raisins, rum they were soaked in, and almonds on the bread and mix well. Add egg mixture to the bread mixture and mix together well. Pour into the caramel-lined casserole dish and place in a large pan half filled with hot water. Bake for 1 hour and 30 minutes, or until a knife inserted in the center comes out clean.

Bread Pudding of Hope

Pudín de Pan Esperanza

This is very much the queen of all puddings in most Hispanic communities. Even when stale and dry, the coarse Cuban bread used in this recipe retains its rich flavor. This is one of my favorite desserts because of the delightful aroma that permeates the household.

Some of my friends like to prepare it with half evaporated milk and fresh whole milk because of the creamy caramelized flavor it lends the pudding.

Serves 8 to 10

    6 cups diced day-old Cuban bread,
      crusts removed
    1 quart whole milk
    6 large eggs, slightly beaten
    1 cup granulated sugar
    4 tablespoons butter or margarine, melted
    1 teaspoon lime zest
    ½ teaspoon ground cinnamon
    ½ teaspoon grated nutmeg
    1 teaspoon vanilla extract
    Pinch of salt
    ½ cup raisins, soaked in 3 tablespoons
      dark rum
    ⅔ cup toasted blanched slivered almonds

Preheat the oven to 350° F. Caramel-line a 2-quart casserole dish according to directions on page 25.

Traditional Flan

Flan de Leche

F*lan de leche* is without a doubt the most popular Cuban dessert. This is an easy recipe, but it is important that directions are carefully followed in order to produce a perfectly textured flan. Use a good vanilla and fresh eggs; they will make a difference. It may take a bit of practice, but a few tries and you'll be a pro.

Serves 6

½ cup sugar, for caramelizing custard cups
2 cups whole milk
¼ teaspoon salt
6 large eggs
⅓ cup granulated sugar
1 teaspoon vanilla extract

Caramel-line 6 custard cups according to instructions on page 25. Preheat the oven to 300° F.

In a medium saucepan over medium-high heat, add milk and salt and scald. Remove from heat.

In a medium mixing bowl, add eggs, ⅓ cup sugar, and vanilla, and beat well (about 35 seconds) until light and foamy. Add the scalded milk to the egg mixture, stirring continually. Strain the egg mixture equally into the caramel-lined custard cups. Place cups in a shallow pan set on the middle oven rack, then pour warm water into the pan (*bain marie*) so that it reaches about two thirds up the side of the cups.

Cook about 1 hour, or until custard achieves a golden yellow crust (not brown) and is set. Do not allow water in pan to boil. If water begins to boil, add cold water to end the boiling. Shake the pan, and if custard is not firmly set, it is not done. Or test for doneness by inserting a toothpick or cake tester in the center of the custard. When it comes out clean, the flan is done. Remove from oven (and the *bain marie*), and allow to cool to room temperature.

After the flan has cooled to room temperature, cover with wax paper or plastic wrap and refrigerate until chilled. Run a sharp knife around the edge of each cup, then shake each cup slightly. Invert cups onto individual desert plates. Pour caramel over all so that it drapes down the sides to form a sauce.

Banana Flan with Coconut Rum Sauce

Flan de Guineo con Salsa de Ron Coco

This recipe is a variation on one that is served at the Heritage Grille, a Caribbean-style restaurant in St. Petersburg, on the West Coast of Florida. It's quick, easy, and delicious.

Serves 8

> 3 cups heavy cream
> 8 eggs, beaten
> 1 cup superfine sugar
> 1 ounce almond extract
> 1½ ounces banana liqueur
> ¾ cup flaked fresh coconut

RUM SAUCE

> 4 egg yolks
> 1 cup superfine sugar
> 2 tablespoons all-purpose flour
> 1 tablespoon cornstarch
> 1 quart whole milk
> 3 ounces dark rum
> ½ (15-ounce) can cream of coconut
> 1 teaspoon vanilla extract

Caramel-line a 2-quart casserole or mold according to instructions on page 25. Preheat the oven to 300° F.

In a large bowl, mix together the cream, eggs, sugar, almond extract, and banana liqueur. Fill caramelized mold to about ½ inch from the top. Sprinkle with flaked coconut. Place mold in a large shallow pan and pour in hot water halfway up the mold. Bake for about 1 hour.

To prepare the rum sauce, beat together the yolks and the sugar in a medium saucepan until smooth. Add flour and cornstarch and set aside.

Pour milk into a large saucepan and heat until it comes to a boil. Add rum, cream of coconut, and vanilla, then add this to the egg yolk mixture and stir to combine. Bring to a boil and remove from heat. Strain and serve over the flan.

Guava Pudding

Pudín de Guayaba

The aromatic guava is a lovely introduction to the Cuban culinary experience. You can use either pink or yellow guavas. I prefer the sweet taste of the pink variety.

Serves 4 to 6

> ½ cup granulated sugar
> ½ teaspoon ground cinnamon
> ½ teaspoon grated nutmeg
> 2½ cups fresh bread crumbs
> 4 tablespoons butter or margarine
> 2 cups seeded and diced guavas
> ¼ cup water
> 2 tablespoons fresh lime juice

Preheat the oven to 350° F.

Blend together the sugar, cinnamon, and nutmeg. In a separate bowl, mix together 2¼ cups of the bread crumbs with butter, using a fork to stir until crumbly.

Cover the bottom of a buttered 8 × 8 × 2 -inch square pan with the remaining ¼ cup bread crumbs and add 1 cup guavas. Sprinkle with the sugar mixture. Repeat with remaining guavas and cover all with bread-crumb mixture.

Mix together the water and lime juice and pour over entire pudding. Dot with butter or margarine and cover with foil. Bake for 40 to 45 minutes, removing the foil after 20 minutes. Serve with cream and sugar.

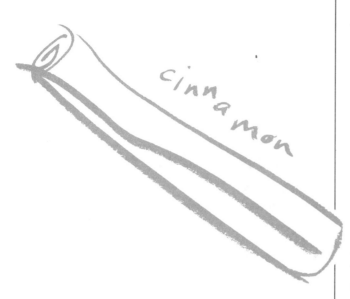

cinnamon

In the top of a double boiler, mix together the cream, sugar, flour, and vanilla with a hand mixer.

Bring the milk just to a boil. Pour the hot milk into the cream mixture and beat well until very smooth. Cook in the top of a double boiler until mixture thickens.

In a mixing bowl, beat the yolks until smooth. Pour the hot mixture into the yolks, stirring fast. Return the mixture to the double boiler and add the butter. Continue to cook for about 30 minutes, stirring frequently to prevent burning. Pour into a 2-quart rectangular Pyrex serving dish. Place in the refrigerator to cool.

For the topping, combine sugar with the cinnamon and sprinkle evenly over top of cooled custard. To caramelize, place under the broiler until sugar is melted and browned. Cut into brownie-size squares and serve with guava paste slices on the side.

*See page 10.

Cream Squares with Guava

Panelitas de Crema Varadero

con Guayaba

These classic custard squares, named after the beautiful Varadero Beach in Cuba, require a good deal of mixing, but the result is well worth the effort. The creamy texture of the custard combined with a small slice of the guava paste makes a tantalizing and richly fruity treat. Your success will depend on how carefully you cook the custard.   **Serves 6**

    1 cup light cream
    1 cup superfine sugar
    ¼ cup all-purpose flour
    1 teaspoon vanilla extract
    3 cups whole milk
    8 egg yolks
    1 tablespoon butter or margarine
    ¼ cup granulated sugar
    1 tablespoon ground cinnamon
    Guava paste (purchased or homemade),*
      sliced

Whim of Havana

Capricho Habanero

This rich presentation, once popular in Havana, is topped with meringue and relished by many Cubans. It's a winner.

Serves 8

MERINGUE

3 egg whites, at room temperature
½ teaspoon vanilla extract
¼ teaspoon cream of tartar
6 tablespoons granulated sugar

FILLING

3 eggs yolks, at room temperature
¾ cup granulated sugar
2 cups evaporated milk
1 cinnamon stick
1 teaspoon vanilla extract
10 slices heavy white bread, such as day-old Cuban bread, crusts removed
1 cup guava marmalade or other fruit marmalade

To prepare meringue, beat egg whites until whipped. Add vanilla and cream of tartar and beat until soft peaks form. Very gradually add the sugar, beating until stiff and all sugar is completely dissolved. Set aside or, if using later, refrigerate.

In a saucepan, beat the yolks with sugar over low heat for a few minutes. Add milk and cinnamon stick and cook a few minutes until thick. Add vanilla and let cool. Remove cinnamon stick.

Preheat the oven to 350° F.

Soak bread slices in yolk mixture until saturated. Place 4 whole slices and 1 slice cut in half on the bottom of a 13 × 9 × 2-inch Pyrex baking dish. Spoon marmalade over to cover. Place the other 4 slices of bread and 1 slice cut in half on the marmalade, then spread meringue over bread pieces, sealing meringue to the edges of the dish.

Place in the oven and bake until meringue peaks turn golden brown, about 12 minutes. Cool and refrigerate until ready to serve.

Guava Fool

Loca de Guayaba

The word *loca,* or fool, once was a term denoting love and affection. The meaning has changed over the years, but the dessert has remained a favorite. **Serves 6 to 8**

10 ripe guavas, trimmed and sliced into 1-inch pieces
3 to 4 tablespoons sifted confectioners' sugar
½ cup heavy whipping cream, whipped
Mint leaves and chopped blanched slivered almonds, for garnish

Put the guavas and 2 tablespoons of the sugar into the container of a food processor. Purée for 10 to 12 seconds, or less, depending on the ripeness of the guavas. Add the remaining sugar (according to sweetness desired) and purée the mixture for a few more seconds.

Push the mixture through a food mill or a wire strainer, then pour into a glass bowl and chill for at least 1 hour. Fold the whipped cream into the guava purée, making an attractive swirling pattern.

Garnish with mint leaves and chopped slivered almonds. Serve chilled.

Fried Milk with Pineapple Sauce

Leche Frita con Salsa de Piña

Fried milk is a creamy custard with a crunchy exterior, served alone or with a sauce. The pineapple sauce in this version adds a distinct combination of flavors. In preparing this dessert, it is important to allow time for the mixture to chill. After chilling, it only takes about 15 minutes to complete.   **Serves 4 to 6**

2 cups whole milk
¼ cup cornstarch mixed with
  1 tablespoon milk
½ cup plus 1 tablespoon granulated sugar
1 teaspoon almond extract
½ cup all-purpose flour
1 egg, at room temperature
4 tablespoons butter or margarine

PINEAPPLE SAUCE

2 tablespoons granulated sugar
1 tablespoon all-purpose flour
1 egg, slightly beaten
3 tablespoons cold water
¾ cup unsweetened pineapple juice
½ cup orange juice
2 tablespoons lime juice
½ cup water

In a medium saucepan, heat the milk, cornstarch mixture, sugar, and almond extract. Stir constantly with a wooden spoon until thickened.

Pour into an 8 × 8 × 2-inch glass pan. Chill to almost freezing so that pudding is well set.

When ready to serve, cut into small squares. Sprinkle with flour, then dip into egg to coat, and fry in butter or margarine.

To prepare pineapple sauce, mix sugar and flour together. Combine egg with water and beat slightly. Add egg combination to sugar-flour mix-

ture. In a medium saucepan, combine pineapple, orange, and lime juices over low heat. Slowly add egg mixtures to juices and cook over low heat until thickened. Serve warm over fried milk squares.

Brazo Gitano

This traditional custard roll contains a typical cast of island characters: rum, fresh lime, sugar, and fresh shaved cinnamon. This elegant dessert is often prepared for special occasions and is considered a very "important" dessert in the minds of most Cubans.

Egg yolks and *natilla* add a very special richness; only a small slice is necessary. This variation on a recipe by Clarita Garcia, who once owned the Las Novedades restaurant in Ybor City, has fewer eggs than most, but is just as delicious.

Serves 6 to 8

8 egg whites
8 tablespoons granulated sugar
8 egg yolks
5 tablespoons all-purpose flour
½ teaspoon salt
1 teaspoon lime juice mixed with ½ teaspoon lime zest
¼ cup confectioners' sugar

SYRUP

½ cup granulated sugar
½ cup water
¼ cup rum

NATILLA

1½ cups whole milk
3 tablespoons cornstarch
4 tablespoons granulated sugar
Pinch of salt
1 teaspoon vanilla extract
Peel from 1 lime
1 cinnamon stick
2 egg yolks

CREAMY MERINGUE

3 egg whites
½ pint heavy whipping cream
4 tablespoons granulated sugar

GARNISH

Freshly ground cinnamon
Chocolate curls
Fresh mint leaves

Prepare a 15 × 10 × 1-inch jelly roll pan by lining with waxed paper. Grease paper liberally with margarine. Preheat the oven to 350° F.

Chill a mixer bowl and beaters, then beat egg whites until soft peaks form. Gradually add the sugar, beating continually until the texture of meringue. In a separate bowl, beat the egg yolks slightly, then pour over the meringue and fold in until well combined.

In another bowl, combine the flour and salt and sprinkle over mixture and fold in until well combined. Stir in the lime juice and zest. Pour mixture into the jelly roll pan, spreading evenly.

Bake for 20 to 25 minutes, or until a toothpick inserted in the center comes out clean. Cool.

Dampen a kitchen towel and then sprinkle with the powdered sugar. When cake is cool, invert it onto the towel and gently peel off the wax paper.

With a very sharp knife, cut off any edges that have become too crisp. Starting at the wide end, roll up the cake with the aid of the dampened towel. Set aside while preparing the syrup.

Put sugar and water in a small saucepan. Bring to a boil, and when sugar becomes totally dissolved, add the rum, blending thoroughly. Pour into a Pyrex bowl and set aside to cool.

For the *natilla,* combine the milk and cornstarch in the top of a double boiler. Beat with an electric beater or whisk until the cornstarch is completely dissolved. Add the sugar, salt, vanilla, lime peel, and cinnamon stick. Stir to blend well, then place the pan over low direct heat and cook, stirring continually, until mixture thickens. Be careful to stir so mixture will not stick to pan.

In a bowl, beat the egg yolks until light, then add a little of the hot mixture to the eggs, stirring briskly to avoid curdling, then return to hot mixture in the double boiler. Cook about 5 minutes, stirring, until mixture becomes creamy and thick. Remove the lime peel and cinnamon stick and discard. Cool mixture completely.

Prepare the meringue by combining the egg whites with the whipping cream in a chilled mixing bowl. Beat until light and creamy. Slowly add the sugar, beating constantly until mixture is thickened.

Unroll the cooled cake and sprinkle lightly with half the rum syrup. Spread the cooled cream over the cake to within 1 inch of the edges. Dust with cinnamon, then very carefully reroll the cake and place on a colorful platter with the seam on the bottom. Dribble with the rest of the syrup, or to desired consistency. Some prefer their cake drier than others.

Using a steel spatula, coat the roll with the meringue and sprinkle with chocolate curls. Slice and serve with fresh mint leaves.

Fresh Mango-Coconut Cake

Torta con Nevado de Mango y Coco

Ever since I was a little girl I have loved the frosting much better than the cake. Perhaps that's why I've sought out unusually delicious toppings. Since this frosting will be only as good as the ingredients it's prepared with, it is of utmost importance to use fresh coconut. You'll know it's fresh if the flesh is white and oily and smells fruity and pleasant.

You can make your own pound cake for this recipe if you prefer, but purchasing the cake saves lots of time and effort that you can put toward the rest of the menu.   **Makes 1 cake**

   2 tablespoons all-purpose flour
   1 cup 2% milk
   ¼ pound butter or margarine, softened
   ¾ cup granulated sugar
   1 teaspoon vanilla extract
   1 cup toasted blanched slivered almonds, chopped
   1 cup grated fresh coconut
   1 pound cake
   ½ cup sliced fresh mangoes*

In a medium saucepan, whisk flour into a small portion of the milk, then add the remaining milk and cook over medium heat, stirring, until thick. Let cool.

In a medium bowl, cream the butter with the sugar. Add the cooled milk mixture and beat well until fluffy. Add vanilla, almonds, and coconut. Combine thoroughly. Cover pound cake with frosting and top with fresh mango slices.

*See page 23 for how to cut a mango.

Rum Balls

Bolitas de Ron

These unbaked traditional rum balls are a lovely ending to a fine Cuban meal. Using a good quality cocoa will ensure the best results.   **Makes about 2½ dozen**

   1 cup finely crushed vanilla wafers
   1 cup confectioners' sugar
   1½ cups chopped pecans
   1 tablespoon cocoa
   ¼ cup corn syrup
   ¼ cup white rum
   Superfine sugar

In a large mixing bowl, combine the wafer crumbs, sugar, 1 cup of the pecans, and cocoa. Add the corn syrup and rum and mix together until it holds together well; it will be sticky. Add more syrup if necessary. Scoop by teaspoonfuls then roll into balls.

Roll half of the balls in superfine sugar and the other half in remaining ½ cup chopped pecans. To store, pack loosely in an airtight container and keep in a cool place.

Coconut Bars with Guava Jelly

Barras de Coco con Guayaba

When you taste this distinct combination of flavors, you may gain a new appreciation of each of the ingredients. The sweet coconut meat is enhanced by equally sweet almonds, while the guava jelly rounds out this toothsome trio. **Makes 12 squares**

PASTRY

¼ cup granulated sugar
¼ pound unsalted butter, softened
½ teaspoon vanilla extract
4 egg whites
1½ cups cake flour

FILLING

½ cup guava jelly*
1 cup packaged sweetened coconut
½ teaspoon freshly grated nutmeg
¼ teaspoon ground allspice
¼ cup blanched slivered almonds, chopped
1½ teaspoons ground cinnamon
¼ teaspoon vanilla extract
2 tablespoons water

MERINGUE

4 egg whites, at room temperature
⅓ cup granulated sugar

Preheat the oven to 375° F.

To prepare the pastry, cream the sugar with butter and vanilla. Add egg whites and flour and blend until smooth. Pour the batter into an 11 × 7 × 2-inch pan and smooth evenly with a rubber spatula. Bake 10 to 15 minutes, or until golden brown. Remove and cool for a few minutes. Turn oven up to 400° F.

Using a spatula, evenly coat the top of the baked pastry with guava jelly. Combine remaining filling ingredients and pour on top of jelly, but do not mix into it. Carefully spread coconut filling to cover jelly. With your hands, lightly press down on filling.

Chill the bowl and beaters.

Prepare the meringue topping by beating the egg whites until frothy. Slowly add sugar and beat until very stiff.

Spread meringue on top of coconut filling. Using a teaspoon, make peaks of frothy eggs whites. Or pipe meringue on top. Bake for about 5 minutes at 400° F, or until lightly browned. Cut into squares to serve, hot or cool.

*Available at most Hispanic supermarkets and Hispanic sections of your supermarket. You can substitute strawberry, orange, or any other fruit jelly.

Caramel, Chocolate, and Almond Squares

Panelitas de Caramelo, Chocolate, y Almendras

Here is a special-occasion dessert I invented that is made sensational by my addition of white chocolate and Kahlúa. These squares are also a perfect complement to an afternoon tea.   **Makes 32 squares**

    2 cups all-purpose flour
    2 tablespoons powdered milk
    1 tablespoon baking powder
    ½ teaspoon salt
    ½ pound butter or margarine, softened
    2 cups extrafine light brown sugar
    2 eggs, slightly beaten
    1 teaspoon vanilla extract
    1 tablespoon Kahlúa or other liqueur
    1 (10-ounce) package Hershey's milk
      chocolate chunks
    ¾ cup toasted blanched slivered almonds

Preheat the oven to 325° F. Lightly grease two 8-inch square Pyrex baking pans or 1 larger pan.

Sift flour and powdered milk together with the baking powder and salt. Put aside.

In a separate large bowl, beat the butter until smooth. Add brown sugar, eggs, vanilla, and liqueur and beat well. Add sifted ingredients and the chocolate chunks and pour mixture into pans. Spread evenly. Decorate top with almonds. Bake for about 30 minutes, or until top is golden brown (inside will be moist). Cool and cut into squares.

CALABAZA

Kisses

Besos

Meringue kisses are often prepared for very special occasions. I added the pecans and coconut to provide even more flavor. The secret to the success in this recipe is the baking time—the kisses must bake for 1 hour and then sit in the oven for another 2 hours. Don't cheat! Keep the oven closed until the indicated time is over.   **Makes about 30 squares**

    8 egg whites, at room temperature
    2 cups granulated sugar
    1 teaspoon cream of tartar
    1 teaspoon vanilla extract
    ½ cup packaged sweetened coconut
    1 cup chopped pecans

Preheat the oven to 275° F. Lightly grease a 13 × 9 × 2-inch baking pan.

Whip the egg whites in a nonaluminum bowl until foamy. Slowly add the sugar and continue to whip until stiff. Add the cream of tartar and beat until well combined. By hand, fold in the vanilla, coconut, and pecans.

Pour mixture into prepared pan. Bake until meringue becomes hard on the outside, about 1 hour or more. Turn off heat and let dry with oven door closed for at least 2 hours. Remove from oven and carefully cut into small squares.

Calabaza Pie

Pastel de Calabaza

W hile calabaza is usually served as a vegetable, with the right seasonings it can also be the base of a savory pie. The flavor and texture of this dish make it a distant cousin to our own pumpkin pie. **Makes 1 (10-inch) pie**

1½ cups peeled, cooked, and mashed
 calabaza
¼ cup light brown sugar
¼ cup granulated sugar
½ teaspoon salt
1 tablespoon ground cinnamon
1½ teaspoons ground ginger
1 teaspoon ground nutmeg
½ teaspoon ground cloves
2 eggs, slightly beaten
1¼ cups whole milk
1 (14½-ounce) can whole evaporated milk
1 unbaked 10-inch pie shell
Whipped cream, for garnish
Ground cinnamon, for garnish

Preheat the oven to 400° F.

In a large glass bowl, combine the calabaza, sugars, salt, cinnamon, ginger, nutmeg, and cloves. Mix well. Blend in eggs, milk, and evaporated milk. Pour into unbaked pastry shell. Bake for 50 minutes, or until a knife inserted halfway between center and edge comes out clean. Cool.

Serve with a dollop of whipped cream and a sprinkle of cinnamon.

Baked Mango Treat

Postre Camaguey

T his traditional Cuban favorite is very rich; you may want to serve only small pieces.
Serves 8 to 16

MERINGUE

4 egg whites
½ teaspoon vanilla extract
¼ teaspoon cream of tartar
1 tablespoon granulated sugar

2 cups granulated sugar
2 (12-ounce) cans plus 1 cup evaporated milk
4 eggs yolks
1 cinnamon stick
1 teaspoon vanilla extract
1 sponge cake
2 cups very ripe sliced mangoes with juice, or
 2 (17-ounce) cans sliced peaches, drained

Chile the bowl and beaters.

To prepare meringue, beat egg whites with vanilla and cream of tartar until soft peaks form in bowl. Gradually add the sugar, beating until stiff and all sugar is completely dissolved. Set aside.

In a large saucepan, combine sugar, milk, egg yolks, and cinnamon stick. Cook over medium-high heat, stirring continually so that mixture does not burn. When the pudding reaches a thickened consistency, remove from heat. Remove cinnamon stick. Add vanilla and combine well.

Preheat the oven to 350° F.

Cut sponge cake in half crosswise, then cut each half again lengthwise.

Place a layer of the thickened milk mixture in two 8½ × 4 × 2½-inch Pyrex baking dishes. Fit 2 of the sponge cake portions on top of the milk mixture, then a layer of mangoes or peaches. Add the meringue over all and bake for about 12 minutes, or until meringue becomes golden brown.

Fried Yuca-Malanga Puffs

Buñuelo de Yuca y Malanga Amarilla

These crisp fritters with the anise-flavored sugar syrup are easily addictive and have become staple items at many Cuban cafés in Hispanic areas throughout the United States. Here's a variation on a recipe from Victor's in New York.   **Serves 5 to 6**

3 pounds yuca, peeled, cut into 5-inch
   chunks, boiled, and cubed
1 pound yellow malangas, peeled, cut into
   chunks, and boiled
Olive oil or other vegetable oil, for frying
1 egg, beaten
¼ teaspoon aniseed
½ teaspoon salt
¼ cup anise-flavored sugar syrup

SYRUP

1½ cups granulated sugar
½ cup water
2 star anise*
1½ teaspoons lime zest
½ teaspoon lime juice
1 tablespoon Curaçao liqueur
Dash of vanilla extract

Finely grind yuca and malanga in a meat grinder or with a mortar and pestle. Heat oil in a deep-fryer to 350° F.

In a large bowl, mix the yuca and malanga with the egg, aniseed, and salt. While working the dough with your hands, add the anise-flavored syrup gradually to soften, then roll small amounts of dough into a figure eight. Fry a few at a time until golden brown. Drain on brown paper bags or paper towels.

To prepare the syrup, combine all ingredients except the Curaçao and vanilla extract in a medium-size heavy saucepan. Bring to a boil and then simmer until slightly thick, at the point where syrup coats the back of a spoon. Add the Curaçao

and vanilla and blend well until hot. Pour a small pool of the syrup on top of each fritter. Serve piping hot.

*A commonly used spice and tea flavoring, but also used to flavor liqueurs.

Babalu Banana Fritters

Friturus de Guineo Babalu

Fritters are made using a variety of fruits prevalent in Cuban cuisine, but banana fritters are probably served most often. Be sure to use unbruised ripened fruit and light olive oil that won't mask the flavor of the bananas.

Serves 6 to 8

Light vegetable oil, for deep-frying
1½ cups sifted all-purpose flour
½ cup granulated sugar
½ teaspoon salt
2 teaspoons baking powder
1 large egg, beaten
⅓ cup whole milk
2 teaspoons light olive oil
4 medium-size ripe bananas, peeled and cut
   crosswise into quarters
Ground cinnamon, for sprinkling

Heat vegetable oil in deep-fryer to 375° F.

Sift 1 cup of the flour together with the granulated sugar, salt, and baking powder. Beat egg and milk together well. Add to flour mixture by beating in with a whisk until smooth. Add oil.

Carefully roll bananas in remaining ½ cup of flour so that all sides are covered, then dip into batter. Deep-fry for 4 to 6 minutes. Sprinkle with cinnamon and serve with vanilla yogurt.

Pickled Pineapple

Piña Encurtida

Cubans love pineapple, most often fresh cut into small pieces, but they also enjoy the canned variety. This recipe calls for canned pineapple because its sweetness and thicker juice lends itself to the pickling process.

Serves 4 to 6

2 (1-pound 4-ounce) cans pineapple slices
   with juice
½ cup granulated sugar
2 cinnamon sticks
¾ cup cider vinegar
8 whole cloves
Pinch of salt

Drain juice from the pineapple into a medium saucepan. Set pineapple slices aside. Add sugar, cinnamon, vinegar, cloves, and salt to saucepan. Bring to a full boil. Add pineapple slices and bring to a second boil. Cool. Refrigerate and serve cold or heated. You can also serve this as a side dish at dinner.

Bread Fritters

Torrejas

Equally at home on the breakfast menu or as a dessert, these rich fritters are flavored with sherry. Topped off with maple syrup, you'll not be able to resist.   **Serves 4**

Vegetable oil, for, deep-frying
4 (1-inch) slices stale Cuban bread,
   crusts removed
4 tablespoons dry sherry
1 (14-ounce) can sweetened condensed milk
   mixed with 1 tablespoon whole milk
3 eggs, well beaten
1 cup confectioners' sugar
2 teaspoons ground cinnamon
Pure maple syrup

Heat vegetable oil in a deep-fryer to 325° F, or use a heavy skillet.

Place the bread slices in a large flat dish. Pour 1 tablespoon of sherry onto each slice, spreading evenly. Dip slices in the milk, coating thoroughly, then dip each slice in the beaten eggs, coating each piece well. Deep-fry until golden brown. Drain on paper towels or brown paper. Sprinkle each piece with sugar, cinnamon, and syrup.

Fresh Mango-Almond Bake

Mejunje de Mango y Almendras

This dessert is perfect for last-minute planning because it is so simple to prepare. It's similar to our traditional apple crisp, but the lovely almonds and cinnamon make it a show stopper rather than an old standby.

Serves 6 to 8

1 cup unsifted all-purpose flour
1 cup plus 2 tablespoons granulated sugar
½ cup toasted blanched slivered almonds
1½ teaspoons ground cinnamon
1 egg, well beaten
3 pounds fresh mangoes, peeled and cut
  into 1-inch pieces*
¼ pound butter or margarine, melted

Preheat the oven to 375° F.

In a medium glass bowl, combine flour, 1 cup sugar, almonds, cinnamon, and egg and mix until crumbly. In a separate bowl, mix mango pieces with 2 tablespoons of sugar.

Place mangoes in an 8 × 12-inch baking pan and sprinkle flour mixture over all. Drizzle the melted butter over the crumbs. Bake for about 30 minutes, or until top is brown and crusty. Serve warm with frozen vanilla yogurt.

*See page 23 for how to cut a mango.

Stewed Guava Shells with Cream Cheese

Cascos de Guayaba con Queso Crema

Fruit and cheese finales to a fine dinner are common in most cuisines, but in this relationship, the smooth texture of the cream cheese plays beautifully against the piquant flavors of the lime juice and guava shells. Use the Mexican variety of guava with egg-size fruit and pink or white centers, the Catley, with small fruit in yellow or dark red, or the more common plum-size guava with pink centers. The best varieties to look for have few seeds and generous pulp.

Serves 4

12 ripe whole guavas
1 cup water
¼ cup fresh lime juice
Grated rind of 1 large lime
½ cup granulated sugar
1 (8-ounce) package cream cheese, softened

Rinse guavas well and remove blemishes. Remove bud end with the point of a sharp knife. Halve guavas, then scoop out seeds and pulp. Put water in a saucepan and bring to a boil. Add lime juice, zest, and sugar. Add guavas and cook, turning, for 6 to 9 minutes, until limp and soft. Refrigerate in syrup for a few hours to let flavors meld. Fill shells with cooked guavas and softened cream cheese, or cut in half and serve with hunks of cream cheese cut into 1-inch pieces. Pour remaining syrup over all.

Fruit Compote with Sparkling Wine

Compota de Frutas con Cava

This hot compote may seem a strange mix, but the sweet blends with the tart with the help of a lovely *cava*, or sparkling wine.

Serves 4

2 mangoes, peeled and thinly sliced*
1 pineapple, peeled and thinly sliced
2 Granny Smith apples, peeled and thinly sliced
4 ripe plums, thinly sliced
1 tablespoon butter or margarine, chopped into small pieces
1 (750 ml) bottle sparkling white wine, preferably a Spanish cava
Fresh mint, for garnish

Preheat the oven to 475° F.

Place fruit on a large piece of heavy aluminum foil and dot with butter. Fold up the edges tightly to make a pouch, so that juices will not come out. Pour the wine over all then seal the pouch. Place foil-wrapped fruit in a metal pan. Bake for 25 to 30 minutes. Carefully unwrap fruit mixture and pour into compote glasses. Serve immediately, garnished with fresh mint.

*See page 23 for how to cut a mango.

Tropical Cobbler

Bebida de Vino y Frutas Tropicales

This is a refreshing *nuevo Cubano* dessert and the recipe can be used as a framework for any combination of tropical and native American fruit.

Serves 6

1 teaspoon ground cinnamon
½ teaspoon grated nutmeg
½ teaspoon ground allspice
½ cup plus 1 tablespoon granulated sugar
1 teaspoon cornstarch
4 ripe mangoes, peeled and diced*
3 sweet carambola (star fruit),† diced
1 pint blueberries
1 teaspoon lime juice
¼ pound butter or margarine
½ cup whole milk
1 egg, slightly beaten
1½ cups all-purpose flour
1 tablespoon baking powder

Preheat the oven to 375° F. Generously grease a 9 × 12-inch baking pan.

In a small bowl, blend the cinnamon, nutmeg, allspice, 1 tablespoon sugar, and cornstarch. Add fruits and lime juice and toss together until thoroughly blended. Spread fruit evenly in prepared pan.

To prepare the topping, melt butter in a saucepan. Add milk, the remaining ½ cup sugar, and egg and beat well. In a bowl, blend the flour and baking powder together. Add to butter-egg mixture and blend completely. Spread evenly over fruit mixture. Bake for about 30 minutes, or until a toothpick comes out clean. Serve with a scoop of vanilla or mango ice cream.

*See page 23 for how to cut a mango.
†Available at most supermarkets.

Mango Dumplings

Pastelitos de Mango

These delightful light mango dumplings will take time to make, but the surprise inside is worth it.

Makes 8 generous servings

PASTRY

2 cups all-purpose flour, sifted
Salt, to taste
¼ pound butter or margarine plus 3
    tablespoons shortening*
¼ cup water

FRUIT AND CINNAMON MIXTURE

2 cups diced fresh ripe mango†
⅔ cup granulated sugar
2 teaspoons freshly ground cinnamon
½ teaspoon freshly grated nutmeg
½ teaspoon ground allspice
1 teaspoon lemon juice
Butter or margarine

SYRUP

1⅓ cups granulated sugar
2¾ cups water
4 tablespoons butter or margarine
1 teaspoon ground cinnamon
½ teaspoon freshly grated nutmeg

To prepare the pastry, pour flour and salt into a medium bowl. Cut in the butter and shortening with a pastry blender. Using a tablespoon, sprinkle water over the mixture, about 1 tablespoon at a time, until all is moistened. Roll into a ball on a floured board. Divide the ball into 8 equal portions. Form into 8 squares, using a sharp knife to make the edges even.

Preheat the oven to 425° F.

To prepare the fruit blend, combine the diced mango with the cinnamon mixture ingredients, except the butter, and mix well.

Fill the center of each pastry with 2 tablespoons of the fruit mixture. Dot with butter or margarine and twist the pastry to enclose the filling.

Prepare the syrup by combining all the syrup ingredients in a saucepan. Boil for 3 to 4 minutes. Pour over pastry. Bake for 40 to 60 minutes, or until pastry browns. Serve with a scoop of ice cream on the side, garnished with mint sprigs.

*May use margarine or lard as some Cubans do.
†See page 23 for how to cut a mango.

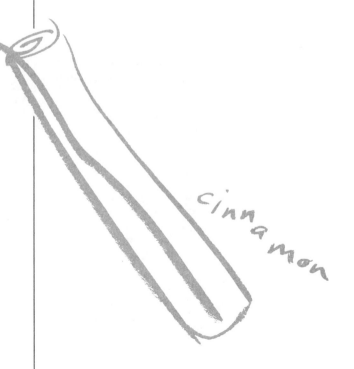

cinnamon

Honey-Baked Plantains

Plátanos con Miel Horneados

This recipe displays· the versatile robust plantain at its best. You can serve it as a sweet side dish with ham or pork, or by adding a scoop of ice cream or yogurt, as a rich dessert. Use the best honey, fresh orange juice, and blackened plantains for best results.   **Serves 4**

**4 very ripe plantains, peeled and cut in half
   lengthwise***
**1 tablespoon butter or margarine, melted,
   with 1 teaspoon pure olive oil**
¼ cup honey
1½ tablespoons orange juice
½ teaspoon lime juice
½ cup chopped pecans
½ cup heavy cream, whipped (optional)

Preheat the oven to 375° F. Using a pastry brush, coat plantains with butter-oil mixture and place cut side down in an ovenproof 13 × 9 × 2-inch dish.

In a small bowl, combine honey with orange and lime juices. Mix together well to incorporate the thick honey with the juices. Pour mixture over plantains. Sprinkle with pecans. Bake for about 20 minutes, turning plantains over and coating with the juice mixture several times during baking. Serve on warmed dessert plates, pouring baking juice over all. Add a dollop of whipped cream on the side.

*See page 23 for how to peel plantains.

Soursop Star Mousse

Mousse de Guanábana

This dessert can be spotted at the most fashionable Cuban restaurants in Florida. Soursop, a cigar-shaped black fruit with a bright green skin covered with soft thorns, has a sweet-sour flavor with a lovely aroma. Fresh soursop appears occasionally in shops, but you can almost always find it frozen in Hispanic markets.

This is a variation on a recipe given to me by Luis Zalamea, a native Colombian married to my friend Beba, who grew up in Havana.   **Serves 4**

1 (16-ounce) package frozen soursop
½ cup heavy cream
¼ cup fresh lime juice
2 egg whites
Pinch of salt
⅓ cup granulated sugar
1 sweet carambola (star fruit), thinly sliced*

Thaw soursop and pour into the container of a blender. Purée with the heavy cream. Add lime juice.

In a chilled deep nonmetallic mixing bowl, beat egg whites until they become frothy. Add salt and sugar and continue to beat until peaks are formed. Add in soursop mixture and then spoon into small bowls or champagne glasses. Garnish each with a slice of the carambola. Refrigerate for at least 3 hours before serving.

*There are a number of varieties of this star-shaped fruit. Ask your produce manager to help you find a sweet one, as many of them are sour.

Plantains with Rum Caramel

Plátanos con Ron Acaramelado

Here's a simple yet elegant dessert that is rich with the flavors of the island. For this recipe the plantains should be totally black and slightly wilted. When peeled, the pulp will have a golden red color; this indicates a very high concentration of natural sugars. Be careful not to overcook, because at this stage the plantain will become almost liquefied.   **Serves 4**

    6 tablespoons unsalted butter
    ¼ cup granulated sugar
    ⅓ cup fresh orange juice
    1 tablespoon grated orange rind
    ⅓ cup aged dark rum
    4 ripe plantains, peeled and cut diagonally
        into slices*

Cook butter and sugar in a large skillet over low heat for about 5 minutes, or until sugar begins to caramelize and separates from the butter. Add orange juice, rind, and dark rum to pan. Shake the pan to deglaze the caramel. Add plantain slices and cook, turning once, until they are tender and golden brown. Serve while warm with vanilla ice cream or frozen yogurt.

*See page 23 for how to peel plantains.

Mamey Sapote Ice Cream

Mantecado de Mamey Sapote

Mamey sapote, also known as *sapodilla*, is usually large with a rough, brownish outside. Its flesh is a beautiful salmon color with the consistency of an apple. When it ripens, it becomes very sweet and tastes like a combination of pears and brown sugar.

This fruit Cubans are so very fond of is not easy to find fresh, so many people settle for a frozen version found in most Hispanic markets. It is rarely cooked and most often served fresh or in cold preparations, such as this ice cream, and in *mamey batidos,* the Cuban answer to the milkshake.

It's important to serve this classic-style ice cream immediately. It does not store well.

Serves 4

    ½ cup granulated sugar
    ½ cup corn syrup
    Dash of salt
    1 cup whole milk
    1 cup puréed mamey sapote*
    Juice of 1 lime
    2 eggs
    1 cup heavy whipping cream
    Fresh lime slices, for garnish

Mix together sugar, corn syrup, salt, and milk. Add the mamey sapote purée and lime juice and mix well. Beat the eggs, add to the fruit mixture, and mix thoroughly. Whip the cream and fold in. Pour into ice cube trays, cover, and freeze. Stir a few times during the freezing process. Serve garnished with fresh lime slices.

*Available at most Hispanic markets.

Fresh Mango Ice Cream

Helado de Mango Fresco

Mangoes possess a spicy peachlike flavor, yet more intense and perfumy. Choose one that is about as tender as an avocado when ripe.

Makes about 16 (1-cup) servings

4 cups mashed mango pulp*
1 cup granulated sugar
Juice of 1½ limes
5 eggs
1 tablespoon cornstarch
1½ pints half-and-half
1 teaspoon salt
3 cups heavy cream
2 teaspoons vanilla extract
Fresh lime slices, for garnish

Mix mango pulp, sugar, and lime juice. Refrigerate.

Make a custard by mixing the eggs, cornstarch, half-and-half, and salt together in the top of a double boiler and cook, stirring occasionally, until it becomes thick enough to coat a spoon. Remove from heat and cool. Place in refrigerator for 1 to 2 hours.

When ready to make the ice cream, whip the cream with the vanilla and combine with the custard and mango pulp. Mix well and freeze in a 13 × 9× 2-inch pan. Serve while still fresh tasting. Garnish with fresh lime.

*See page 23 for how to cut a mango.

Mango Yogurt Ice

Sorbete de Yogur de Mango

Since mango comes in many degrees of sweetness, it is best to sample a piece of the fresh fruit before you start adding the sugar in the following *nuevo Cubano* recipe.

Serves 4 to 6, depending on size of molds

2 mangoes, peeled and cut into chunks*
2 cups plain vanilla yogurt
½ cup granulated sugar, or to taste
Fresh mint sprigs, for garnish

Purée mango chunks in a blender to a smooth thick consistency.

Measure about 1½ cups of the mango purée into a mixing bowl. Add yogurt and mix well. Add sugar and mix again. Pour into individual molds. Freeze until firm. Run warm water over bottom of molds and invert onto plates. Serve garnished with fresh mint.

*See page 23 for how to cut a mango.

Beverages

Bebidas

Its bountiful gifts of fresh fruits and excellent rum have made Cuba an important source of distinctive cocktails. Everyone has enjoyed a daiquiri or a glass of sangria on a hot summer day. Less well known is the *mojito,* a fashionable Cuban libation consisting of fresh lime juice and rum with sprigs of mint.

It is no surprise that nearly every Cuban drink has some kind of rum in it. There is sugarcane, from which rum is distilled, in many of the Caribbean islands. Each island has its own distillate, hence Jamaican rum is pungent, dark, and sweet, while Cuban and Puerto Rican rums tend to be lighter and drier. There are also golden rums, spiced rums, and fruit-flavored rums, with the added aroma of tropical island fruits such as coconut and banana.

The same fruits and many others also contribute to the variety of nonalcoholic drinks that have become an integral part of the Cuban way of life.

Also essential to the Cuban way of life is rich, thick, dark coffee. Whereas American coffee is roasted fifteen minutes per one-hundred-pound coffee bag roaster, *café Cubano* is roasted twenty minutes per one-hundred-pound coffee bag roaster and is about double the strength of the coffee we're used to.

Free Cuba

Cuba Libre (Mentirita)

Contrary to popular belief it was Americans, not the Cubans, who invented this drink. It was first introduced in Havana's American Bar when the U.S. intervention forces brought in the first bottled cola drinks. The name comes from the pro-independence cry of Cuba's Mambi fighters against Spanish rule in the 1800s.

Serves 1

2 tablespoons fresh lime juice
Rind of ½ lime
2 ounces light rum
4 to 6 ounces Coca-Cola*
Lemon and lime wedges, for garnish

Combine lime juice and rind with the rum in a tall glass filled with ice cubes. Fill with cola and stir well. Garnish with lemon and lime wedges.

*In Cuba today, this drink is still popular but is prepared with Tropicola, the locally produced soda.

Original Daiquiri Cocktail

Coctel Daiquiri Original

The daiquiri is considered the most popular cocktail made with light or white rum. While the cocktail is a purely American drink, the daiquiri was named after the Daiquiri Iron Mines near Santiago, Cuba, in the late 1890s.

Serves 1

Cracked ice
3 ounces light or white rum
1 tablespoon fresh lime juice
1 teaspoon superfine sugar
Slice of lime, for garnish

Fill a cocktail shaker with cracked ice. Add rum, fresh lime juice, and sugar. Shake well and strain into a chilled cocktail glass. Add a slice of lime that has been cut halfway through so it can be attached to the rim of the glass.

Ernest Hemingway Special

El Especial de Ernest Hemingway

Antonio Meilan, the bartender at the famous Floridita Restaurante in Havana, served this drink on many occasions to Papa Hemingway. Antonio made it for me the exact way he prepared it for the writer.

If you have trouble finding maraschino liqueur, substitute cherry-flavored brandy. The resulting drink will be more tart but just as refreshing. **Serves 1**

2 ounces light or white dry rum
1 teaspoon grapefruit juice
1 teaspoon maraschino liqueur
1 tablespoon fresh lime juice
2 cups shaved ice
Sprig of mint, for garnish

Place all ingredients except garnish in the container of a blender. Blend until frothy. Pour into a large chilled cocktail glass. Garnish with mint.

Cuban Mojito

Mojito Cubano

Ernest Hemingway was not only a great writer but also a friend of Cuba and Cubans. He used to sit around and drink *mojitos* at Bodeguita del Medio, and then take a short stroll down the narrow street in Old Havana to the Floridita Restaurante, where he drank his favorite daiquiris. **Serves 1**

2 fresh mint sprigs
Juice and rind of 1 lime
1 teaspoon granulated sugar
1½ ounces white rum
Ice cubes
Soda water

Place mint, lime juice, rind, and sugar in a glass. Blend with a long spoon, crushing leaves. Add rum, ice cubes, then soda water to top. Stir. Add another sprig of mint. Stir again. Serve with a straw.

Perfectly Perfumed Island Rum

Ron Isla Perfumado a la Perfección

While you can purchase spiced rum, its taste will never compare to your own distinctive "house brand." It is quite simple to prepare; just be sure to choose a very good dark rum.

Makes 1 bottle

    1 (750 ml) bottle aged dark rum
    3 whole cloves
    1 star anise*
    3 whole allspice berries
    1 vanilla bean, split lengthwise
    2 cinnamon sticks

Combine all ingredients well in a large glass bowl. With a ladle, pour into a sterilized glass bottle. Cork well. Allow to age for at least 3 months.

*A commonly used spice and tea flavoring, but also used to flavor liqueurs.

Almendares

Light dry rum combined with pineapple juice, grenadine, and maraschino liqueur produce a coral-colored drink that captures the colors of a tropical island sunset.

Serves 1

    ⅛ teaspoon (5 drops) grenadine
    ⅛ teaspoon (5 drops) maraschino liqueur
    1½ ounces pineapple juice
    1½ ounces light or white dry rum
    1 cup cracked ice
    Maraschino cherry, for garnish

Place all ingredients except garnish in the container of a cocktail shaker. Shake and strain into a chilled cocktail glass. Garnish with cherry.

Archer

Arquero

Try this elegant blend of fresh mint, orange juice, and dry rum instead of its poor cousin, the Mimosa, at your next brunch.

Serves 1

    ½ teaspoon granulated sugar
    ⅓ teaspoon fresh orange juice
    ⅔ ounce light or white dry rum
    Mint leaf
    1 cup cracked ice

Place sugar, orange juice, and rum in a cocktail shaker. Cut mint leaf into small pieces and add to the shaker. Add ice, shake well, and strain into a chilled cocktail glass.

Baracoa Special

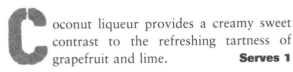

Baracoa Especial

Coconut liqueur provides a creamy sweet contrast to the refreshing tartness of grapefruit and lime.   **Serves 1**

½ ounce light or white dry rum
1 ounce fresh grapefruit juice
1 teaspoon coconut liqueur
2 teaspoons fresh lime juice
2 teaspoons extra-aged rum plus additional,
   for garnish
1 cup cracked ice

Place all ingredients into the container of a blender. Blend until smooth and pour into a chilled cocktail glass. Sprinkle additional rum on top.

Crusta

This stunning, tall drink is served in a sugar-rimmed glass—hence its name.   **Serves 1**

½ teaspoon granulated sugar (plus extra to
   rim glass)
3 dashes of maraschino liqueur
2 dashes of Angostura bitters
½ ounce fresh lime juice
2 ounces light or white rum
Soda water
Orange peel, for garnish

Dip rim of a chilled 10-ounce glass in a container holding a small amount of sugar. Fill the glass with ice cubes and all ingredients except the soda water and garnish. Stir and fill with soda water. Garnish with orange peel.

Small Cuban

Cubanito

This Cuban version of the standard Bloody Mary uses rum and fresh lime juice instead of lemon.   **Serves 1**

1 ice cube
¼ ounce fresh lime juice
Salt, to taste
1 teaspoon Worcestershire sauce
Dash of hot sauce
1½ ounces light or white rum
3 ounces tomato juice

Place ingredients in an 8-ounce glass and stir.

Joyce Special #2

On my first visit to the Tropicana Cabaret in Havana, manager José Cartaya, a most gracious host, prepared a special drink for me. Dubbed Joyce Special #1, the first drink was a bit too sweet. But Joyce #2 was just right—a chocolaty, minty libation.   **Serves 1**

½ ounce dark cocoa liqueur
½ ounce crème de menthe
½ ounce seven-year-old Añejo rum
1 teaspoon 151-proof rum, to flambé

Carefully, in order given, pour into poussecafé glass the cocoa liqueur, crème de menthe, and añejo so that each ingredient floats on preceding one. Colors should be separate and not mixed. Float 151-proof rum on top. Ignite the rum and serve.

Saoco

This simple, imaginative mixture of rum and coconut milk or water is traditionally served in a coconut shell. In Cuba, these days, it's most often made with *aguardiente*, the rawest form of rum, about 40 proof.

This drink is refreshing and wonderfully rich. Place coconut milk in the refrigerator, gather together enough coconut shells for a party, and have a ball.   **Serves 1 (or 2)**

2 ounces light or white rum
4 ounces coconut milk*
Ice cubes
1 coconut shell

Pour rum and coconut milk over ice cubes in a coconut shell. Stir and serve with a straw (or two).

*May be purchased or prepare your own (page 32).

Little Horse

Caballito

This drink looks like a Manhattan and tastes like a mint julep, Cuban style.
        Serves 1

1 teaspoon granulated sugar
3 mint leaves, crushed
¼ ounce fresh lime juice
1½ ounces light or white rum
½ ounce sweet vermouth
1 cup cracked ice
1 maraschino cherry, for garnish

Place all ingredients except the garnish in a cocktail shaker. Stir well and strain into a chilled cocktail glass. Garnish with the cherry.

Soroa

The apricot brandy and dry rum are magic with the pineapple juice. Mix the ingredients in the order listed.   **Serves 1**

¼ ounce apricot brandy
¼ ounce fresh lime juice
1½ ounces light or white dry rum
1 ounce pineapple juice
1 cup cracked ice
Slice of pineapple, for garnish

Place all ingredients except garnish in a cocktail shaker. Shake well and strain into a chilled cocktail glass. Garnish with a pineapple slice.

Cuban Spanish Wine Punch

Sangría de Cuba

N o cookbook about the cuisine of a major nation in the Spanish-speaking world would be complete without a recipe for sangria. This fruit-flavored punch is prepared in pitchers and is a traditional way to enjoy wine.

Serves 8 to 10

¼ cup granulated sugar, or to taste
1 cup water
½ cup fresh orange juice
½ cup fresh lime juice
1 Valencia or other juicy orange, thinly sliced
1 lime, thinly sliced
1 cup sliced canned peaches
1 apple, sliced
¼ cup maraschino cherries
1 (750 ml) bottle Burgundy wine
½ cup light or white rum
1 cinnamon stick
6 ounces soda water

Dissolve sugar in water in a large pitcher. Add fruit juices, fruit, wine, rum, and cinnamon stick. Add a dozen or more ice cubes and stir gently with a wooden spoon until cold. Cover pitcher and allow to stand at least 1 hour in the refrigerator. Remove cinnamon stick. Add soda water. Stir lightly and serve in chilled red wine glasses, putting a portion of each fruit in each glass.

Malecon Moon

Luna del Malecon

I n Havana, a popular place for young and old to gather is the Malecon waterfront, which gives this drink its name. Festivities there go on until all hours of the morning, accompanied often enough by this superior drink.

Serves 4

1 ounce fresh lime juice (plus extra to rim glasses)
Salt to rim glasses
8 ounces tequila gold
2 ounces triple sec liqueur
4 cups shaved ice
Fresh lime slices, for garnish

Dip rim of each cocktail glass in a container holding a small amount of lime juice. Dip rim of each glass into a plate of salt. Place glasses in refrigerator freezer to chill.

In the container of a blender combine lime juice, tequila, and triple sec. Blend on low speed until smooth (about 10 seconds). Add shaved ice, 1 cup at a time, and blend on high speed until frosty, or about 10 seconds between each cupful. Pour into chilled cocktail glasses and garnish with lime slices.

Lime Juice Cocktail

Coctel de Jugo de Limón Verde

Here's a refreshing nonalcoholic cocktail that's sure to quench your thirst. It's also pleasant made with Key lime juice, which is more tart. **Serves 1**

¼ cup lime juice
2 tablespoons grapefruit juice
2 tablespoons fresh orange juice
⅔ cup ginger ale
Sugar, to taste
Crushed ice
Lime slice and maraschino cherry, for garnish

Place all ingredients except the ice and garnish ingredients in a cocktail shaker and shake vigorously. Pour over crushed ice. Garnish with a slice of lime and maraschino cherry.

Mango-Banana-Peach Shake

Batido de Mango, Banana, y Melocotón

Batidos, with their use of fresh, ripe, tropical fruits, are a popular drink with most Cubans, who often stop for such a refresher in the middle of the day. They're the Cuban version of our popular milkshake and they come in a variety of flavors and colors.

Serves 1

1 cup whole milk
½ cup peeled and diced ripe mango
½ cup sliced banana
½ cup peeled and diced ripe peach
½ cup crushed ice

Place all ingredients in the container of a blender. Process for a few seconds until smooth. Serve in a tall frosted glass.

Mango-Orange Eye Opener

Abre-Ojo de Mango y Naranja

Your family will look forward to waking up to this frothy combination of both tart and sweet juices. **Serves 1**

1½ cups puréed ripe mangoes
2 tablespoons honey
2 cups orange juice
¼ cup grapefruit juice

In the container of a blender, combine all the ingredients and blend for a few seconds. Chill. Pour over chunked ice in a 4-ounce glass.

Mango Shake

Batido de Mango

Although it's best made with fresh pulp, this popular drink can be made with the canned or bottled variety of mango found in most supermarkets.   **Serves 1**

½ cup puréed mango
1 cup whole milk
2 tablespoons granulated sugar
½ cup crushed ice
Fresh mint sprig, for garnish

Place the mango purée and whole milk in the container of a blender. Add sugar and ice. Blend until smooth and frothy. Pour into a tall chilled glass and garnish with a mint sprig.

Mamey Shake

Batido de Mamey

When I am in Miami, where I lived for a number of years, I always stop at the Varadero Supermarket on Coral Way to stock up on Hispanic food and drink. While there, I visit the little take-out eatery in the market and order a *batido de mamey* made with mamey sapote, a tropical, sweet, salmon-colored fruit. You will probably have to purchase frozen mamey purée because fresh is difficult to find in many areas.   **Serves 1**

1 cup whole milk
1 cup mamey sapote purée*
2 tablespoons granulated sugar, or to taste
½ cup crushed ice

Place all ingredients in the container of a blender. Process for a few seconds until smooth. Serve in a tall frosted glass.

*Use fresh or frozen. Available at most Hispanic markets.

Easy Orange-Mango Shake

Batido Fácil de Naranja-Mango y Leche

You can cut calories by using skim milk and vanilla ice milk in this recipe.
Serves 4

3 cups whole milk
1 cup puréed mango
½ cup fresh orange juice
1 cup vanilla ice cream
1 cup crushed ice
Fresh mint leaves, for garnish

Pour milk and mango into the container of a blender or food processor. Add the orange juice, ice cream, and ice and blend for about 30 seconds, or until smooth. Pour into tall chilled glasses. Garnish with mint leaves and serve immediately.

Cuban Almond Drink

Cubana Horchata

Here's a refreshing drink that's perfect for a hot summer's day.　**Serves 4**

¼ cup blanched almonds
4 cups whole milk
1 cup granulated sugar
2 drops almond extract
1 vanilla bean, split
Crushed ice

With a mortar and pestle, pound nuts into a paste, or use prepared almond paste. Put in a medium-size heavy saucepan and add milk and sugar. Stir well over medium heat, bring to a boil, then reduce to a simmer. Cook for about 5 minutes. Remove from heat, add the almond extract and vanilla bean, and allow to sit for about 10 minutes. Mix well, reheat, then remove from heat. Strain. Cool. Serve over ice.

Guava Punch

Ponche de Guayaba

Here's a pleasurable nonalcoholic punch with the true flavor of the islands.

Serves 12 to 20

1½ cups granulated sugar
4 cups water
3 cups guava juice or guava nectar
3 cups fresh orange juice
1 cup fresh lime juice
1 cup finely chopped pineapple
Zest of 1 orange
Zest of 1 lime or 3 Key limes
Cracked ice
Fresh mint leaves, for garnish

Boil sugar and water for about 4 minutes. Cool. Add guava, orange, and lime juices, pineapple, and zests and mix well. Pour over cracked ice. Garnish with fresh mint leaves.

Party Coffee Smoothies

Cafés Zalameros

This is a good finish to a great dinner. The better the blend of coffee, the better the smoothie.   **Serves 8**

2 pints French vanilla ice cream, softened
4 ripe bananas, peeled and sliced
4 cups strong cold Cuban coffee
8 fresh mint sprigs, for garnish

Place ice cream in the container of a blender. Add bananas and coffee and process until thick and smooth, 20 to 30 seconds. Serve in chilled glass coffee mugs and garnish with a sprig of fresh mint.

Cuban Espresso

Espreso Cubano

Many Cuban families still make their espresso in a small stovetop maker, which seems to suit them fine.

Cold water
1 tablespoon espresso coffee grounds per demitasse cup of water

Fill the lower chamber with fresh cold water, almost all the way up to the small steam valve.

Fill the basket with espresso coffee grounds. Set the basket on top of the lower chamber.

Screw the top chamber tightly. Place pot on burner and brew over medium-high heat until bubbling sound stops and top chamber is full. Remove pot from heat.

Pour coffee into demitasse cups about three quarters full, leaving enough space to add sugar. Mix well to achieve a frothy top on the coffee. Coffee is always served steaming hot.

CAFÉ CON LECHE

Pour an equal amount of milk that has been brought to a boil into hot brewed espresso. Sweeten as desired.

CORTADITO

Heat together two parts milk to 1 part freshly brewed espresso. Remove from heat as soon as it begins to boil. Sweeten as desired.

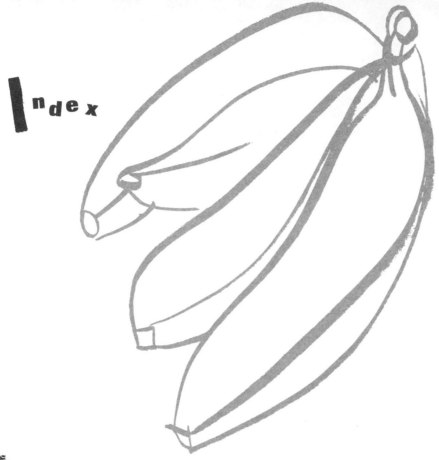

Index

OKRA

CALABAZA

CUBANELLA
PEPPER

YUCA